Knowledge Economy in the Megalopolis

In recent decades urban regions around the world have engaged in a new process of development based on the creation of new knowledge. Amidst the globalization of economic activities and the arrival of transformative technologies, knowledge has become the key driver of competitiveness and is profoundly reshaping the patterns of economic growth and activity. This book offers a comprehensive new model of the rise of a Knowledge Economy and its evolutionary development in the Megalopolis.

These regions are developing new institutions and governance mechanisms to adapt, disseminate, and utilize available knowledge to promote continuing development of their Knowledge Economies. However, such developments are accompanied by increasing inequalities in incomes and in urban services. This book examines the resilience of some urban regions and their recent emergence as vibrant Knowledge Economies. It also reviews the recent renewal and growth in the Megalopolis—stretching along the Atlantic Seaboard along the metropolitan areas of Boston, New York, Philadelphia, Baltimore, and Washington DC.

This book will appeal to researchers and professionals interested in urban and regional development, and to business groups interested in economic development.

T.R. Lakshmanan is Emeritus Professor and Director of the Centers of Energy, Environment, and Transport, Boston University, USA.

William P. Anderson is Director of the Cross-Border Institute, University of Windsor, Canada.

Yena Song is Assistant Professor, Department of Geography, Chonnam National University, Korea (ROK).

Routledge Advances in Regional Economics, Science and Policy

Knowledge Economy in the Megalopolis

Interactions of innovations in transport, information, production and organizations

T.R. Lakshmanan,
William P. Anderson,
and Yena Song

LONDON AND NEW YORK

First published 2016 by Routledge

2 Park Square, Milton Park, Abingdon, Oxfordshire OX14 4RN
52 Vanderbilt Avenue, New York, NY 10017

Routledge is an imprint of the Taylor & Francis Group,
an informa business

First issued in paperback 2019

British Library Cataloguing in Publication Data
A catalogue record for this book is available from the British Library

Library of Congress Cataloging in Publication Data
Lakshmanan, T. R., 1932-
Knowledge economy in the megalopolis : interactions of innovations in
transport, information, production and organizations / T.R. Lakshmanan,
William P. Anderson and Yena Song. -- First Edition.
pages cm
Includes bibliographical references and index.
1. Knowledge management. 2. Technological innovations. I. Anderson,
William P. (William Peter), 1954- II. Song, Yena. III. Title.
HD30.2.L345 2015
306.4'2--dc23
2015019531

ISBN: 978-0-415-85951-6 (hbk)
ISBN: 978-0-367-86792-8 (pbk)

Typeset in Times New Roman
by GreenGate Publishing Services, Tonbridge, Kent

Contents

Figures

Tables

Boxes

1   Introduction and Overview

Over the last three decades or more, a number of urban regions around the world have engaged in a new process of economic, social, and spatial development based on the creation of knowledge and the harnessing of that knowledge to spur further growth, competiveness, and wealth creation. Spurred by the arrival of some transformative general purpose technologies and the globalization of economic activities, knowledge has clearly become the key driver of competitiveness and is now profoundly reshaping the patterns of economic growth and activity. At the same time these regions are developing new institutions and governance mechanisms to adapt, disseminate, and utilize available knowledge to promote continuing development of their "Knowledge Economies."

Knowledge and innovation have always played a crucial role in economic and social development in history. In the late Neolithic period, the development of new knowledge related to agriculture—in the form of seeding of plants, ploughing practices, metal works, better tools, etc.—paved the way to the agricultural revolution and to the rise of urban centers in the river valleys of Egypt, Mesopotamia, India, and China. That fund of knowledge was expanded in many dimensions, codified, and transmitted in the succeeding centuries, forming the basis of major civilizations in many parts of the world. Indeed, this process continued to support the development of society till the late medieval period, when Europe laid the foundations of the *Renaissance movement*. That movement was built on the recovery of Greco-Roman knowledge (lost during the Dark Ages) and the acquisition of the knowledge base accumulated by Arab, Indian, and Chinese cultures and resulted in an explosion of art, science, and other branches of knowledge. Subsequently, the Industrial Revolution rose and flowered initially in Great Britain and subsequently in the United States, Europe, and Japan with the development of new scientific and technical knowledge, the emergence of general purpose technologies like steam power and electricity, and the linking of dynamic entrepreneurship with sources of new knowledge and invention. This era of the industrial economy—stretching from the nineteenth century to well into the twentieth century—has been the basis of structural transformation, socio-economic development and modernization, and rising affluence in Europe, North America, and Japan and, in recent times, in many other parts of the world.

However, in the latter half of the twentieth century, there has been a maturing and progressive decline of the traditional industrial sectors of these high income economies in North America, Europe, and Asia. In the last three decades, however, in some large urban regions of these countries, a "Knowledge Economy"—comprised of production and service sectors based on knowledge intensive activities which promote an accelerated pace of technological and scientific improvements as well an equally rapid obsolescence—appears to be rising.

More generally, this emerging Knowledge Economy is characterized by its ability to generate, share, analyze, and utilize knowledge in the creation of value and wealth. The focus is not merely on expansion of knowledge, but also on *the effective harnessing of different types of knowledge in various sectors of the economy to secure competitive advantage and improved performance*. Knowledge represents cognitive ability which can transform the vast information made available by new information technology (IT) into *competitive advantage* to economic social and political actors and enterprises in various economic activities. Consequently, there is, in the emerging Knowledge Economy, an increasing relative shift in investment from physical assets (such as machinery, buildings, etc.—typical of the industrial era) to knowledge-based assets such as R&D, software, design and development, process innovations, and human and institutional capital. Further, the emerging Knowledge Economy is operated by an increasingly educated, well-qualified and flexible labor force. In this context, the rise and expansion of knowledge intensive economic sectors—from professional services, finance and insurance, health and educational services, to high tech manufacturing—is a story being played out in several rising new economies in metropolitan regions. Knowledge-based economic sectors and knowledge related occupations are providing in the last three decades dominant portions of new jobs in this emerging economy.

These emerging Knowledge Economies thus represent a major emerging structural change and socio-economic evolution from the prior declining industrial economies. How do such contemporary Knowledge Metropolises emerge and make the transition from the decline and malaise of post-industrial society? How do they unravel the complexities and dead ends of industrial economic decline and become vibrant new economies based on the generation and use of knowledge in the creation of value and wealth? What kinds of *resilience*—the capacity to reorganize their systems to deal with change and continue to grow and develop—do these large urban areas display?

This book aims to address such questions in the context of the ongoing structural change and economic evolution towards the new Knowledge Economy.

First, it ascertains how this transition from a declining industrial economy to a vibrant Knowledge Economy comes about. What kinds of new technologies and other innovations have arrived to promote economic, social, and spatial processes that enable this structural transition to the Knowledge Economy? For such a transition to be successful, major economic, political, and social actors in a metropolitan region would have also to unravel the complexities of change and initiate strategies of structural change. Such actors would have to shift mindsets and change behavior of various urban and metropolitan private, public, and social sector agents in evolving and sustaining innovation, and in maintaining the dynamics of change—innovating new institutions and organizations to facilitate such change. In other words, this book aims to address such issues and offer a broad analytical framework underlying the rise and evolution of the new Knowledge Economy.

Second, this book attempts to apply the resulting analytical framework of the rise and evolution of the Knowledge Economy to the socio-economic developmental experience in recent decades in the very large mega-urbanized region of the Megalopolis—stretching from the Boston Metropolitan region in the north to the Washington DC metro region in the south. The book will review the observed patterns of structural change and the economic evolution in the last three decades in the Megalopolis and its five major metropolitan areas (Boston, New York, Philadelphia, Baltimore, and Washington DC) and assess the degree of coherence between those observed patterns and the scope and predictions of the model of the rise of the Knowledge Economy presented here.

The Megalopolis

Megalopolis was a term coined by Jean Gottmann (1957, 1961) to describe the urbanized Northeast of the US, "an almost continuous stretch of urban and suburban areas from southern New Hampshire to Northern Virginia and from the Atlantic shore to the Appalachian foothills" with a population of 31.9 million in 1950.[1] Gottmann built upon Bogue's (1951) innovative idea of a "metropolitan state economic areas," where "the non-agricultural economy is a closely integrated unit and is distinctly different from the economy of areas which lie outside the orbit or close contact with the Metropolis." Gottmann (1957) deduced "the continuity of a *metropolitan economy*" from a little north of Boston to a little south of Washington—the contemporary corridor from the Boston Metropolitan region in the north to the Washington Metropolitan Region in the south (the BOSWASH corridor).

The Megalopolis region has evolved over more than three centuries in the Northeast United States. The early European settlements in the United States began as trading posts and harbor settlements more than three centuries ago in the Atlantic seaboard and over time coalesced into towns in the mercantile era and subsequently into large urban regions—such as Boston, New York, Philadelphia, and Baltimore—in the industrial era. By the mid-twentieth century, these large urban regions clearly extended beyond an individual city region with complex linkages among the various urban and regional economies. It is in this context that Jean Gottmann advanced his notion of the Megalopolis as a region in the Northeastern seaboard of the US, stretching from Southern New Hampshire and Maine to Northern Virginia across metropolitan areas of Boston, New York, Philadelphia, and Baltimore-Washington DC and bounded by the Appalachian Mountains to the west and the Atlantic Ocean to the east (1957, 1961).

Gottmann (1961) postulated the notion of a continuous metropolitan economy in a region extending from a little north of Boston to a little south of Washington. He wanted to proceed beyond the traditional notion of a city as a tightly packed spatial unit of people, structures, and activities in a small area clearly separated from its non-urban surroundings. By the mid-twentieth century, these large cities clearly extended beyond an individual city region. The Megalopolis concept recognizes this fact and suggests a new geography to highlight emerging complex linkages among the various urban and regional economies. Thus Gottmann viewed the Megalopolis as a clustered network of cities, a poly-nucleated interactive network rather than a centralized urban system. In other words, Gottmann proceeded beyond the limited image of the traditional large early twentieth century urban area, and suggested a new geography to highlight emerging complex linkages among the various urban and regional economies. Megalopolis is thus viewed as a clustered network of cities, a poly-nucleated interactive network rather than a centralized urban system—viewed as a thriving industrial region and the densest mega urban region in the US by the mid-twentieth century with a population of over 30 million around 1960. Gottmann noted that this relatively small area contained the most prosperous, well-educated, productive, and serviced population, the largest and most important centers of financial and governmental power, and its greatest concentrations of wealth in the nation.

Gottmann also indicated that this region "may be considered the cradle of a new order in the organization of inhabited space" (1961, p. 9) and "an incubator of important socio-economic trends" (1987, p. 2). Further, Gottmann (1961) stated: "In spite of the relative lack of local natural riches, this seaboard has achieved a most remarkable concentration of labor force and of wealth" (p. 46). He attributed this phenomenon to the region's "network of overseas relationships," and from maintaining the "reins of direction of the national economy." Gottmann also indicated that this region "may be considered the cradle of a new order in the organization of inhabited space" (1961, p. 9) and "an incubator of important socio-economic trends" (1987, p. 2).

This Megalopolis region, with its demonstrated history of *resilience and reinvention*, has emerged in the last three decades as a "Knowledge Economy."

In the more than five decades since Gottmann identified the Megalopolis, a variety of demographic and economic evolutionary changes have occurred in this region and in the country. First, there was a demographic and economic shift regionally from the "Manufacturing Belt" (Megalopolis and sections of the Midwest) to the south and west of the country. Second, the population shifted locally from large cities to suburbs, though at a much slower rate during the 1980s and 1990s than earlier. While some cities in the Megalopolis declined continuously and also experienced either an above-average loss of population to their surrounding suburbs or else below average metropolitan area growth, some large metropolitan areas in the Megalopolis tended in the most recent quarter century to *reverse population declines* both by slowing population losses to surrounding suburbs as well as by increasing metropolitan area growth.

However, in the *subsequent* three decades to the present day, there has been a remarkable reversal of regional economic decline and indeed a notable economic resurgence in several metropolitan areas of the Megalopolis. The region accounted in 2010 for 17 percent of the national population and 20 percent of the country's GDP. A variety of knowledge intensive production and service sector enterprises have arrived and continue to grow in the several metro areas of the Megalopolis, which now represent large concentrations of high quality human, cultural, and organizational capital, and of some vibrant contemporary "Knowledge Metropolises."[2]

How did these contemporary Knowledge Metropolises in the Megalopolis make the transition from the malaise of post-industrial society, unraveling the complexities and dead ends of industrial economic decline and managing the transformation to the contemporary post-industrial thriving knowledge society? How are the old industrial metros of Boston and New York— well advanced currently in this transition to Knowledge Economies—and Washington DC metro (with a large public sector and rich scientific, technical, and cultural resources) accomplishing such a transformation?[3]

What broad economic and social processes are at play in the region and in the country in stimulating and facilitating the creation and diffusion of new "useful knowledge" (Kuznets 1965; Mokyr 2002) and its high degree of incorporation into economic activity, which in turn promotes structural changes in the operation of the Megalopolis economy and its continuing evolution? Why are these change processes more advanced in one metropolitan region than another, and take the form they do?

This book on this large Knowledge Economy emerging in the Megalopolis addresses these questions, suggesting that:

a) the recent transition of the Megalopolis from a mature industrial economy and structural evolution towards knowledge intensive activities can be traced to the cumulative consequences of *four broad classes of technologies and processes, and their interactive and cumulative effects*;

b) the recent economic growth and evolution of the knowledge intensive production and service activities of major Megalopolis metros (e.g. Boston, New York, Washington DC) are consistent with the predictions of the underlying structural change mechanisms identified in a) above;

c) the Megalopolis Knowledge Economy is evolving into new patterns of regional spatial organization in terms of new and varied spatial patterns, and the emergence of the Megalopolis as a *functional economic region*; and

d) the rapidly evolving global organization of economic activities in the Megalopolis and its major metropolitan areas paves the way to the *sharply rising income inequalities* in the Megalopolis.

Two of these four classes of innovations (noted in a) above) can be termed as "General Purpose Technologies" (GPT). The GPTs are technologies initially with limited uses that evolve over time into complex technologies with a very broad range of uses across the economy and a large range of economic output they help to produce (Lipsey et al. 2005; Lakshmanan and Chatterjee 2006; Basu and Fernald 2006). Steam power and electricity were such general purpose technologies of the industrial era.

Two such GPTs critical to the contemporary knowledge era are:

1. *Transport Innovations*: such innovations appeared in recent decades in the form of new key physical technologies (Interstate Highway System, Containers, and Jet aircraft) and major institutional innovations pertaining to overall economic governance of transport (deregulation, privatization, and modified physical transport flows and border controls). This combination of physical and institutional innovations in the transport sector have combined in the last three decades to greatly reduce transport times and costs and promote a broad range of transport logistics capacities—which in turn greatly enhance *physical connectivity* between economic actors and enterprises, thereby enabling goods to be sourced and produced, and markets serviced over vast distances and indeed globally (Lakshmanan 2011; Lakshmanan and Anderson 2002).[4]

2. *Information and Communication Technology (ICT)*: the central feature of these innovations is the increasing ability to collect, manipulate, store, and transmit large quantities of information at low and ever dropping costs. ICT is also pervasive in its impacts on goods and services, and on various business processes, from R&D, production, distribution, and marketing. Consequently, the knowledge intensity of economic activities in the economy is constantly on the rise. Further, ICT improvements, by reducing the *costs of access* to information and knowledge, not only speed up the creation, use, and diffusion of the knowledge base (Lakshmanan and Chatterjee 2006); ICT improvements are dramatically further increasing the levels of *connectivity* (across vast distances— indeed globally) between individuals and enterprises and between ideas and actors. New technology derives from new combinations of ideas (or innovations), and with enhanced connectivity the number of potential new combinations increases also. Finally, ICT affects human cognition, including the way workers and consumers think about and interpret their environment (Mokyr 2002).

The joint effect of these two GPTs (Transport and ICT) in recent decades is the enabling of low cost long distance personal and freight transport and sharply declining costs of access to information and knowledge and its utilization. The internet and low cost powerful computers have led to global information networks that make much of the Knowledge Economy possible, finding their way into most aspects of production and service processes, and sharply lowering transaction and investment costs across vast distances. These developments, in the context of recent global trade-enhancing *institutional innovations* such as reduced barriers to trade and investment, deregulated product markets, and international capital flows in many countries, have led to *globalization*. Economic globalization involves increasing flows of capital across national boundaries and around the world, an explosive expansion of cross-country economic interactions and division of labor, complex value-adding chains of production of goods and services, *and a globally distributed production system and vastly expanded markets*. Such a territorial dispersal of the globalized economy has been enabled also by the emergence of global corporate integration functions in some large cities in the Megalopolis and elsewhere (Sassen 2001). These corporate central organizational service functions (financial, legal, accounting, and other business and professional services) permit business operations by global network corporations in multiple countries around the world. In short, the GPT innovations of transport and information provide *infrastructures* that facilitate economic globalization and the distributed Knowledge Economies of large urbanized regions such as the Megalopolis (Lakshmanan and Chatterjee 2006).

The third class of *Innovations* underlying the rise of the Knowledge Economy relate to the emergence of processes which *a) nurture and commercialize new industrial products and operations and b) promote the structural evolution towards a Knowledge Intensive Service Economy*. There is a vast and growing literature drawn from many disciplines over the last three decades on the emergence of new knowledge intensive production, which focuses largely on what may be described as innovation networks that nurture and commercialize innovation and industrial adaptation in various regions (Saxenian 1994; Scott 1998; Storper 1995; Feldman 2000; Gertler 2003; Camagni 2004; Malecki and Moriset 2008; Cooke et al. 2011; Capello 2011). Further, in the US and specifically in the Megalopolis, where the transition to the service economy is advanced, the share in the economy of business services has grown monotonically over the past two to three decades, as the share of the manufacturing sector has been dropping. These business services (particularly, Knowledge Intensive Business Services, KIBS) have contributed heavily to the Megalopolis and US economic growth, in terms of employment, productivity, and innovation. A direct growth contribution stems from the business services sector's own remarkably fast growth, while an indirect growth contribution is caused by the positive knowledge and productivity spillovers from KIBS to other industries (Kox and Rubelcaba 2007; Stehrer et al. 2012; Bryson and Daniels 2007).

Institutional Innovations represent the fourth class of innovations, which support the transition to the Megalopolis Knowledge Economy. A major example pertains to the rise and evolution of a *new economic institution* which underlies the Knowledge Economy. Since economic institutions are constrained by the social context in which they are embedded (Polanyi 1944; Granovetter 1985), the advent of a new economy is facilitated by the evolution towards a *new economic institution*. With the arrival of knowledge-rich technologies in this economy in various aspects of production—design, fabrication, input and output logistics, marketing, after-sales services—enterprises seek to add value to their core competencies by taking advantage of complementary assets and capabilities of other enterprises. Further, these firms become concerned with the reduction of a new class of costs that they confront in this Knowledge Economy. These are *adaptive costs* incurred by the firm as it monitors the environment for changes in technology and products, creates competitive strategies, and implements such strategies fast enough to retain or improve market share—typically utilizing *physical, relational, and institutional proximity* to relevant enterprises (Alter and Hage 1993; Lakshmanan and Button 2009). This combination of the criticality of innovator and entrepreneur and adaptive cost reduction shapes the nature and structure of incentives for economic actors. It requires new competences on the part of economic actors, and an institutional framework that facilitate such new patterns of interactions among economic actors, who are functionally interdependent but autonomous. *Networks* represent a new institutional form developed in response to this changing context of desired economic interactions among economic agents in innovative regions (Lakshmanan and Button 2009). Networks differ from the traditional (industrial era) hierarchical coordination of the firm since each enterprise has autonomy, because networks have "visible hands" in the form of complex decision-making groups at multiple levels. Networks comprise sometimes only firms, at other times of firms, public sector actors, and social sector actors. A regional economy of networks becomes increasingly a system of cooperative interactions among economic actors or a web of links between individuals, firms and organizations—with links based on knowledge assets and evolving through cooperative learning processes.

The book also describes a variety of other institutional changes which have made possible a) the many facets of global trade, investment, distributed production, and consumption, and b) innovative "urban governance models" to manage the structural change of physical systems (infrastructure, land use, etc.) in the large urban areas (as in the Megalopolis), serving as key poles of the new economy (Chatterjee and Lakshmanan 2005).

Further, the book highlights the *joint and reinforcing effects* of the four different types of innovations noted above in shaping the rise and evolution of the Knowledge Economy, and illustrates this experience in the mega region of the Megalopolis. The empirical record in terms of the economic growth and structural change in the last several decades in the major metro areas (Boston, New York, Philadelphia, Baltimore, and Washington) will be described and interpreted in the light of the explanations offered here for the rise of the Knowledge Economy.

Finally, the book will characterize the emerging Megalopolis Knowledge Economy in two other ways:

1. Identification of the *changing spatial evolution and structure* of dynamic economic activities in the Megalopolis region over the last two to three decades, in terms of economic clustering and agglomeration patterns, and evolution of the entire Megalopolis as a *functional economic region*;
2. Identification of the adverse distributional consequences associated with the rising Knowledge Economy—consequent on the increasing globalization and the associated labor market polarization of the Megalopolis economy in the last two decades. The rise of "tradable" and "nontradable" sectors (Spence and Hlatshwayo 2011) in the globalizing Megalopolis and their differential economic performance in terms of how value-adding chains in an economic sector are structured by global trade requirements and affect employment and value added per employee by sector. The analysis of the performance of these two classes of sectors in the Megalopolis metropolitan areas, which have high levels of knowledge intensive manufacturing and service sectors, and of global trade participation suggests an evolution of the Megalopolis Knowledge Economy towards an "hourglass profile"—more high wage jobs at the top, more low wage jobs at the bottom, and fewer in the middle—with adverse income distribution implications of this two sector economic evolution and widening income inequalities in the Megalopolis metro areas.

The remainder of the book is structured as follows. Chapter 2 of the book offers a survey of the demographic, urban, and economic evolution over recent decades in the Megalopolis. An analysis of urban development patterns in the I-95 Corridor stretching from southern New Hampshire (in the Boston Metro) to Northern Virginia (in the Washington Metro) over a long time period (six decades) suggests different patterns of urban development— *urban decline followed by resurgence*. This evolution ranges from the dense and compact *industrial era spatial pattern* (pre-1957—manufacturing production and working class households concentrated in dense central cities) to the *Decentralized Spread City* (1957 to the early 1980s—suburban expansion of population and employment in an increasingly affluent economy), to the contemporary (post 1985) *trends towards agglomeration, demographic and economic resurgence of central cities and metropolitan clustering of "Knowledge Economy" activities* along the large metropolitan regions in the Megalopolis.

The multiple century demographic, urban, and economic evolution of the Megalopolis is identified in Chapter 2, which starts with an identification of the changes in the magnitudes and dimensions of such changes from the colonial era to recent decades. Particular attention is given to the evolution of contiguous metropolitan counties in the BOSWASH corridor in the recent historical period. The evolution of the major metropolises in the corridor is described utilizing the data on the multiple designations used by the

US Census Bureau over the period, namely MSA (Metropolitan Statistical Area), CMSA (Consolidated Metropolitan Statistical Area), and PMSA (Primary Metropolitan Statistical Area). Large metropolises such as New York and Boston in this corridor are experiencing a demographic resurgence in the last two decades.[5] Statistical and cartographic representations of this urban-metro evolution document in detail the demographic changes and the continuing development and deepening of the mega regional coherence anticipated by Jean Gottmann in the Megalopolis. Finally, this chapter provides a multidimensional portrait of the economic changes over several decades in the Megalopolis. It delineates the nature and scope of economic evolution of the Megalopolis over the last several decades into the world's largest mega urban region. This portrait will be drawn from the economic statistics on the changes in the magnitudes of employment, value added, output, and productivity, and in terms of shifts in the composition and locations of different industrial and service sectors.

Chapter 3 focuses on the recent phase of the rise and evolution of two GPTs—Transport and ICT—in the Megalopolis. Over recent decades, US transport systems have undergone a major transformation, induced by new transport technologies and major institutional reforms pertaining to overall economic governance of transport, in the context of new IT. Recent investments in transport links and terminals directly provide additions to flow or throughput capacity in the form of new lanes and facilities, safer and speedier movement, and operational improvements. In turn, these improved infrastructure attributes get translated into highly enhanced freight transport infrastructure attributes (e.g. capacity, safety, access, etc.) and lower freight service characteristics such as travel costs, freight travel times and their variability, and logistical services. Logistics refers to the integrated analysis and management of a firm's overall supply chain and embraces processes of transportation, warehousing, inventory maintenance, order processing, and administration. Transport enterprises coordinate with other processes precisely in order to permit lower levels of inventory, warehousing, handling, errors, and waste. Taking advantage of the service and process innovations involved in logistical restructuring and the substitutability of transport and inventory carriage, there has been reorganization of the logistics with an overall reduction of total logistics costs, estimated at 40 percent for an average American enterprise (Lakshmanan et al. 2009). Further, the steeply dropping time and money costs of personal and goods travel—in the context of ICT improvements noted earlier—yield a situation where goods can be sourced, produced, marketed, and serviced globally.

Chapter 3 also offers an elaboration of the central feature of the second GPT (ICT), namely its increasing ability to collect, manipulate, store, and transmit large quantities of information at low and ever dropping costs. Further, ICT improvements, by reducing the *costs of access* to information and knowledge, promote the creation, use, and diffusion of the knowledgebase, and heighten the knowledge intensity of economic activities in the economy. Finally, the central feature of ICT is its attribute of a GPT, namely that it leads to fundamental changes in the production process of *industries using new IT* (see, e.g. Helpman and Trajtenberg 1998).[6] Indeed, the availability of cheap ICT capital allows firms to deploy their other inputs in radically different and productivity-enhancing ways (Basu and Fernald 2006). Further, Chapter 3 describes the joint effect of these two GPTs (Transport and ICT) in recent decades in enabling a) low cost long distance personal and freight transport and sharply declining costs of access to information and knowledge and b) *economic globalization* and the functional and spatial reorganization of activities of multinational corporations (Lakshmanan and Chatterjee 2006).

Chapter 4 focuses on a) the reinvention of major metro areas in the Megalopolis in recent decades as Knowledge Economies or hubs of creativity and b) the various interactive technical and institutional changes underlying this transformation of the metro regions. The literature on such economic transformation processes is highlighted here in terms of 1) current theoretical formulations of the rise of the "knowledge production economy," 2) the contributions that the growing KIBS make in the form of positive knowledge and productivity spillovers thereby augmenting the productivity of major service sectors, and 3) the emergence of new institutions—networks, new urban governance models—that facilitate the transition to the knowledge society. A comprehensive analytical framework of the rise of the Knowledge Economy is offered.

Chapter 5 offers an empirical survey of a) the reinvention over recent decades of the Megalopolis and component major metro areas (Boston, New York, Philadelphia, Baltimore, and Washington) as Knowledge Economies or hubs of creativity in production and service sectors and b) an interpretive assessment of the recent economic evolution in these metros of the Megalopolis in the light of the various interactive technical, institutional, and the two general purpose technologies identified in this book as underlying the rise of the Knowledge Economy in the mega region of Megalopolis.

Chapter 6 offers some evidence of increasing *spatial concentration* in those knowledge intensive service industries that are growing most rapidly, particularly in the Megalopolis corridor metropolitan areas. Specialization in financial, business, and legal services extend throughout this entire corridor. There is a growing concentration of the finance industries in the Boston-Washington Corridor during the years 1977–1987. Over the next 18 years to 2005, there is further strengthening of the finance sector, with our spatial analysis indicating the strong linkages between these financial clusters and the Interstate highways. The Megalopolis (Boston-Washington) is the pivotal region in the nation for the many innovations and new developments in this capital services industry, which have promoted rapid growth and the globalization activities. The analysis of clustering patterns and the location of "hot spots" in the I-95 Megalopolis Corridor suggests an interesting *pattern of spatial spread of service activities over time which is shaped by the layout of the*

Interstate highway system. Thus the "hot spots" for financial services spread out along the I-95 Corridor over three time periods. In 1977, the hot spots are limited to major cities, such as Boston, Philadelphia and the broader region around New York. By 1987, additional hot spots appear in New Jersey, and by 2005, they extend into central Massachusetts and Southern New Hampshire. Parallel analyses of the spatial patterns of evolution of business and legal services are also reported. Essentially, the Interstate system provides a spatial conduit through which some (lower value-adding) components of these knowledge intensive service activities spread out—just as older dynamic manufacturing activities spread out in the 1950–1970 period from the central cities of the I-95 Corridor metropolitan areas. This transfer of dynamic activities from the center towards the periphery (accessible enough for daily interactions) seems to be occurring at the larger spatial level of the Megalopolis.

Further, this analysis of the evolving spatial configuration of the Megalopolis Knowledge Economy sheds some light on the issue of whether the contemporary Megalopolis is evolving as a functional economic region. An earlier study indicated that the I-95 transport corridor in the Megalopolis behaved like a functional economic region, when goods movements were analyzed through a gravity model (Lakshmanan et al. 2006). Goods flows (even after controlling for distance and the sizes of origins and destinations) within the corridor are greater than flows across the corridor borders. *This suggests a high level of economic integration in the associated fabrication activities.*

Chapter 7 implements for the Megalopolis the Spence and Hlatshwayo (2011) national analysis of economic performance in the last two decades of "tradable" and "non-tradable" sectors to capture their differential economic performance in terms of how value-adding chains in an economic sector are structured by global trade requirements—with increasing losses of low and medium wage jobs—thus affecting employment and value added per employee by sector. The performance of these two classes of sectors in the Megalopolis metropolitan areas, which have high levels of knowledge intensive manufacturing and service sectors, and of global trade participation is presented. An increasing "hourglass profile" of incomes is emerging, with increasingly adverse income distribution implications and widening income inequalities in the Megalopolis metro areas.

Chapter 8 concludes the book.

Notes

1 Megalopolis was an ancient (fourth century BC) Greek city, planned on a grandiose scale on the Peloponnese Peninsula to accommodate the population of 40 local villages (Baigent 2004). The residents of that city have been described as "Megalopolitan."

2 Gottmann's book (1961) had a prescient chapter on "The White Collar Revolution," with an emphasis on the "office industry" whose "essential raw material is information." To some extent, his discussion in this book is relevant to the

contemporary transition from an industrial to a Knowledge Economy (a transition well underway now in the Megalopolis), as noted in this chapter and elaborated in Chapter 4 of the book. Further, Jean Gottmann's work was highly influential, promoting work on large city regions. At a time when social commentators such as Patrick Geddes and Lewis Mumford weighed in against large urban agglomerations and their "uncontrolled and undesirable growth," Gottmann (1961) celebrated urban size and growth, expressed his faith in the Boston-Washington DC region's robust entrepreneurialism (Baigent 2004). He believed that the dense metropolitan areas of the Megalopolis provided opportunities for experimentation, exchanges of ideas and knowledge, promoting cross-fertilization of new ideas and innovations. Gottmann's view—expressed five decades ago—of the dynamism of the Megalopolis and its role as an incubator of new economic trends has been prescient.

3 Other examples of such creative regions or Knowledge Economies are: Bay Area and Silicon Valley, Los Angeles, Seattle, London, Paris, Tokyo, Milan, Munich, Stockholm, Sydney, etc.

4 Further, the multivalent and multimodal transport system resulting from this combination of physical and institutional transport innovations in turn unleashes various economic mechanisms and processes which govern the broader economic consequences of transport investments in the region. Such economic mechanisms— gains from trade, technology diffusion, and gains from agglomeration induced by transport—enhance total factor productivity and gross regional product over time in the Megalopolis (as elaborated in Chapter 3).

5 Anticipating the findings in Chapter 5, this can be traced to the rise of the Knowledge Economy and knowledge intensive financial, business, professional, and technical services greatly enhanced economic and demographic opportunities in the Megalopolis. New York, Washington DC, and Boston have been particular demographic beneficiaries from these favorable economic developments.

6 For example, Chandler (1977) discusses how railroads, in an earlier time period, transformed retailing by allowing nationwide catalog sales. David and Wright (1999) also discuss historical examples of transformation of economies by GPTs.

References

Alter, C., Hage, J., 1993. *Organizations Working Together*, Newbury Park, CA: SAGE Publications.

Baigent, E., 2004. Patrick Geddes, Lewis Mumford, and Jean Gottmann: divisions over Megalopolis, *Progress in Human Geography*, 28, 687–700.

Basu, S., Fernald, J., 2006. *Information and Communication Technologies as a GPT: Evidence from US Industry Data*, Federal Reserve Bank of San Francisco, Working Paper, 2006-29.

Bogue, D., 1951. *State Economic Areas*, Washington DC: US Bureau of the Census.

Bryson, J.R., Daniels, P.W., 2007. *The Handbook of Service Industries,* Northampton, MA: Edward Elgar.

Camagni, R., 2004. Uncertainty, social capital, and community governance: the city as a Milieu. In Capello, R., Nijkamp, P. (eds) *Urban Dynamics and Growth: Advances in Urban Economics*, Amsterdam: Elsevier, pp. 121–149.

Capello, R., 2011. Innovation and productivity: local competitiveness and the role of space. In Cooke, P., Asheim, B., Boschama, R., Martin, R., Schwartz, D., Tödtling, F. (eds) *Handbook of Regional Innovation and Growth*, Northampton, MA: Edward Elgar, pp. 107–119.

Chandler, A.D., 1977. *The Visible Hand.* Cambridge, MA: Harvard University Press.

Chatterjee, L., Lakshmanan, T.R., 2006. The Fashioning of Dynamic Competitive Advantage of Entrepreneurial Cities: Role of Social and Political Entrepreneurship. A chapter of the *Festschrift for Borje Johansson* (eds) Åke Andersson and Charlie Karlsson, Northampton, MA: Edward Elgar.

Cooke, P., Asheim, B., Boschama, R., Martin, R., Schwartz, D., Tödtling, F., 2011. *Handbook of Regional Innovation and Growth*, Northampton, MA: Edward Elgar.

David, P.A., Wright, G., 1999. General purpose technologies and surges in productivity: historical reflections on the future of the ICT Revolution. Presented at the symposium on economic challenges of the 21st century in a historical perspective, Oxford, 2–4 July 1999.

Feldman, M.P., 2000. Location and innovation: the new economy geography of innovation, spillovers, and agglomeration. In Clark, G., Feldman, M., Gerler, M. (eds) *The Oxford Handbook of Economic Geography*, Oxford: Oxford University Press, pp. 373–394.

Gertler, M.S., 2003. Tacit knowledge and the economic geography of context, or the undefinable tacitness of being (there). *Journal of Economic Geography* 3(1), 75–99.

Gottmann, J., 1957. Megalopolis or the urbanized Northeastern seaboard. *Economic Geography* 33(3), 189–200.

Gottmann, J., 1961. *Megalopolis: The Urbanized Northeastern Seaboard of the United States*, Cambridge, MA: MIT Press.

Gottmann, J., 1987. *Megalopolis Revisited: 25 Years Later*, College Park, MD: The University of Maryland, Institute for Urban Studies.

Granovetter, M., 1985. Economic action and social structure: the problem of embeddedness. *American Journal of Sociology* 91(3), 481–510.

Helpman, E., Trajtenberg, M., 1998. Diffusion of general purpose technologies. In Helpman, E. (ed.) *General Purpose Technologies and Economic Growth*, Cambridge, MA: MIT Press.

Kox, H.L.M., Rubalcaba, L., 2007. *Business Services and the Changing Structure of European Economic Growth*, CPB Memorandum 183, CPB Netherlands Bureau for Economic Policy Analysis.

Kuznets, S.S., 1965. *Economic Growth and Structure*, New York: Norton.

Lakshmanan, T. R., 2011. The broader economic consequences of transport infrastructure investments. *Journal of Transport Geography* 19(1), 1–11.

Lakshmanan, T.R., Anderson, W.P., 2002. *Transport Infrastructure, Freight Services Sector and Economic Growth: A White Paper*, prepared for the US Department of Transportation.

Lakshmanan, T.R., Anderson, W.P., Song, Y., Li, D., 2009. *Broader Economic Consequences of Transport Infrastructure: The Case of Economic Evolution in Dynamic Transport Corridors*, Boston University Center for Transportation Studies, Working Paper.

Lakshmanan, T.R., Button, K.J., 2009. Institutions and regional economic development. In: Cappello, R., Nijkamp, P. (eds) *Advances in Regional Economics*, Cheltenham: Edward Elgar, pp. 443–460.

Lakshmanan, T.R., Chatterjee, L.R., 2006. The entrepreneurial city in the global marketplace. *International Journal of Entrepreneurship and Innovation Management* 6(3), 155–172.

Lakshmanan, T.R., Kuhl, B., Anderson, W.P., Chatterjee, L., 2006. *Highway Development Corridors: Evidence of Growth Effects Along US Interstate Corridors. Phase I Study Report.* A report prepared for the US Department of Transportation, Federal Highway Administration. Office of Policy Analysis. March 2006.

Lipsey, R.G., Carlaw, K.I., Beker, C.T., 2005. *Economic Transformations: General Purpose Technologies and Long Term Economic Growth*, Oxford: Oxford University Press.

Malecki, E.J., Moriset, B., 2008. *The Digital Economy: Business Organization, Production Processes and Regional Developments*, Abingdon & New York: Routledge.

Polyanyi, K., 1944. *The Great Transformation: Political and Economic Origins of Our Time*, New York: Beacon Press.

Mokyr, J., 2002. *Useful Knowledge as an Evolving System: The View from Economic History*, Paper presented at the Conference on The Economy as an Evolving System, Sante Fe, NM.

Sassen, S., 2001. *The Global City: New York, London, Tokyo*, Princeton, NJ: Princeton University Press.

Saxenian, A.L., 1994. *Regional Advantage: Culture and Competition in Silicon Valley and Route 128*, Cambridge, MA: Harvard University Press.

Scott, A.J., 1998. *Regions and the World Economy: The Coming Shape of Global Production, Competition and Political Order*, Oxford: Oxford University Press.

Spence, M., Hlatshwayo, S., 2011. *The Evolving Structure of the American economy and the Employment Challenge,* Working Paper, Council on Foreign Relations, Maurice R. Greenberg Center for Geoeconomic Studies.

Stehrer, R., Foster, N., de Vries, G., 2012. *Value Added and Factors in Trade: A Comprehensive Approach*, Working Paper No. 80, The Vienna Institute for International Economic Studies.

Storper, M., 1995. The resurgence of regional economies, ten years later: the region as a nexus of untraded interdependencies. *European Urban and Regional Studies* 2(3), 191–221.

2 Demographic, Urban, and Economic Evolution in the Megalopolis

1. Introduction

The French geographer, Jean Gottmann (1957, 1961), pioneered the conceptualization of the urbanized northeast seaboard of the United States—stretching from Southern New Hampshire and Maine to Northern Virginia across metropolitan areas of Boston, New York, Philadelphia, and Baltimore-Washington DC and bounded by the Appalachian Mountains to the west and the Atlantic Ocean to the east—as the Megalopolis. Gottmann built upon Bogue's (1951) innovative idea of "metropolitan state economic areas," where "the non-agricultural economy is a closely integrated unit and is distinctly different from the economy of areas which lie outside the orbit or close contact with the Metropolis." Gottmann (1961) deduced "the continuity of a *metropolitan economy*" from a little north of Boston to a little south of Washington. Gottmann recommended the abandonment of the idea of a city "as a tightly settled agglomeration of persons, economic activities in a small geographical area clearly separated from its non-urban surroundings."

Gottmann (1961) exhaustively mapped and characterized the string of cities from Boston to Washington, including New York, Philadelphia, Baltimore, and several smaller cities, not as independent metropolitan centers, but as an integrated urban system, linked together by a high density of transportation and communication infrastructure and flows. This multinucleated urban field, which he called "Megalopolis," predated the Interstate Highway system, but the construction of the I-95 connecting all of its major centers reinforced its integrity. His contribution (1961) lies in his recognition of the "urban character" of Megalopolis. What began as trading posts and harbor settlements in the Atlantic seaboard well over three centuries ago had coalesced into many urban centers in the Mercantile Era and subsequently into large cities such as Boston, New York, Philadelphia, and Baltimore in the subsequent industrial era. By the mid-twentieth century, these large cities clearly extended beyond an individual city region. The Megalopolis concept recognizes this fact and suggests a new geography to highlight emerging complex linkages among the various urban and regional economies. Thus Gottmann views the Megalopolis—as noted earlier—as a clustered network of cities, a poly-nucleated interactive network rather than a centralized urban region.

The Megalopolis makes up only a very small fraction of the US land mass. The entire region, which extends from Southern New Hampshire and Maine to N. Virginia, includes only about 50 thousand square miles, less than 2 percent of the nation's land area—smaller than the state of Illinois, with its 57,915 sq. miles. However, this region accounted in year 2010 for 20 percent of the nation's Gross Domestic Product and 17 percent of its population. From the time of the American Revolution the Megalopolis has been the richest and most powerful region of the United States. This relatively small area contains the most prosperous, well-educated, productive, and serviced population, its largest and most important centers of financial and governmental power, and its greatest concentrations of wealth.

In the four decades following the 1950s, Gottmann's Megalopolis has experienced many demographic and economic changes—growth, decline, evolution, and spatial spread of its urban areas. The demographic evolution of the Megalopolis region over several decades reveals several interesting *urban* aspects. The progression of urban development in the Megalopolis over the period from 1945 to 1990, as revealed in Figures 2.1 and 2.2, indicates *different stages of urbanization process* in the Megalopolis. In 1945, at the end of World War II, one notices the *industrial era urban pattern*. This phase of urbanization is characterized by manufacturing production and working class households concentrated in dense cities. Such cities are sharply differentiated from the surrounding rural areas. Figure 2.1 shows this urban-rural differentiated settlement pattern of the industrial era in the Megalopolis at the end of World War II. Figure 2.2 displays the quite different spatial patterns of urbanization toward the end of the twentieth century. The advent of the massive Interstate Highway System in 1957 made cheaper land available at the urban peripheries, which combined with rising affluence and tax policies promoting home ownership in the US led to extensive suburbanization, central city decline, and expansion of cities into extensive metropolitan regions and "edge cities."

Figure 2.3 presents the fine-grained urban evolution along the Megalopolis, differentiating the urban growth over the decades from 1950 to 2000 (Morrill 2006). There is in this half century a modest growth (approximately 75 percent) of urban population, and a 300 percent increase in the urbanized area—the consequent dropping urban density reflecting the growth of suburbs and exurbs. In the three decades from 1972 to 2002, the five major metro areas in the Megalopolis had a modest growth in population. But this period actually comprised two different sub periods. The first half (1972–1987) was a more or less a stationary period for the four large metro areas and one of even population loss for the largest metro area of New York. As elaborated below, with their economies dominated (in the 1960s to the 1980s) by declining manufacturing industries, both metropolitan Philadelphia and Baltimore were nearly stationary, and New York suffered population loss. Boston—which

Figure 2.1 Urban Centers in the Megalopolis

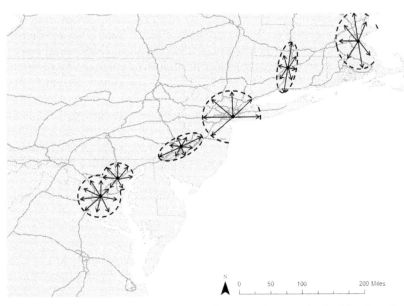

Figure 2.2 Suburbanization and Metropolitan Development in the Megalopolis

Source: adapted from Bergstrom (2007).

Figure 2.3 Population and Urbanized Area Growth in the Megalopolis, 1950–2000

Source: Morrill (2006).

had entered the phase of its industrial decline earlier than the other metro areas and had begun to restructure itself—registered a minor population growth. In the subsequent period (1987–2007), the rise of the knowledge intensive production and financial, business, professional, and technical services greatly enhanced economic and demographic opportunities in the Megalopolis. New York, Washington DC, and Boston have been particular demographic beneficiaries from these favorable economic developments.

In the time frame of the 1960s to the 1980s, the Megalopolis region also experienced a parallel decline and restructuring of manufacturing industries which had dominated the region's economy for the previous century. The Megalopolis began experiencing progressively declining shares of national manufacturing employment as such activities migrated to the lower cost locations in the US and the world. Employment in manufacturing industries grew in the Megalopolis in the 1960s and 1970s at a slower rate than in the nation and *declined* by close to 25 percent by 1992 and even by a steeper pace by 2007 (Table 2.1). The nation's decline in manufacturing industries appears to have started later than in the Megalopolis and has proceeded at a gentler pace.

Table 2.1 Evolution of Manufacturing Industries in the Megalopolis and the US, 1963–2007

	Megalopolis				US			
	1963	1977	1992	2007	1963	1977	1992	2007
Number of employees (1,000)	3,316	3,517	2,860	1,650	16,961	19,590	18,205	13,396
Value added* ($ millions)	226,165	307,862	307,885	271,833	1,226,069	1,885,857	1,983,207	2,244,264

* 2005 dollars.

Sources: US Census Bureau, Census of Manufacturers, Washington DC, 1963, 1977 and 1992; Economic Census 2007.

However, in the most recent three decades to the present day, there has been a remarkable reversal of regional economic decline and indeed a notable economic resurgence in the metropolitan areas of the Megalopolis. While employment in many economic sectors of the industrial era continued to decline, a variety of knowledge intensive production and service sector enterprises have arrived and continue to grow in the several metro areas of the Megalopolis.[1] These enterprises represent *first*, a shift away from production that is dependent on material resources, physical capital, and low skill labor to one which increasingly exploits knowledge as the key ingredient of competitiveness and innovation, and *second, the emergence of* knowledge intensive business services (KIBS), which exploit the economies of scale in human capital, and which promote knowledge dissemination and productivity effects in other parts of the economy. These economic clusters now represent large concentrations of high quality human, cultural, and organizational capital, and of some vibrant "Knowledge Metropolises" (e.g. Boston, New York, Philadelphia, Washington-Baltimore, etc.). Indeed, these metropolises have become large constellations of knowledge intensive production and service activities, *yielding rising levels of output per capita and the mega knowledge region of Megalopolis* (Figure 2.4).

Figure 2.4 The Megalopolis Region

Megalopolis refers in this study to metropolitan areas lying on the I-95 corridor stretching from Lewiston-Auburn MSA to Washington-Arlington-Alexandria MSA. Following the MSA definition by Census Bureau in 2005, there were 29 MSAs in this area.

   With a population of over 52 million in 2010, the Gross Regional Product of the Megalopolis has climbed up to 2.92 trillion dollars. Indeed, if the Megalopolis in 2010 were an independent country, its economy would be the *sixth largest in the world*, right after that of Germany—which has a larger population (Table 2.2).

   The aim of this chapter is to offer an empirical and discursive profile of the Megalopolis region in terms of the demographic, urban, and economic evolution—rise and fall of cities and metropolises, deindustrialization, economic restructuring, and resurgence as a Knowledge Economy—over the last five plus decades since Gottmann's christening of the region. In this period the Megalopolis experienced a multi-decade industrial decline and restructuring, but has recently been able to innovate and create a new vibrant economy, where knowledge is the source of value and wealth.

   The next section offers a brief survey of the rise of growth of settlements, ports, towns, and economic activities in pre-industrial (seventeenth century to early nineteenth century) Megalopolis. Section 3 highlights the rise and rapid growth of an innovative industrial economy in the Megalopolis, an early industrializing region of the world. Section 4 offers an interpretive account of the recent half century of deindustrialization and the transformation of Megalopolis into the contemporary Knowledge Economy.

2. Pre-Industrial Megalopolis

Native American groups were, prior to the arrival of European traders and settlers, the inhabitants of the space comprising present day Megalopolis and

Table 2.2 International Rank of the Megalopolis Economy, 2010

Ranking	Country/Region	Gross Domestic Product (Purchasing Power Parity—$)
1	USA	14.991 Trillion
2	China	10.105 Trillion
3	Japan	4.327 Trillion
4	India	4.122 Trillion
5	Germany	3.079 Trillion
6	MEGALOPOLIS	2.970 Trillion (Gross Regional Product)

Sources: World Bank WDI Historical GDP, 1/31/2014, America 2050 www.america2050.org.

subsisted through a combination of agriculture and hunting and gathering. To the early arrivals into the region from Europe—the Dutch and the English traders—the various Indian tribes provided trading opportunities and access to the riches that lay west of the Appalachian Mountains. However, as European settlement picked up its pace over time and expanded further west, further economic and political participation of the indigenous people in the country's development weakened and faded.

The Megalopolis region was favorably located for economic growth under the system of colonial trade that existed in the seventeenth and eighteenth centuries. It had numerous safe harbors, most with navigable rivers connecting to hinterlands with great agricultural potential. These became the economic and political centers of the colonies: Boston, New York, Philadelphia, and Baltimore—which, along with Charleston, were the largest cities along the coast—and smaller centers such as Providence and Portland (Figure 2.5).

After independence from Britain, the US expanded in earnest to the regions west of the Appalachian Mountains. In this process, low cost access to the Great Lakes, Midwest, and beyond became a critical factor for further economic expansion and city growth. New York with its excellent and extensive harbor and easy low cost access to the Great Lakes and the Midwest, via the Hudson and Mohawk rivers and the Erie Canal (and later the New York Central Railroad), won out over Philadelphia, Baltimore, and Boston in this race to the dominance among cities in terms of the economy and population (Figure 2.5). By the middle of the nineteenth century, New York had double the combined population of Philadelphia and Boston to become the dominant city in the nation in the pre-industrial era United States—a position it continues to retain today.

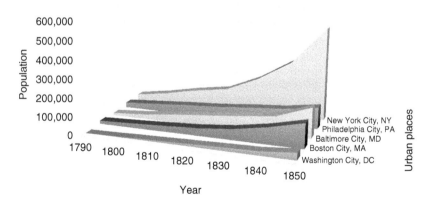

Figure 2.5 Major Urban Centers in Pre-Industrial Megalopolis

Source: US Census, population of the 100 largest cities and other urban places in the United States, 1790–1990.

3. Rise and Evolution of the Industrial Era in the Megalopolis

At the beginning of the nineteenth century, most residents of the Megalopolis resided in farms producing much of the food they ate. By the last quarter of that century, however, a high proportion of workers in the Megalopolis (and the majority in New England, the first industrializing region in the US) were wage laborers toiling in and buying their food in urban markets. This shift of a large number of people in the Megalopolis from agricultural activities to industry, from older to newer modes of production, transport, and communications, and from rural to urban locations is the process of *industrialization* of the Megalopolis. Commercial cities became industrialized and new manufacturing cities grew rapidly. More broadly, industrialization involves the capacity of a society to innovate, create, and to make the relevant economic and social investments and to engage in self-transformation, a capacity driven by technical and social knowledge (Lakshmanan 1993).

Several geographical factors encouraged industrial development in the nineteenth century in the cities of Megalopolis. Many cities were ports, facilitating international trade. Further, many had developed access to raw materials and markets in the interior through investments in transport (sail and steam shipping) and communications (telegraph and cable). Such access was augmented by the railroads that came into common use after the 1830s radiating from cities such as New York, Boston, Philadelphia, and Baltimore to the Great Lakes and the Corn Belt. The Megalopolis also possessed abundant water power in New England, and especially along the *Fall Line*, which represents the head of navigation of many eastern rivers and the transition between the Atlantic coast and the Piedmont. Major industrial centers—New York, Trenton, Philadelphia, and Baltimore—are located along the Fall Line (Figure 2.6).

The rise of New York in the early nineteenth century—resulting from the Hudson-Mohawk-Erie canal route—was further accelerated by technological changes that moved ocean shipping from a point-to-point system to a hub and spoke system early in the nineteenth century; New York's geography made it the natural hub of this system in the east coast (Glaeser 2005). As a major transhipment point between inland water, rail, and marine transportation, New York was a point of high accessibility to material inputs and markets, making it a favorable location for manufacturing. As transportation networks became increasingly focused on New York, its manufacturing industries gained scale economies, reinforcing its dominance in both trade and production.

Philadelphia first grew as a trading center, exporting agricultural produce from its rich hinterland to markets along the coast and across the ocean. A trade embargo during the war of 1812 may actually have provided impetus for a shift from trade to production activities. Philadelphia soon became an important manufacturing center in paper-related and leather footwear industries. Connections to coal and iron mines via new roads, canals, and railroads

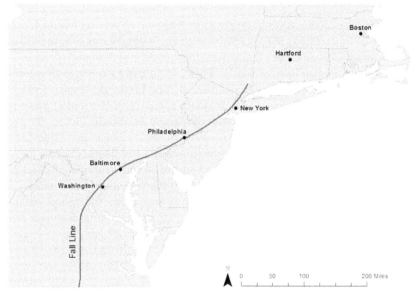

Figure 2.6 Cities Along the Fall Line

in the nineteenth century gave Philadelphia a locational advantage as manufacturing industries shifted to steam driven technologies and metals-based products.

A useful way to highlight the key features of and the factors underlying the arrival, growth, and evolution over time of modern industries in the entire Megalopolis region is to offer a synoptic view of the major dimensions of the industrialization process from the early nineteenth century to middle twentieth century in New England—the pioneering industrializing region in America.

In the pre-industrial era, New England exhibited a relatively diverse economy with many small mills and shops producing wood and metal products and apparel. From this base of small-scale industry, a large scale and technologically advanced manufacturing sector was to emerge.

New England possessed in the early nineteenth century a relative abundance of institutional and human capital supportive of industrialization (Lakshmanan 1993; Temin 1999). *First*, the region's institutional environment (derived from the Anglo-American culture and Puritanical roots)—in the form of stable government and laws and predictable judicial processes—supported new enterprises, allowing them to sprout and flourish. *Second*, the New England states pioneered and invested early and heavily in education and human capital development, creating a highly productive labor force. Labor productivity of the better educated industrial workers in New England by the mid-nineteenth century exceeded that of industrial workers in England, the pioneer industrializer (Temin 1999). Some of the New England industrial entrepreneurs in this context made successful transitions from old to new industries, from small to large firms, from old to new technology, and implemented innovations in the areas of finance, management, and the use of a more educated labor force.[2] The synergy between the skill of industrial leaders and of the educated hard-working operatives (mostly women in the textile industry) promoted rapid industrialization in New England (Temin 1999).

The early success of a large scale modern industry in the textile plant in Lowell, Massachusetts represented a convergence of several factors. It was a new technology (the power loom), which made possible very large scale operations and the consequent economies of scale. To realize such scale economies, several operational innovations were instituted in terms of efficient procedures of mill operation, improved methods of training and management of labor, and procedures to keep the mill machinery in good repair. The raising of the large amount of capital needed for such large factories was facilitated by a financial innovation, namely, *the joint stock company*. Finally, the US government provided tariff protection for this "infant industry."

A major industrial innovation developed in New England in the nineteenth century was the production process known as *the American system of manufactures*, based on the use of interchangeable parts. While the textile industry was a dominant sector, it paved the way for the rise and rapid growth of a variety of machinery industries. The work experience gained from keeping the cotton textile factory machinery in good repair led to spinoffs of enterprises which developed machine tools that cut, shape, and finish manufactured products. Thus, New England firms branched into making of machinery for sectors such as firearms, paper, locomotives, clocks, and watches (Browne 2003).[3]

The rise of the machinery industries (and indeed the diverse industries in New England) was facilitated by the American system. The core idea behind this system is to break down a complex product (e.g. a rifle or a clock) into many components, each of which can be fabricated on a large scale by machinery and reassembled for the market at lower overall costs. Temin (1999) notes that this technical innovation in the form of higher *quality of machinery* conferred on New England workers in the nineteenth century higher levels of labor productivity as compared to industrial labor in England. Based largely on its burgeoning manufacturing industry, by the mid-nineteenth century New England was one of the most prosperous regions of the country—and the world.

The rise and growth of industrial activities in the Mid-Atlantic towns of Megalopolis from the mid-nineteenth to the middle of the twentieth century was also quite robust. Further, the overall industrial and economic performance of the Megalopolis in this period was greatly enhanced by physical linkages and market expansion made possible by the expansion of railroads to the Midwest.

The expansion of US railroads from the Megalopolis all the way to the west coast in the second half of the nineteenth century triggered an economic feedback effect. Railroads made possible things like commercial agriculture, expanded postal services, wholesaling, and other activities, which in turn expanded demand for more and better rail service. Figure 2.7 highlights some of these parallel technical, market, and institutional developments that yielded additional economic effects. The cumulative effects set in motion by rail transportation technology transformed the economies not only of the American interior and west, but also of the Megalopolis (Fishlow 1965; Chandler 1965).

Only a selective listing of the cascade of the economic stimuli that arose from cost and time savings due to railroad expansion in nineteenth century from the Northeast US to the Midwest first and later to the rest of the country is possible here. As the producers, consumers, and labor experienced lower costs and increased accessibility due to railroads a successive series of economic impacts ensued. These include expansion of settlements and agriculture in the Midwest, which in turn led to market expansion and regional integration. There was regional specialization in agriculture and industry and the gains from trade, promotion of volume production, and the realization of scale economies. The railroads promoted the rise of a wholesaling sector, leading to a logistical revolution. Such were the general equilibrium effects of railroad investments.

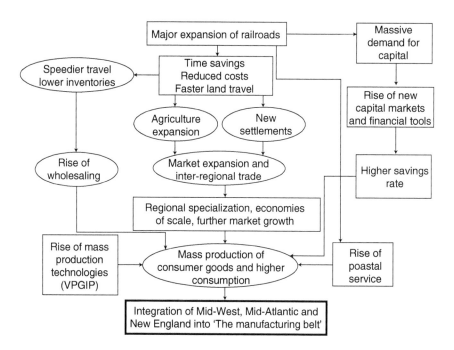

Figure 2.7 US Railroad Expansion and the Rise of the "The Manufacturing Belt"

Not only did railroad expansion promote new markets and services, the huge capital requirements for railroad growth induced the development of financial institutions providing investment opportunities that increased the national savings rates. With increasing capacity to move industrial inputs and outputs over long distances, mass production techniques such as VPGIP (Volume Production of Goods with Interchangeable Parts) developed, first in New England industries such as firearms, but eventually expanded into a broad range of goods, thereby expanding markets, income, and consumption. Railroads also promoted the complementary communication service (US Postal Service). All this led to a regime of mass production, distribution (mail order retailing), and consumption of goods. In the longer term, railroad expansion made possible the integration of the Megalopolis to the Midwest to form the "Manufacturing Belt" of the US (Chandler 1965; Lakshmanan and Anderson 2007; Kim and Margo 2003).

The economic growth in the industrial era was accompanied by rapid urbanization in the Megalopolis. Table 2.3 shows the steady growth of population over a century in the five major industrializing crowded central cities of the Megalopolis.

4. Deindustrialization and the Rise of Knowledge Economy in the Megalopolis

In the quarter century following Jean Gottmann's designation of the Northeast as the Megalopolis (1957, 1961), that region and its metropolitan centers experienced industrial decline and restructuring with declining regional shares of national manufacturing output and employment, and the spatial spillovers of population and economic activities from central city to suburban and exurban space, to other regions in the US, and abroad (Tables 2.4, 2.5, and 2.6). The variety of factors underlying this decline of output and employment in manufacturing, the spatial spread and spillover

Table 2.3 Population of the Central Cities in the Major Metro Areas of the Megalopolis in the "Industrial Era"

	1800	*1850*	*1900*	*1950*
New York City, NY	60,515	515,547	3,437,202	7,891,957
Philadelphia City, PA	41,220	121,376	1,293,697	2,071,605
Baltimore City, MD	26,514	169,054	508,957	949,708
Boston City, MA	24,937	136,881	560,892	801,444
Washington City, DC	3,210	40,001	278,718	802,178

Source: US Bureau of the Census. population of the 100 largest cities and urban places in the US, 1790–1990, www.census.gov/population/www.census.gov/econ/census.

Table 2.4 Megalopolis' Population Share to National Population, 1970–2010

1970	1975	1980	1985	1990	1995	2000	2005	2010
20.2	19.3	18.2	17.9	17.6	17.1	16.9	16.6	16.2

Table 2.5 Population Growth in Selected MSAs (Population Growth as % Change)

MSA	1970–1980	1980–1990	1990–2000	2000–2010
New York	−4.16	3.12	8.67	3.09
Philadelphia	−1.63	3.84	4.56	4.89
Boston	0.45	4.84	6.41	3.56
DC	8.34	21.22	16.49	16.35
Baltimore	5.18	8.49	6.98	6.14
Megalopolis	0.46	6.46	8.10	5.58
US	11.49	9.86	13.05	9.62

Table 2.6 Megalopolis' Employment and Earnings Share to National Level, 1970–2010

		1970	1975	1980	1985	1990	1995	2000	2005	2010
Employment	Manufacturing	22.25	19.98	19.27	18.79	16.10	14.07	13.43	12.16	11.95
	All	21.33	19.74	18.92	19.20	18.52	17.21	17.02	17.03	17.29
Earnings	Manufacturing	22.96	20.79	19.39	19.70	18.52	16.58	16.42	14.06	14.17
	Private non-farming	24.49	22.21	20.76	22.18	23.12	21.69	21.85	21.68	22.47

of urban industries and population from central cities to suburban space are well documented. Such factors include the lowered monetary and time cost of access to metropolitan and national locations provided by the Interstate Highway System, the emerging land-intensive layouts of factories, and the lure of lower labor and land costs in urban peripheries and outside the Megalopolis (as compared to high wage/income Megalopolis). The economic fortunes of central cities declined as compared to those of the suburbs and exurbs in the expanding metropolitan areas (Figure 2.3).

Figure 2.8 shows that population growth has been relatively slow in the Megalopolis region, with all metro areas except Washington DC growing more slowly than the US as a whole in all decades from the 1970s to 2010. Figure 2.8 shows the progression over four decades (1970–2010) of population, employment (manufacturing, and all non-farming sectors), and total earnings (manufacturing and all non-farming sectors) in the Megalopolis in terms of national shares. The Megalopolis share of national population declined steadily in the first two decades, but this decline is at a gentler pace in the last two decades (Figure 2.9). There is a similar pattern to the national shares of total employment, except that total employment shares in the Megalopolis are always higher than that of population—showing an upward shift in per capita levels of employment in the Megalopolis as compared to the nation.

However, the manufacturing employment of this region relative to the nation drops sharply since 1990, indicating sharper regional decline of the manufacturing sector. However, the earnings shares of the Megalopolis in the manufacturing sector stay higher than the employment shares in the entire period (and more so in the last two decades). In the last two decades, the earnings per manufacturing worker in the Megalopolis are higher, suggesting a higher proportion of high value-adding (more knowledge intensive) sectors remaining in the region—as compared to the sector components being outsourced to the rest of the world.

The Megalopolis shares of national total (non-farm) earnings have dropped in the 1970–1990 period, but have since held more or less steady, reflecting the faster growth in the knowledge intensive higher wage service sectors. However, the Megalopolis shares of total non-farm earnings remains

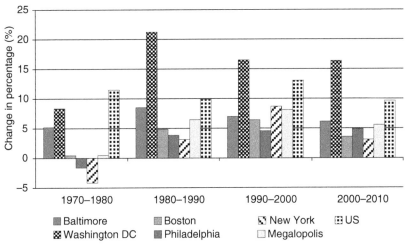

Figure 2.8 Population Change in the US and Five MSAs in the Megalopolis, 1970–2010

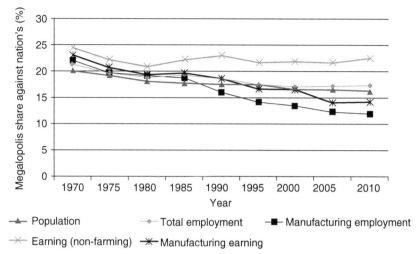

Figure 2.9 Megalopolis: National Shares of Population, Employment, and Earnings

Source: Bureau of Economic Analysis, US Department of Commerce.

high—6 percent higher than population shares in 2010—suggesting that earnings per employee are higher in the Megalopolis than in the nation.

Recent Transition to the Knowledge Economy in the Megalopolis

As noted above, many metropolitan areas in the Megalopolis have experienced economic decline in the recent past, as their manufacturing sectors lost their competitive edge. They had to confront the dislocations of post-industrial society and the dead ends of economic decline. However, some of the urban regions in the Megalopolis (e.g. Boston, New York, and Washington DC) have, in the most recent quarter century, reinvented themselves as hubs of creativity and development, creating jobs utilizing knowledge in technical, economic, social, and cultural fields.

The combination of physical and natural resources and low to moderate skill labor characterized the mid-twentieth century industrial economy. The Knowledge Economy emerging in the late twentieth century Megalopolis, in contrast, exhibits an increasing role of knowledge as a factor of production and its impact on human capital, production, organization, and innovation. The central feature of IT and knowledge revolution—namely the very low (virtually zero marginal) cost of collecting, storing, and transmitting information—leads to the *pervasiveness and application* of knowledge to very many aspects of the economy, particularly in the context of a globalizing economy of the Megalopolis.

Further, the Knowledge Economy is promoted by its location in knowledge and production networks in the spatial urban clusters in the major metropolises. In view of the increasing complexity, rising cost, and the expanding scope of emerging technologies, firms increasingly collaborate and supplement their capabilities in technology-based alliances. Further, enterprises co-locate in these urban agglomerations to take advantage of the ability to share understanding (tacit knowledge) and generate further knowledge. Thus locations such as large metropolitan areas that are attractive to knowledge assets are crucial to the economic growth and vitality of a region like the Megalopolis. Finally, information, unlike physical goods, is *non-rival*—not destroyed in consumption—and can be utilized repeatedly. Hence, the social return on investment in the generation of knowledge can be vastly enhanced through its diffusion.

It is in this context, in the last three decades to the present day, a remarkable *reversal* of regional economic decline and indeed a notable economic resurgence have occurred in the metropolitan areas of the Megalopolis. A variety of knowledge intensive production and service sector enterprises have arrived and continue to grow in the several metropolitan areas of the Megalopolis. The old industrial metros of Boston and New York are well advanced in this transition to Knowledge Economies and Washington DC (with large public, health, and scientific sectors) is emerging as a vibrant creative region. These metropolises, representing large concentrations of high quality human, cultural, and organizational capital, are the vibrant contemporary "Knowledge Regions," which jointly make up the mega region of the Megalopolis.

The proliferation of such economic structural changes characterizes the passage from a declining regional industrial economy to an emerging Knowledge Economy in the Megalopolis. This book argues that the passage to the Knowledge Economy requires the rise and development of a *knowledge infrastructure*, comprising of four interacting components. The first two, a) transport and b) ICT infrastructure, physically and virtually link activities and provide low cost access for economic actors. The resulting combination of enhanced links among and improved and heightened access to economic agents in a globalizing economy promotes economic structural changes. The passage to the Knowledge Economy requires, in addition, two other components of the knowledge infrastructure. One is c) innovations in *production and service technologies that nurture and commercialize new industrial products and operations and the structural evolution toward a Knowledge intensive Service Economy*. The emergence of new knowledge intensive production occurs largely in what may be described as innovation networks which nurture and commercialize innovation and industrial adaptation in various regions. The final component is: d) *Institutional Innovations*—which support *physical, relational, and institutional proximity* among far-flung economic agents—promote new knowledge and value generation in enterprises in the Megalopolis

Atkinson and Andes (2008) have constructed a variety of economic indicators, which jointly capture the key aspects of such a transition in the nation to the new *Knowledge Economy*. Their construction of such indicators is based on the number and variety of knowledge jobs, globalization, economic dynamism, level of transfer to the digital economy, and technical innovation capacity. From such indicators, Atkinson and Andes have also fashioned an *aggregate knowledge score* at the state level for each of the 50 states in the nation for 2008.[4]

Table 2.7 identifies the top ten Knowledge Economies in the nation based on the aggregate knowledge scores.[5] *The top six and the eight of the top ten "knowledge-rich states" in the nation (as measured by the aggregate knowledge scores) are in the Megalopolis*—the rest of the Megalopolis states are in the top 20 states in the nation in terms of the evolution toward the Knowledge Economy. Clearly, the Megalopolis represents a relatively advanced Knowledge Economy in the nation.

In the Megalopolis states listed in Table 2.7, the knowledge-rich economic sectors are clustered in large metropolises centered on Boston, New York, Philadelphia, Baltimore, and Washington DC Large clusters of highly educated workforce operating in knowledge-rich sectors and interacting, with workers with similar and complementary capabilities (often face to face), generate and utilize new "useful knowledge" in productive economic activities.

In these large knowledge-rich metropolitan areas, the share in the economy of business services has grown monotonically, as the share of the manufacturing sector has been dropping. These business services (particularly KIBS) contribute heavily to the Megalopolis and US economic growth, in terms of employment, productivity, and innovation (as detailed in Chapter 4). There are two reasons for this. First, the rapid growth of the KIBS sector contributes to aggregate growth, and second KIBS yield benefits to other sectors by increasing their productivity and promoting innovation (Kox and Rubelcaba 2007; Bryson and Daniels 2007).

Table 2.7 Top Knowledge Economies in the US (Defined by Aggregated Knowledge Scores)

2008 rank	State	2008 Aggregated Score
1	Massachusetts	17.31
2	Connecticut	16.94
3	Virginia	15.82
4	Maryland	15.28
5	New York	14.75
6	Delaware	14.37
7	Washington	14.06
8	Minnesota	13.68
9	New Jersey	13.48
10	New Hampshire	12.34

Source: Atkinson and Andes (2008, p. 18).

Finally, the various processes noted here as governing the rise and growth of knowledge intensive economic activities yield two new location patterns of the Megalopolis Knowledge Economy activities. First, a variety of KIBS benefit and grow from the agglomeration economies of central locations inside large metros such as New York, Boston, and Washington. Indeed, a high proportion of the earnings in these knowledge intensive sectors occur in the core areas of the metro areas. This spatial agglomeration of KIBS within large metropolitan areas is evident in the cases of Manhattan in New York and Boston-Suffolk County in the Boston Metro region (Table 2.8).

Table 2.8 Producer Services Earnings by Industry in New York and Boston, 1988 and 2000 (2000 Billion Dollars)

Industry	US		New York		Manhattan (New York County)		Boston		Suffolk County	
	1988	2000	1988	2000	1988	2000	1988	2000	1988	2000
Banking	75.2	148.5	12.2	19.8	8.6	12.7	NA	4.2	1.0	2.1
Security	41.1	174.8	19.8	83.2	17.7	65.8	1.6	8.8	1.4	7.0
Insurance carriers	47.6	96.9	5.8	11.3	2.7	5.0	1.4	2.4	0.9	1.2
Insurance agents, brokers, and services	30.1	49.2	3.4	5.7	1.4	2.5	0.8	1.1	0.2	0.3
Holding and other investment offices	16.2	49.3	3.5	12.2	2.7	7.7	NA	2.1	0.2	1.1
Business services	136.8	490.9	18.9	46.0	8.5	21.2	5.1	18.9	1.1	3.2
Motion pictures	12.9	34.0	2.1	5.4	1.8	3.6	0.2	0.3	0.9	0.1
Legal services	70.5	127.6	11.1	16.9	7.4	10.0	2.0	3.9	1.3	2.6
Engineering and management services	103.2	253.6	13.5	26.3	6.6	12.6	4.5	11.9	1.5	3.8
Miscellaneous services	9.9	23.1	1.6	1.7	1.1	1.1	0.2	NA	0.5	0.2
All producer services	543.3	1447.9	92.0	228.6	58.5	142.0	15.8	53.7	7.8	21.6
% of US total producer services	100.0	100.0	16.9	15.8	10.8	9.8	2.9	3.7	1.4	1.5

Second, another emerging development of certain knowledge intensive activities is their *economic and spatial interaction and integration across metro areas.* The urban areas of Megalopolis share a common economic history, a shared economic geography, transport (I-95 highway, Amtrak and Acela rail links, multiple airports), and educational infrastructure. The different urban centers often exhibit many similarities and complementarities, which can generate mega-regional economic clusters. The Department of City and Regional Planning, University of Pennsylvania (2006) has mapped such a functional and geographical organization of the pharmaceutical sector.

Figure 2.10 shows the functional components of the pharmaceutical sector and how they are spatially separated and functionally integrated across five metropolitan areas.

Box 2.1 Northeast Pharmaceutical Cluster

The pharmaceutical and medical cluster is one of several leading economic sectors with potential to take advantage of mega-regional scale. It has the unique advantage of having the largest agglomeration of pharmaceutical firms in the world, four of the top ten biotechnology clusters in the country, access to the necessary venture capital, and strong clusters of chemical manufacturing, insurance, medical device manufacturing, hospitals, and research institutions. In addition, the industry has the advantage of reorganizing its vertical and horizontal structure in such a way as to promote greater diversification across a larger geographic area. Where previously large pharmaceutical firms held a majority of their operations in close proximity to headquarters, now certain functions are located in areas that have improved access to resources, workforce, and lower cost. For example, independent biotechnology firms are now generators of new drug patents. Successful biotechnology clusters tend to locate near strong universities and venture capital markets, not pharmaceutical headquarters. Other trends include the outsourcing of drug marketing and clinical trials. As a result of these trends, a New Economic Geography (NEG) has emerged, in which this whole industry and its network of interconnected firms and job sectors are distributed over the Megalopolis. This geographic dispersal has an underlying connection based on shared infrastructure resources and labor force that bind it to the region.

Source: University of Pennsylvania (2006).

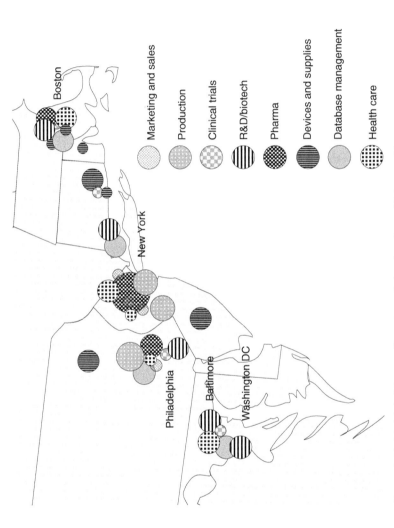

Figure 2.10 Multiple Metropolitan Knowledge (PHARMA) Sector Cluster

Source: University of Pennsylvania (2006).

Notes

1 For example, the 3.316 million manufacturing jobs in the Megalopolis in 1963 has been reduced to 1,150 million in 2007. By contrast, Megalopolis contains about 1 in 2 US workers in the financial services and insurance sectors, and over 80 percent of national securities intermediation employees.
2 In the industrial era of the nineteenth century, the Boston region reported the highest average education levels, exceeding those of Meiji Japan, Scandinavia, Prussia, and England (Lakshmanan and Chatterjee 2009). To keep wages low, the textile industry used a predominantly female labor force.
3 Indeed, The Lowell Machine Shop became a manufacturer of locomotive engines.
4 Most state economies represent a composite of the many component regional economies, which may differ in the degree to which their economic evolution corresponds to that of the "Knowledge Economy" factors.
5 The "knowledge jobs" indicators in this table measure seven aspects of knowledge-based employment: 1) employment in IT occupations in non-IT sectors; 2) the share of the workforce employed in managerial, professional, and technical occupations; 3) the education level of the workforce; 4) the average educational attainment of recent immigrants; 5) the average education attainment of recent US interstate migrants; 6) employment in high value-added manufacturing sectors; and 7) employment in high-wage traded services.

References

Atkinson, R.D., Andes, S., 2008. *The 2008 State New Economy Index: Benchmarking Economic Transformation in the States,* Washington DC: The Information Technology and Innovation Foundation, The Kauffmann Foundation.

Bergstrom, K., 2007. *Economic Development and Place-Making.* Lecture at the Graduate School of Design/Executive Education Course, Harvard University. June 10.

Bogue, D., 1951. *State Economic Areas*, Washington DC: US Bureau of the Census.

Browne, L., 2003. *Emergence of Manufacturing in 19th Century*, Boston, MA: Federal Reserve Bank of Boston.

Bryson, J.R., Daniels, P.W., 2007. *The Handbook of Service Industries,* Northampton, MA: Edward Elgar.

Chandler, A.D. Jr., 1965. *The Railroads: The Nation's First Big Business*, New York: Harcourt, Brace & World.

Fishlow, A., 1965. *American Railroads and the Transformation of the Ante-bellum Economy*, Cambridge, MA: Harvard University Press.

Glaeser, E.L., 2005. *Urban Colossus: Why is New York America's Largest City?* NBER Working Paper, WP05-05.

Gottmann, J., 1957. Megalopolis or the urbanized Northeastern seaboard. *Economic Geography* 33(3), 189–200.

Gottmann, J., 1961. *Megalopolis: The Urbanized Northeastern Seaboard of the United States*, Cambridge, MA: MIT Press.

Kim, S., Margo, R.A., 2003. Historical perspectives in US economic geography. In Henderson, V., Thisse, J-F. (eds) *Handbook of Regional and Urban Economics*: Volume 4. *Cities and Geography*, Amsterdam: Elsevier, pp. 2981–3019.

Kox, H.L.M., Rubalcaba, L., 2007. *Business Services and the Changing Structure of European Economic Growth*, CPB Memorandum 183, CPB Netherlands Bureau for Economic Policy Analysis.

Lakshmanan, T.R., 1993. Social change induced by technology: promotion and resistance. In Ackerman, N. (ed.) *The Necessity of Friction*, Heidelberg: Physica Verlag, pp. 135–158.

Lakshmanan, T.R., Anderson, W.P., 2007. Contextual determinants of transport infrastructure productivity: the need for model reformulation. In Karlsson, C., Anderson, W.P., Johansson, B., Kobayashi, K. (eds) *The Management and Measurement of Infrastructure: Performance, Efficiency and Innovation*, London: Edward Elagar, pp. 25–46.

Lakshmanan, T.R., Chatterjee, L.R., 2009. New governance institutions in the entrepreneurial urban region. *Innovation: The European Journal of Social Science Research* 22(3), 371–391.

Morrill, R., 2006. Classic map revisited: the growth of Metropolis. *Professional Geographer* 58(2), 155–160.

Temin, P., 1999. *The Industrialization of New England: 1830–1880,* NBER Working Paper Series on Historical Factors in Long Run Growth, Historical Paper 114.

University of Pennsylvania, 2006. *Megalopolis Unbound*, College Park, PA: Department of City and Regional Planning.

3 General Purpose Technologies of Transport and ICT and the Emergence of the Globalized Economies

1. Introduction

This book argues, as noted earlier, that the contemporary era of technological progress towards a Knowledge Economy and the consequent economic evolution in the Megalopolis is driven by four types of technologies and their interactive and cumulative effects. These four technologies are: *transport technologies*, *ICT*, *production technologies*, and *institutional innovations*.

This chapter will describe the nature and evolution of the first two of these technologies—Transport and ICT—in the nation and in the Megalopolis in recent decades. These technological changes have arrived in the form of new physical and organizational innovations in transport and ICT. This chapter will further argue that such transport and information innovations function as GPTs, which support and undergird a variety of *production and organizational technologies*—which jointly drive structural change and economic evolution towards the Knowledge Economy in the Megalopolis.

GPTs are a few key technologies which appear to drive critical eras of technical progress and economic growth (Breshnehan and Trajtenberg 1992; David and Wright 1999; Carlsson 2003). GPTs become pervasive in the economy in certain periods, as they are utilized as inputs by a large number of downstream sectors and with considerable potential for technical improvements and innovation. Thus, as technological progress embodied in GPTs induces productivity growth in a large variety of industries, the productivity of the whole economy is raised. The steam engine and the electric motor are commonly regarded as critical GPTs of the industrial era (David 1990; Rosenberg and Trajtenberg 2004).

Contemporary space-shrinking transport technologies and ICT, as elaborated in this chapter, facilitate the rise of global systems of investment, production, markets, and the organization of enterprises. Further, the enhanced connectivity offered by ICT among economic and social actors and ideas across great distances increases (in the sense of Schumpeter 1934) the potential for new combinations of goods and services, input sources, markets, and organizations—in other words, *technical change*.[1] Thereby, transport and ICT technologies (viewed here as GPTs) set the stage for the evolution in production and organizational technologies, which in turn pave the way to the ongoing structural evolution of the Megalopolis from a mature industrial economy towards a vibrant, globalized Knowledge Economy (as detailed in Chapter 4).

2. Physical and Organizational Transport Innovations

New Physical Technologies of the US Transport System

New physical technologies have been influential over history in the development of transport systems. A National Academy of Engineering survey of engineering breakthroughs in the twentieth century listed the automobile as the second, airplane as the third, and the interstate Highway system as the eleventh of such breakthroughs.[2]

We focus here on three transport technical innovations—in water, land, and air modes—crucial in the economic evolution of the Megalopolis in the last third of the twentieth century. The first is in water transport, namely, the development and rapid expansion of *containers* in the transport of general cargo. Innovated for international service in 1966 in a Megalopolis port by US lines on North Atlantic routes, containerized shipping tonnage has rapidly grown on the Europe–Asia and North America–Asia routes to account for 55 percent of general cargo by the mid-1990s (Hummels 1999). Containerized shipping has greatly enhanced shipping efficiency, substantially reducing port labor costs, lowering ship's port dwell time, increasing cargo holding capacity per ship ton and ship speed, and promoting intermodal inland transport of freight. While ocean shipping costs were erratic from the 1950s to the early twenty-first century—owing in part to variations in fuel costs and other factors—evidence suggests that the effect of containerization on liner costs was negative and that the effect on the efficiency of ports and inland distribution was positive (Hummels 2007).

The second technical innovation is in the area of land transportation. This is the *Interstate Highway System* (often called the largest public works project in the US) initiated in 1957 and expanded greatly over the next two decades. The Interstate offered a divided well banked highway surface that was in effect a new road technology and an improvement over prior roads—permitting speedier (65–70 miles per hour) and safer travel. This system vastly enhanced interurban and intra-urban mobility at the same time as it offered a steep drop of time and out-of-pocket costs of passenger and freight movements. The economic benefits of the Interstate accrue directly to the trucking industry, to the broader economy from improved quality of freight service, and to the final consumers (households and government). Keeler and Ying (1988) focused on just one segment of these beneficiaries—Class I trucking industry—and found that the benefits to that segment of the trucking industry ($12.84 billion) alone would have repaid (under some assumptions) 72 percent of the total costs of the Interstate Highway System.[3]

There have been a number of econometric studies assessing the broader contribution of highway capital to the productivity of the American economy (Lakshmanan and Anderson 2001). The most definitive of these studies uses a cost function (specified in a flexible functional form) to compute the rate of return of highway capital as compared to the return on private capital and the interest rate (Nadiri and Mamuneas 1996). It is high initially at around 37 percent until 1968—well above the rate of return to private capital—during a period of introduction of the new technology of high speed, safe, divided highways of the Interstate System and a period of rapid network expansions with its nonlinear effects (Figure 3.1). In the latter years, the rates of return to highway capital drops to levels closer to that of private capital, as the interstate highway system gets completed and a significant and increasing proportion of annual highway investments is intended for maintenance.

The third major technical development is the jet aircraft and the consequent technical evolution in the aviation sector and the sharp drops in the air passenger and freight prices. First, the advent of the jet aircraft greatly shortened the travel time—typically from a "block" speed of 210 miles per hour in 1954 to 433 miles per hour in the 1972–89 period—with 2.37 hours of time savings per trip (Figure 3.2). Gordon (1992) estimated the value of resultant time savings in the economy in 1989 at $182.4 billion. Second, as technical improvements in aircraft and air navigation have continued, air freight prices have continued to drop, enabling an increasing number of high value added goods being shipped by air (Table 3.1).

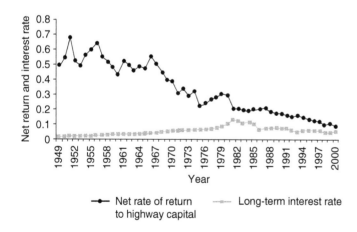

Figure 3.1 Rate of Return on Highway Capital

Source: Mamuneas and Nadiri (2003).

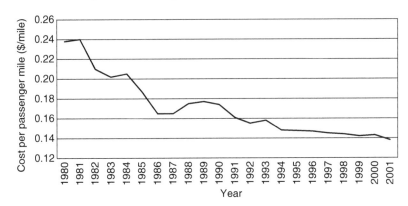

Figure 3.2 Passenger Cost of US Airline Industry, 1980–2000 (in current US $)

Source: Gang Gong (2005).

Table 3.1 Changing Air Freight Rates in Developed Nation Routes (Annualized Growth Rates)

Routes	Shipping Prices/Kg (1990s) 1973–1993	Ad-Valorem Air Freight Rate 1973–1993
North Atlantic	–2.22	–4.16
Mid Atlantic	–1.26	–3.22
South Atlantic	–1.13	–3.06
North and Mid Pacific	–2.39	–4.33
South Pacific	–1.74	–3.69
All Routes	–1.53	–3.48

Source: adapted from Hummels (1999).

Transport Organizational Innovations and the "New" Transport Networks

Reforms of transport policy initially in the US (and in many other countries since the 1980s) and the consequent supporting environment of new economic incentives and competition have led to proliferation of freight innovations. The two elements of the changing transport public policy pertain to a) overall economic governance (e.g. deregulation, privatization), and b) those governing transport physical flows (e.g. vehicle size/wt. rules, reinvented border inspection processes, etc.). Both of these policy sets influence the freight services powerfully; first, deregulation and liberalization policies, by changing economic incentives and releasing competitive forces, have enabled and motivated service and process innovations and logistical improvements; second, the changes in transport physical flow rules—less restrictions on vehicle size/ weight attributes and improved ports/ customs rules, etc.—have influenced transport capacities on transport routes and terminals and logistical potential (Lakshmanan et al. 2001). The variety of service innovations and process innovations in freight services, enabled by this combination of transport and IT and public policy reforms, promotes in turn a new set of freight service attributes and the subsequent restructuring of business logistics, as transport infrastructure attributes evolve.

There are two aspects of these transformational changes in US transportation. The first aspect deals with the major changes in the technologies, functions, and spatial reach of the production and consumption activities in the US and in the larger global economy, which define the *context* in which the transport industry operates and evolves. The second element of this literature focuses on the qualitative changes in the *scope* of the expanded and new services developed by the freight industry in response to this emerging context. Taking advantage of new technologies of transportation and information, transport institutional and policy reforms, and transport infrastructure investments, a new world of freight transport— that is a vastly transformed landscape with many elements of discontinuity and novel and profound changes from the past—has emerged in the last decade and a half (e.g. Chatterjee 2001; Lakshmanan and Anderson 2000; Lakshmanan et al. 2001).

As noted earlier, a variety of technological, socio-economic, and business factors in the last two decades have combined to erect a globally integrated production system for an increasing number of economic sectors—in the process transforming the freight services sector itself in major ways (Figure 3.3). New developments in the technologies of transportation and ICT are fundamentally transforming the space-time relationships in the US and around the world. Innovations in the complementary technologies of transportation and information have led to sharp reductions in costs, and sharp increases in the service quality (speed, time-definite delivery, high frequency, etc.). This combination of lower costs and broader and better services makes possible the nationwide and indeed worldwide search by production firms for cheaper and better materials, production components, and product marketing. This in turn requires functional integration, management, and coordination of nationally and indeed globally distributed sets of diverse corporate economic activities. The consequence is an increasing division of labor in the production processes as the component activities in many industries are further disaggregated and spatially reallocated in response to labor prices.

Recent changes in public policies in the US and other countries related to trade and transport have also promoted interregional and global economic development processes. The advent of free trade regimes (GATT, WTO, NAFTA, etc.) and liberalization policies promoted by the US has expanded US firms' international trade and capital flows in North America, Europe, Asia, and indeed all over the world. As production and consumption

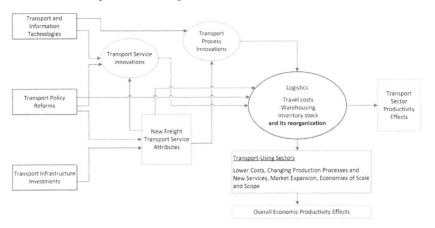

Figure 3.3 Linkages between Transport Policy and Investments, Freight Services Sector, and Overall Economic Productivity

Source: Lakshmanan et al. (2009).

technologies change in this context, production value increasingly derives from knowledge. Materials, products, services, and transportation are becoming more knowledge intensive in an increasingly competitive American and global economy (Chatterjee 2001). To stay competitive in this environment, US production and transportation firms cut costs by broadening the sourcing of raw materials and intermediate products in increasingly interdependent regional and global markets. The growing practice among national and international firms of maintaining lean inventories[4] is only possible if such reliable and timely freight transport capacities exist. Further, the increasing trend towards intra-firm trade (deriving from a division of labor on a regional and global basis within American and other OECD multinational firms), which amounted to $800 billion in the mid-1990s, is possible only with a highly responsive freight transportation system (Lakshmanan et al. 2001).

Infrastructure investments in transport links and terminals directly provide additions to flow or throughput capacity in the form of new lanes and facilities, safer and speedier movement, and operational improvements. In turn, these improved infrastructure attributes get translated into freight services characteristics such as lower travel costs, reduced travel times, and travel time variability. As Figure 3.3 indicates, transport infrastructure attributes (e.g. capacity, safety, access, etc.) influence freight service characteristics such as travel costs, freight travel times and their variability, and other services. It must be clear that freight service characteristics and the service and process innovations mutually influence one another. The service and process innovations possible at a point in time are determined by the freight time and cost characteristics available; similarly, the available service and process innovations influence the new service attributes of the freight system.

Finally, these freight service attributes and technical innovations converge on the central activity in Figure 3.3, namely, the logistics process and its restructuring over time. Logistics refers to the integrated analysis and management of a firm's overall supply chain and embraces processes of transportation, warehousing, inventory maintenance, order processing, and administration. Transport enterprises coordinate with other processes precisely in order to permit lower levels of inventory, warehousing, handling, errors, and waste. Taking advantage of the service and process innovations (noted above), and the substitutability of transport and inventory carriage, there has been reorganization of the logistics with an overall reduction of total logistics costs (estimated at 40 percent for an average American enterprise). This logistics reorganization appears in the form of:

a) Process changes, such as *better management systems* (improved vehicle utilization, handling systems, etc.) and *product flow rescheduling* (use of JIT (just-in-time), quick response system, etc.). These process changes reflect improving efficiency and, through changing load factors and carrying capacity, will influence the total level of goods transport.

b) Service changes, such as *realignment of supply chains* (new patterns of sourcing, vertical disintegration of production value chains, changing markets), and *refashioning of the logistical systems* (the spatial concentration of inventories and production). These service changes underlie the growth in the number of elements in a supply chain and, given the increasing market areas and the spatial dispersion of locations, the growth in the distance over which the freight is carried.[5]

McKinnon (1995) argues that the benefits accrue less in the form of transport cost savings but more in the form of "service opportunities" such as precise scheduling (e.g. just-in-time systems) market expansion and spatial agglomeration. The increasing shift to a service-oriented, knowledge intensive economy and the spatial expansion into a globally organized economy creates a demand for flexible and time-specific transport of high value goods. Organizational developments are enabling a shift from a supplier-driven, inventory-insensitive freight logistics ("push type") logistics to a consumer-focused, time-definite ("pull type") freight logistics system. Hence the recent shift away from the traditional mode-focused transport, and an upsurge in intermodal transport demand and "mode invisible" performance.

Recent Evolution of the Transport System in the US and in the Megalopolis

A broad overview of the national economy and transportation trends appears in Figure 3.4. Over the last four decades of the twentieth century, the US population increased by 57 percent, while the economy, as measured by

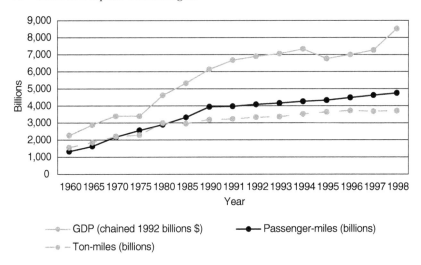

Figure 3.4 GDP and Progress of Transport

Source: National Transportation Statistics 2000, Bureau of Transportation Statistics, US Department of Transportation.

production and GDP (in chained 2000$) rose respectively by 300 percent and 293 percent—leading to sizeable increases in income per capita. Reflecting this real income increase, the passenger-miles traveled shot up by 273 percent. However, the freight flows in that period grew only half as fast—exhibiting a declining income elasticity (0.50) of freight. Tons moved per US $1000 GDP (1992 prices) dropped between 1965 and 1998 by 54 percent. Ton-miles per dollar of US GDP dropped between 1960 and 1998 by 36 percent from 0.69 miles to 0.44 miles (Figure 3.4). The American economy showed a consistent trend in the closing decades of the twentieth century towards lower intensity of freight use and reflects the increasingly lower material intensity and growing knowledge content in the economy.

Both measures of progress of transport over the past four decades reflect the recent transformation of the US economy, with less and less of the GDP deriving from transport activities. The oft-noted increasing shift in the US to a service economy over this period signifies a reduced resource and energy intensity and the consequent lower intensity of goods production for transport. At the same time in this period, transport technology changes continued to lower transport costs sharply. The common measure of shipping costs (the ratio of c.i.f. trade value—measured as cost to the importing country—to f.o.b. trade value—measured as it leaves the exporting country) declined from 9.5 percent in 1950 to about 6 percent in 1990 (Frankel 2000).

Sharp drops in freight rates have pervasive effects. In competitive regions, lower transport costs promote expanded markets and improved export opportunities, which in turn enhance regional output. As "peripheral regions" confront the influx of cheaper goods and the resultant import competition, there is restructuring of activities (with firms arriving and exiting), leading to lower production costs and enhanced efficiency in those regions. The outcome of these processes is greater market integration, as various regions in the US are integrated into the national network of production. In turn, regional specialization of production develops and leads to greater intra-industry and interregional trade and freight movements over an expanded national production space. This scenario is in many ways a stylized description of the incorporation of the Southern and Western States into the US national production system in the 1960s and 1970s—in the context of the emerging transport technologies (Interstate system, jet planes, containers) and the then ongoing brisk shift of population and economic activities from the Snowbelt (e.g. Megalopolis) to the Sunbelt States.

One clear upshot of this regional and national economic integration argument is the longer distances over which goods get transported and the sharper rise of ton-miles of freight as compared to tons moved. More light can be shed on the *underlying structural change*, if we reconsider the freight sector's fortunes for two distinct periods, namely 1960–1980 and 1981–1998 (Table 3.2).

A quick look at Table 3.2 suggests the significant differences between the two periods. The 1960–1980 era witnesses a sharp rise (59 percent) in the ton-miles of freight moved/capita as contrasted with the decline in tons/capita (–5.5 percent), indicating that relatively smaller freight tonnage is hauled over longer average distances and the spatial integration of the national economy is over longer distances (and areas). There is a decline in the freight intensity of GDP, (31 percent on a tonnage basis and 7 percent on a ton-mile basis) indicating the increasing importance of less freight-intensive sectors that make up the GDP.

The second period, 1981–1998, exhibits a markedly different pattern. Reversing the trend in the first period, tons/capita start growing modestly,

Table 3.2 Evolution of the US Freight Sector, 1960–1998

(Percentage Increases)		
Indicator	1960–1980	1981–1998
Tons	11	23
	(1965–1980)	
Ton-miles	92	24
Tons/capita	–5.5	4
Ton-miles/capita	59	4
Tons/$US(000)GDP	–31	–33
Ton-miles/$US GDP	–7	–31

Source: Lakshmanan et al. (2009).

keeping pace with ton-miles /capita growth. The decline in GDP freight intensity is about the same for both tons and ton-miles. Two comments are in order. First, the trend towards longer average freight hauls noted in the first period seems to be abating in the second period. The average distance of freight haul increased in the first period (1960–1980) from 408 to 593 miles and barely afterwards to 597 miles by 1998. Has the process of increasing spatial reach and integration of the US economy, noted in the first period, abated? Second, why does the tonnage moved double its growth rate in the 1981–1998 era (as compared to the 1960–1980 period) at a time when the economy is shifting more towards services and becoming less material-intensive? What changes in the freight services industry and the forces underlying its evolution do these new trends in the 1980s and 1990s suggest?

This different pattern of aggregate freight indicators in the second period of the 1980s and 1990s reflects the operation in this era of new forces underlying the evolution of the freight sector. As noted earlier, a variety of economic, technological, institutional, and policy changes in the 1980s and 1990s have converged to promote major innovations and restructuring in the freight services industry, now offering its users a range of new logistical services at ever dropping costs (e.g. Lakshmanan et al. 2001).

Table 3.3 differentiates the commodities freighted in terms of their value per ton. The value averaged over all modes is $667 in 2002. Rail, pipelines, and water are below this average transporting low value bulk commodities. Clearly, air, freight, and parcel post focus high value time-sensitive cargo, critical in high value adding *knowledge intensive sectors*.

Table 3.3 Value per Ton of US Freight Shipments by Transportation Mode, 2002

Transportation Mode	Value per Ton (Dollars)
All modes	667
Multiple modes	4,892
Single modes	611
Air (incl. truck and air)	88,648
Parcel, USPS or courier	37,538
Truck and rail	1,480
Truck	775
Water	401
Pipeline	240
Rail	198
Other multiple modes	148
Unknown modes	908

Source: Bureau of Transportation Statistics, US Department of Transportation.

Transport Networks of the Megalopolis

The Interstate Highway Network, initiated in 1957 and largely completed in the 1970s, is the major component of the contemporary regional transport network. Figure 3.5 traces the geographic evolution of the Interstate on four dates, from 1958 (the first complete year of its operation), through 1971, 1987, and 2004—utilizing special GIS database created for this study. Figures 3.5 and 3.6 show the spatial patterns of the Interstate Highway system and Class I, as well as the major (Class I) Railroads, while Tables 3.4 and 3.5 display the activity levels of major ports and airports for two recent points in time (see also Figure 3.7).

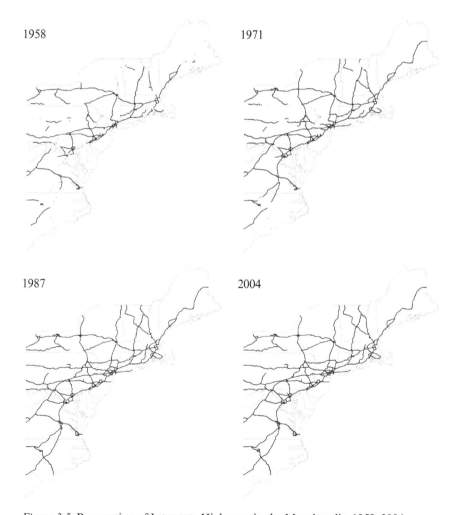

Figure 3.5 Progression of Interstate Highways in the Megalopolis, 1958–2004

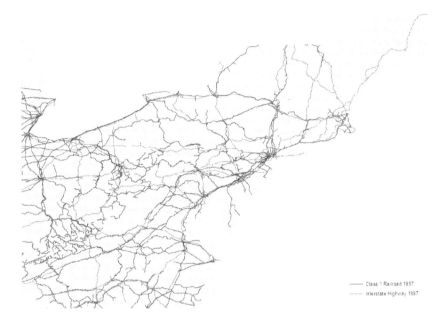

Figure 3.6 Interstate Highways and Class I Railroads in 1997

Table 3.4 Major Ports in the Megalopolis (Total TEUs), 1997–2007

US Custom Ports	New York, NY	Baltimore, MD	Philadelphia, PA	Camden, NJ*	Gloucester City, NJ*	Boston, MA
1997	1,738,613	260,553	90,517	6,833	11,172	62,258
1999	2,027,188	255,378	89,345	7,157	10,275	78,582
2001	2,355,133	273,418	83,408	7,756	6,650	64,078
2003	2,803,036	306,845	103,408	7,739	822	92,609
2005	3,416,622	381,984	159,557	10,710	83	130,547
2007	3,893,491	429,851	197,002	10,370	3,148	158,108

*Camden and Gloucester City are located in the vicinity of the City of Philadelphia, just across the Delaware River.

Table 3.5 Enplaned Passengers at Major Airports in the Megalopolis, 1995 and 2012

	Airport	1995		2012		Percent change of enplanement, 1995–2012
		Total enplaned passengers	National rank	Total enplaned passengers	National rank	
New York	Newark Int'l	11,614,222	11	17,055,993	14	46.9
	John F. Kennedy Int'l	9,234,018	19	24,520,981	6	165.6
	La Guardia	9,665,233	17	12,818,717	20	32.6
Philadelphia	Philadelphia Int'l	7,939,617	24	14,589,337	18	83.8
Baltimore	Baltimore Int'l	5,648,707	28	11,186,444	22	98.0
Boston	Logan	10,460,859	16	14,293,695	19	36.6
Washington DC	Washington Int'l	4,559,895	33	10,816,216	23	137.2
	Ronald Reagan Washington National	6,884,068	25	9,462,231	25	37.5
All airports—Nation		515,722,834		732,953,948		42.1

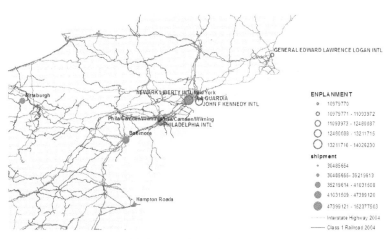

Figure 3.7 Passengers and Shipments in Major Ports and Airports in the Megalopolis, 2004

The decade 1997–2007 was a period of rapid growth of water freight (as measured by TEUs) for the Megalopolis ports, as this region rapidly increased its linkages with other regions in the US and with other countries around the world (Table 3.4). In this decade, the port facilities of New York—with their extensive linkages to the global networks of trade, finance, and business services—increased their TEU shipments by 124 percent, while the other Megalopolis ports (combined) managed to grow by only 85 percent—leading to the further dominance of New York's port in water freight movements.

The progress of air passenger traffic in the Megalopolis metropolitan areas between 1997 and 2012 (Table 3.5) suggests an increasingly rapid growth of air passenger traffic in the Megalopolis. Over these 17 years, air passenger growth nationally was about 42 percent. However, the growth of enplaned passengers in the large airports in the Megalopolis has been significantly larger than the national average—indeed, airports in four of these large five Megalopolis metros evidence double the national growth rates of enplanements. JFK airport in New York reports nearly four times and Dulles in Washington DC three times the national air passenger growth rate; Baltimore and Philadelphia airports report double the national growth rates. As discussed later, this observed higher than national average use of air transport in the Megalopolis reflects the extensive and intensive interactions among economic agents in the globalized Knowledge Economy of Megalopolis in the production and delivery of new goods and services and the associated management and control functions in global network corporations of the region.

Recent Improvements in Metro Transit and Regional High Speed Rail supportive of Growth of Knowledge Agglomerations

As the high value adding economic sectors began to aggregate in the larger Megalopolis metros in the 1990–2010 period of the surging Knowledge Economy, high capacity urban transport modes have begun to respond. In the 2000–2007 period, there was a pronounced shift from earlier patterns in New York from auto commuting to public transportation, an increase in daily subway ridership, and an upsurge in bicycling. It was also a period of considerable growth in New York in the spatially agglomerated knowledge intensive sectors such as finance and professional and business services.

The transport systems in the Megalopolis metros include a variety of multiple-occupancy vehicles. Around 2000, Americans made about 9 billion passenger transit trips—61 percent on buses, 27 percent heavy rail, and 8 percent on commuter and light rail. The urban areas in the Boston-Washington DC Corridor have a disproportionate high proportion of these functioning urban rail systems, which enable the labor force to commute and work effectively in these agglomerations.

This shift to public transportation, while more pronounced in New York City, was evident in the suburbs as well. Figure 3.8 shows the drop in percent of workers who drove alone or carpooled both in the city and the metro area. Correspondingly, the proportion of workers who used public transportation to work increased—significantly in the four largest boroughs (Figure 3.9).

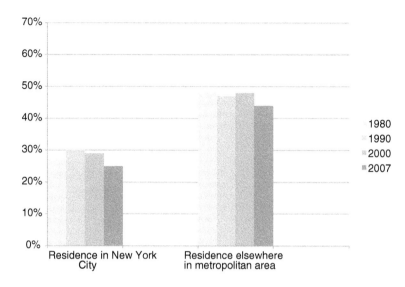

Figure 3.8 Commuter Mode Share: Drove Alone or Carpooled

Source: adapted from New York City Department of City Planning 2008. Changes in employment and commuting patterns among workers in New York City and Metropolitan area, 2000–2007.

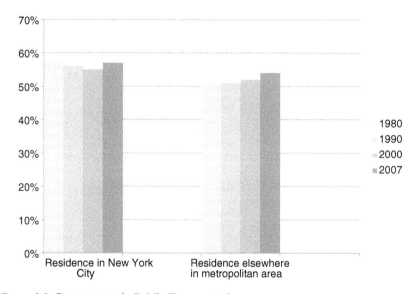

Figure 3.9 Commuters via Public Transportation

Source: adapted from New York City Department of City Planning 2008. Changes in employment and commuting patterns among workers in New York City and Metropolitan area, 2000–2007.

During the 2000–2007 period, there was a pronounced shift from earlier patterns in New York from auto commuting to public transportation, an increase in daily subway ridership (Figures 3.10 and 3.11), and an upsurge in bicycling (Figures 3.12). It was also a period of considerable growth in New York in the spatially agglomerated knowledge intensive sectors such as finance and business services.

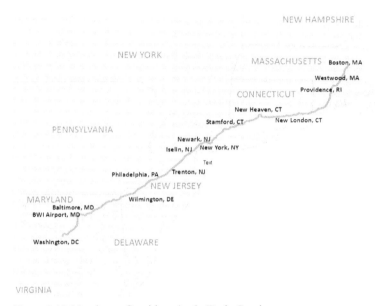

Figure 3.10 Northeast Corridor: Acela Train Service

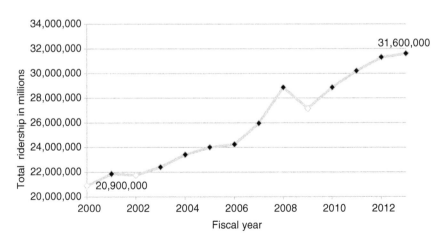

Figure 3.11 Recent Growth of Amtrak Ridership in the Megalopolis

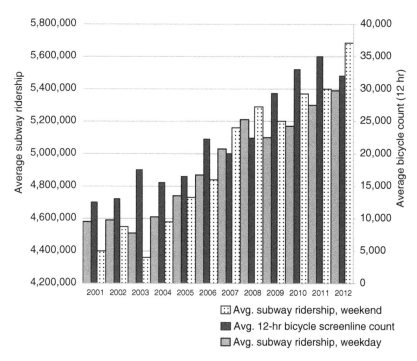

Figure 3.12 Public Transit and Bicycle Trends in New York Metropolitan Area

Over the last decade, a high speed rail service (Acela Express) has operated between Boston and Washington DC with a maximum speed of 241 kph and a daily passenger load of 28,000 (in 2010) along a 585 km, 14 station corridor characterized by an average number of 178,645 jobs and 219,925 residents (2008) within a 5 km range (Murakami and Cervero 2012). Murakami and Cervero's analysis of the economic stimuli provided around High Speed Rail (HSR) stations in the Tokyo-Osaka and the BOSWASH corridors (and in London a major global economy node) appears to support the symbiotic relationships (noted above) between HSR improvements and the location and growth of knowledge intensive economic sectors around major HSR stations in metros such as New York, a top node in the global economy (more on this in Chapter 5).

3. Information and Communication Technology (ICT)

The Rapid Rise and Spread of ICT

ICT pertains to technologies and tools, which individuals and enterprises use to collect information and to communicate with one another (one on one or in groups)—distributing, sharing, and processing that information. While it is frequently used as an expanded synonym for IT, ICT emphasizes the aspect of *unified communications*—among economic and social actors.

In the old industrial economy, flow of information was *physical* in the form of reports, blueprints, cash, checks, invoices, radios, etc. In the contemporary *digital economy*, information flow is digital—in the form of bits stored in computers, tablets, phones, and clouds—and flowing across worldwide networks at the speed of light.[6] People communicate now with one another by using physical devices (hardware), automatic process instructions (software), communication channels (networks), and stored data. Three broad classes of ICTs (all with sharply dropping prices and rapidly enhancing attributes) have been developed: a) *Computers*, vital for processing data and save time and effort, b) *Telecommunication technologies*, and c) *Networking technologies*, the most critical of which is the *Internet*.

Throughout the 1990s, growth in the sale of computers averaged over 28 percent for sales to business and 37 percent for sales to households. Average growth in sales of computer services exceeded 20 percent. These growth rates exceeded those of other industries by a factor of 10 or more, with business investment in computers reaching nearly $180 billion by 1996 (Shapiro and Mathur 2011).

The US ICT sector reached nearly $600 billion in 2009 in direct output and stimulated more than $400 billion in indirect contributions through the benefits other sectors derived from the use of ICT (Shapiro and Mathur 2011).

ICT employment actually declined after 2000, but still accounted for over 3.5 million jobs in 2009. While employment declined slightly total compensation actually rose because of rapidly rising incomes in the sector—by 162 percent from 1991 to 2009, when it reached $107,229. This was over 80 percent higher than the average for all industries (Shapiro and Mathur 2011).

As elaborated below, the combination of investments in IT, Internet, and broadband offers a significantly greater flexibility (than in the past) in organizing the production and delivery of services. The advent of mainframe computers earlier in the 1970s had paved the way to a concentration of computing power of large enterprises, while Internet usage was restricted to mainly academic users. In the last two decades, however, the combination of investments in IT, the Internet, and broadband offers a significantly greater flexibility than in the past in organizing production activities and the delivery of services. The digitalization of information, and the advent of personal computers, phones and tablets (with sharply dropping prices), and the Internet in the last two decades have, however, *democratized the use of IT and accessed IT's enormous potential* for the growth and transformation of the larger economy and society—by allowing vast numbers of people and enterprises to interact across vast spaces in productive ways and by creating value in the process (Figure 3.13).

While the industrial economies are based on controlling the supply of scarce resources, the emerging (ICT) networked economy creates value by

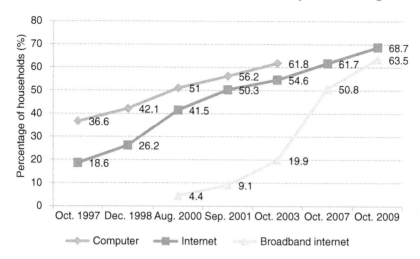

Figure 3.13 Rapid Increases in the Use of Broadband in the United States

Source: Van Ark (2011).

extensively and abundantly connecting individuals, functions, and enterprises across vast spaces around the globe in productive ways and by creating value in the process. As large number of individuals and centers of production and service delivery are connected in this manner, the value of the whole economic network grows exponentially. Further, ICTs are both *drivers and enablers of change*, dramatically altering the ways of work and living. First, the faster information processing allows new ways of communication and interaction with suppliers, customers, and distributors. Second, there is greater flexibility in work practices. Third, by facilitating communication within and across enterprises, the capacity to monitor and better coordinate activities and raise productivity in the enterprises is enhanced.

IT allows manufacturing companies to better coordinate design, production, and management activities to produce more and obtain the synergies from heightened interactions in this process among the workers possessing different types of knowledge in the firms. As new individuals and centers of production and service delivery are widely and intensively connected, the value of the whole economic network grows enormously.

Further, ICT (in combination with recent transport technologies) permit greater flexibility in organizing production, particularly the *geography of production* (Manole and Weiss 2009). As a consequence, there has emerged a finer division of labor in the form of creation of new value adding activities and their geographic distribution across global space (to minimize total production costs)—leading in turn to *global outsourcing*, a globalized system of input sourcing, and global markets for production and service delivery.

4. Contemporary Transport and ICT as GTPs

General Purpose Technologies in the Past

GPTs, as noted earlier, are a few critical technologies which appear to drive some key periods of rapid technical impacts, economic progress, and structural evolution.

Economic historians have suggested that the emergence of key transport and IT have served as GPTs, propelling economic progress and structural change in the past. In the nineteenth century, crucial transport (steamships and railroads) and IT (the telegraph and the cable) vastly increased the speed and reliability and significantly lowered the costs of transport and communications. This in turn made possible a large new national market in the United States. This large market enabled the arrival of capital-intensive, process-oriented industries taking advantage of new production processes which could achieve substantial economies of scale and scope (Chandler 1990). These developments made it possible for large manufacturing plants to produce—using the new production technologies—at far lower costs than smaller units. The advent of large new industrial companies was an economic structural evolution, creating the "Manufacturing Belt"—comprising of the Megalopolis and East North-central region—and leading to the "industrial era," thereby ushering in a century of economic growth (Kim 1995, 1998).

Indeed, students of structural change and economic evolution have suggested that in the period extending from the late eighteenth century (over the last two centuries and more) there have been several periods of economic structural change—driven by new technical innovations—and accompanied by new institutional changes.

Table 3.6 displays a five-period version of that history of economic structural change from 1780 to 1990 from the origin of the Industrial Revolution to the Information Age (Van Ark 2011), listing the critical innovations and the shaping institutional innovations. This chapter argues that the post-1990 period—termed as the "Information Age" in Table 3.6, but designated in this chapter as the "Knowledge Economy"—is driven by two GPTs—Transport and ICT—and the production and institutional Innovations discussed in the next chapter.

Recent Transport Innovations and Economic Evolution in the Megalopolis

The lower time and money costs and increased accessibility due to recent transport technical and organizational transport improvements in the Megalopolis modify the marginal costs of transport producers, the households' mobility, and demand for goods and services. Such changes ripple through the market mechanisms modifying employment, output, and income in the short run. When transport service improvements offer lower costs and improved service to large number of transport-using sectors, a variety of

Table 3.6 General Purpose Technologies in the Past

Timing	Name	Driving Innovations	Salient Institutional Changes
1780–1840	Industrial Revolution	Mechanization of textiles	Factory system
1840–1890	Age of steam power and railways	Application of steam power in factories and railways: machinery	Joint stock companies
1890–1940	Age of electricity and steel	Application of electric power, electrical machinery, application of steel	Rise of the R&D lab, managerial capitalism, Taylorism
1940–1990	Age of mass production	Assembly line, cracking, plastic materials, automobiles	Bretton Woods and Pax Americana; institutionalized labor relations ("Fordism")
1990 onwards	Information Age; Knowledge Economy	(ICT); transport innovations; globalization of production & markets; knowledge-based production & services	Networks: New Regional/Urban Governance Models

Source: modified from Van Ark (2011).

interconnected economy-wide processes are activated. The mechanisms set in motion *dynamic development* effects—in the form of industrial and regional effects—thereby augmenting overall productivity.

The lower costs and enhanced accessibility due to transport technical, organizational, and service improvements allow firms to reach out to ever more distant markets. Market expansion links the economies of different localities and regions, transforming the market for many goods from one of autarky to specialization and trade, leading to productivity growth.

As transport infrastructure and service improvements in the Megalopolis have lowered costs and increased accessibility to various market actors (input suppliers, labor, and customers) market expansion, increased integration, and mutually sustaining growth ensued. Two underlying mechanisms warrant attention:

1. Gains from Trade;
2. Gains in Agglomerations (made possible by transport improvements) within large spatial clusters of firms and individuals in Megalopolis cities—with a variety of endogenous growth effects.

Gains from Trade

Improved transport technology and infrastructure reduce shipment time and costs, thereby expanding the markets of individual transport-using firms. As interregional sale of foods expands, local and regional autarky gives way to increasing specialization and the consequent upsurge in productivity. The US Interstate Highway expansion, the upsurge of jet air travel, the arrival of containers and superefficient ocean ports and new logistical systems all contribute to "Smithian" growth—growth arising due to specialization and trade in the Megalopolis.[7]

Opportunities for exporting and importing goods open up several channels of economic effects both in product markets and in factor markets in the Megalopolis. First, export expansion leads to higher levels of output, allowing higher sales to cover fixed costs of operation, yielding scale economies. Second, competition from imports reduces monopoly rents, further improving efficiency. Schumpeterian dynamics come into play—firms enter, exit, expand, and contract in ways that favor the most efficient and yield aggregate productivity growth. Leaner production processes lower costs and raise productivity, further restructuring of the economy. Third, lower transport costs and increased accessibility enlarge the markets for labor and other factor inputs. Firms may draw labor from a broader area and with a greater variety of skills, improving labor matching and eliminating localized labor shortages. Similar effects in land and other factor markets are likely to open new land for economic activities. Such vastly improved physical connectivity in the contemporary Megalopolis will likely increase contact among economic agents operating in its constituent metro areas. The US Interstate Highway system accelerated suburbanization and air transport improvements helped fill ski, beach, and golf resorts. Vastly improved physical connectivity in the contemporary Megalopolis has increased contact among economic agents operating in its constituent metro areas.

Gains from Agglomeration Supported by Transport

In an increasingly knowledge intensive economy, some urban agglomerations enjoy *increasing returns* in the form of dynamic location advantages, enabling innovation and dynamic competitiveness of these cities. Enquiries into the nature and sources of increasing returns which produce urban agglomeration come from different traditions in economic geography and location economics from the late nineteenth century. In particular, the insights of Marshall (1920), Hoover (1948), Isard (1956), Vernon (1960), Chinitz (1961), Krugman (1991), and Jacobs (1969) are relevant.

Marshall (1920) suggested that firms are able to take advantage of *agglomeration economies* by locating in large clusters. The micro foundations of Marshall's agglomeration economies (in terms of reasons why firms in an industry locate in proximity) suggest a) *input sharing* among firms, enabling a larger input (labor, materials, etc.) supplier market with lower average costs and a larger range of inputs for all firms, b) *matching* in the sense in such large agglomerations, workers with a wider range of skills can be matched with the diverse requirements of employers (further, workers find it less risky in such locations with many employers), and c) *knowledge spillovers or learning*, in the sense that in these dense locations, there are knowledge spillovers, with workers being the primary vehicles of these transfers.[8]

As contrasted with the Marshalian external economies for a particular industry, Jane Jacobs (1969)[9] emphasized the power of industrial diversity in a region on subsequent economic performance. Like historians such as Braudel (1973, 1992), Jacobs argues that the multiplicity and cross-fertilization of "ideas" in variegated environments of a large population and economic cluster stimulate creativity and innovation. Figure 3.14 summarizes our discussion of the various mechanisms and processes underlying the wider economic benefits of transport infrastructure investments, as elaborated in this section.

ICT in the Contemporary Megalopolis

Information and communications technologies have played a unique role in the development and success of the national and regional economies over the last two decades in the US.

1. As noted earlier, ICT, by vastly reducing costs of transaction among economic and social actors distributed around the globe, is expanding explosively the level of connectivity between social and economic actors. The likely results are increasing management efficiency of enterprises and heightened competition paving the way to transparent prices and larger markets. These beneficial impacts will emerge in many economic sectors. Some suggest that the positive impacts are likely to be more pronounced in the "old economy" sectors such as health care and government—by restructuring effectively the flows of information and knowledge and improving productivity (Litan and Rivlin 2001).
2. ICTs act as GPTs and are characterized by:
    a) *Pervasiveness* (ICT sectors are used as inputs by many downstream economic sectors),
    b) *Considerable potential for technical improvements*, and
    c) *Innovational complementarities*, meaning that the productivity of R&D in downstream sectors increases as a consequence of innovation in the ICT (Bresnahan and Trajtenberg 1992). Thus, as ICTs improve they spread throughout the economy, bringing about generalized productivity gains in a variety of sectors. Bresnahan and Trajtenberg (1992) suggest that the semiconductors and the computer are playing the role of GPTs in the contemporary era.

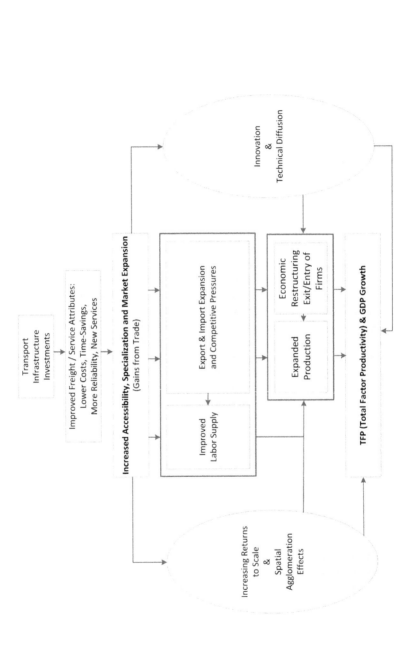

Figure 3.14 Transport Innovations and Economy-Wide Benefits

3. The explosive expansion of the levels of connectivity offered by ICT between actors and ideas (noted above) is likely to have a significant long-term effect on the larger economy (Carlsson 2001). Schumpeter (1934) viewed economic evolution as deriving from new combinations of products, processes, markets, sources of supply, and organizations. Enhanced connectivity through ICT raises the potential for more possible combinations with the potential for conversion of new possibilities into profitable business opportunities—yielding over time technical change and economic evolution (Carlsson 2001).

Transport, ICT and Transformational Effects: Globalization

In recent decades, the space-shrinking technologies of transport and ICT have advanced to a point which offers high levels of physical connectivity and operational linkages and interactions among globally distributed economic and social actors. In the same period, a number of institutional innovations have emerged in the areas of international trade, cross-country investment, and production. Barriers to international trade have steadily fallen. New institutions governing highly open institutional regimes (induced by changing international trade regimes) for trans-border investment, production, and sales have emerged.

This merging of space-shrinking technologies and institutional innovations promoting freer trade and investment makes possible an increasing network of dense economic interactions across the globe among economies, that were until recently separated by high costs of transport and communications and various barriers to trade, production, and finance.

The resulting enhanced interactions among these globally distributed economies are centered in some major metropolitan economies enjoying high levels of global connectivity in the Megalopolis and elsewhere. Taylor and Lang (2005) offer a measure of *global connectivity* based on the location of 100 leading advanced service firms whose presence indicates economic connectedness to other world cities (Table 3.7).

The heightened level of economic interactions among metropolitan areas distributed around the globe has enabled rapidly increasing *globalization of economic activities*.[10] Contemporary globalization represents an explosive expansion of cross-country economic interactions, division of labor, complex webs of production chains, and a globally distributed production system.[11]

A noteworthy feature of the contemporary globalization in the recent three decades is the extent to which the newly industrializing economies (NIEs) of the world are being incorporated in the current global system of investment, production, and trade. The national economies of these NIEs and the affluent industrialized OECD economies (engaged in the global investment, production, and trade) are linked together and integrated in several ways. A key aspect in the organization of production in multiple countries by Global Network Corporations (GNCs) is the spatial organization of

Table 3.7 Global Connectivity of Megalopolis Metro Areas

Metro Region	Global Network Connectivity (Relative GNC)	National Rank
New York	0.976	1
Washington DC	0.418	7
Boston	0.351	8
Philadelphia	0.268	13
Baltimore	0.178	24
Hartford	0.142	32
Wilmington	0.059	40

Source: Taylor and Lang (2005, p. 6).

production activities (Dicken 2000; Dunning 1993; Castells 2000). In the context of the space-shrinking technologies of transport and ICT, the value adding components of production in the OECD economies are divided up increasingly finely and distributed to production locations across the globe by the GNCs—in order to maximize the comparative advantage of locations in terms of value-added and lower factor costs. Finally, the GNCs implement *the functional integration* of such production activities distributed around the globe. Such effective functional integration of the globalized economic activities by GNCs is facilitated (as elaborated in the next chapter) by a new and evolving international financial system and a variety of knowledge intensive professional and business services.

The resulting processes of outsourcing of some production activities and globalization of the production processes play a key role in determining the nature, locations, size, and value added of economic activities of the contemporary Megalopolis and its component major metropolitan areas (as elaborated in Chapters 4 and 6).

Notes

1 The next chapter will focus attention on a) the new *production technologies* which enable the generation and use of new knowledge which supports new knowledge intensive production and service sector activities and b) the emergence of new *institutional technologies* which support the rise and development of new production and service sector activities. Chapter 4 will also note and discuss the interactive and cumulative effects among *all four* types of technologies (noted here) in the rise and evolution of the Megalopolis Knowledge Economy in the last three decades.
2 National Academy of Engineering. National Engineers' Week 2000, February 2000.
3 Under different assumptions of price elasticity of freight carriage and the social discount rate, benefits to Class I trucking would have repaid between 33 percent and 72 percent of the total Interstate investment.

4 Carrying and holding costs represented 25–30 percent of the value of inventories in US firms due to "product, depreciation and interest" (Chatterjee, 2001). In 1998, more than 60 percent of production and sales were processed from direct orders rather than from stock (Gwilliam 1998).

5 By extending just-in-time (JIT) right to the consumer, transport firms not only create a seamless market but also provide value added services to customers. Producers manufacture in response to customers' orders (increasingly by Internet), to which its suppliers of parts and component assemblies have access and respond with appropriate delivery. Transport firms such as FEDEX pre-sort products at points of shipment overseas, distribute direct to US outlets, while informing the US manufacturing firm about the shipment details.

6 Tapscott (1995) suggests: "This new world of possibilities created is as significant as the invention of language itself, the old paradigm on which all physically based interactions occurred."

7 Such efficiency gains from specialization and trade derive from two mechanisms a) the framework of David Ricardo's theory of comparative advantage, whose theoretical extensions are explored in the Heckscher–Ohlin–Samuelson framework, and b) the explanation of gains from trade provided as a benefit to interregional trade via scale economies that are realized as producers target broader markets— as detailed in the NEG (Fujita et al. 1999).

8 It is in this context that Krugman (1991) applied a general equilibrium model to the geography of the economy under conditions of increasing returns to scale and labor mobility and reinterpreted the findings of Marshall on agglomerations. In the resulting NEG model, spatial concentration and dispersion emerge as a consequence of market interactions among individual firms under conditions of scale economies. Over time with lower and lower transport costs, there is a circularity or cumulative causation (especially under conditions of larger local demand in the agglomerations) leading to further strengthening of existing large agglomerations, higher nominal wages, and greater variety of goods.

9 Further, such diversity fosters specialization in inputs and outputs, yielding higher returns (Quigley, 1998). Glaeser et al.'s (1992) analysis of a large number of US cities suggests that industrial diversity in a region is important to subsequent economic performance. Henderson et al. (1995) suggest that that the extent of diversity in manufacturing industries at the start of the period was not important in determining employment and subsequent economic performance.

10 This international distribution of production activities is not novel, having existed from the eighteenth century (with some breaks) in the industrial era. However, in that period while various inputs were sourced around the globe, the industrial products *were fabricated in Europe and North America—UK, Germany, and France, etc.—in national plants and industries* (Hobsbawm 1979). This geographic specialization of production was structured on a *core-periphery basis.*

11 The "first globalization wave" in the nineteenth century was generated by the rise of industrial power in western nations, which resulted in the de-industrialization of the Third World under the dictate of comparative advantage (Baldwin and Martin 1999). In contrast, the contemporary "second wave" has been characterized by the shift of comparative advantage in advanced economies from the industrial production of standardized commodities to the production of goods and services, especially those that incorporate new knowledge. Under the present structure of comparative advantage, the integration of domestic with international markets stimulates the rise of manufacturing activities in the newly industrializing economies—unlike the case of the first globalization wave (Hayami and Godo 2005).

References

Baldwin, R.E., Martin, P., 1999. *Two Waves of Globalization: Superficial Similarities and Fundamental Differences*, NBER Working Paper 6904.

Braudel, F., 1973. *Civilization and Capitalism 15th–18th Century*, New York: Harper and Row.

Braudel, F., 1992. *The Perspective of the World: Civilization and Capitalism 15th–18th Century*, Berkeley, CA: University of California Press.

Breshnehan, T.F., Trajtenberg, M., 1992. *General Purpose Technologies: Engines of Growth?* NBER Working Paper 4148.

Carlsson, S.A., 2001. Knowledge management in network contexts. *Global Co-Operation in the New Millennium*, The European Conference on Information Systems. Bled, Slovenia.

Castells, M., 1996. *The Information Age, Volume 1: The Rise of the Network Society*, Oxford: Blackwell.

Chandler, A.D. Jr., 1990. *Scale and Scope: The Dynamics of Industrial Capitalism*, Cambridge, MA: Harvard University Press.

Chatterjee, L., 2001. *Transportation, Globalization and Competitiveness: Transportation Data Needs for the Twenty-First Century*, report prepared for the Bureau of Transportation Statistics, US Department of Transportation.

Chinitz, B.J. 1961. Contrasts in agglomeration: New York and Pittsburgh. *American Economic Review* 51(2), 279–289.

David, P.A., 1990. The dynamo and the computer: an historical perspective on the modern productivity paradox. *American Economic Review*. 80(2), 355–361.

David, P.A., Wright, G., 1999. *General Purpose Technologies and Surges in Productivity: Historical Reflections on the Future of the ICT Revolution*. Presented at the symposium on Economic Challenges of the 21st Century in Historical Perspective, Oxford, 2–4 July.

Dicken, P., 2003. *Global Shift: The Internationalization of Economic Activity*, 4th edn, New York: Guilford Press.

Dunning, J.H., 1993. *The Globalization of Business: The Challenge of the 1990s*, London: Routledge.

Frankel, J.A., 2000. Globalization of the economy. In Nye, J., Donahue, J. (eds) *Governance in the Globalizing World, Visions of Governance Project,* Washington DC: Brookings Institution Press, pp. 45–71.

Fujita, M., Krugman, P., Venables, A.J., 1999. *The Spatial Economy*, Cambridge, MA: MIT Press.

Gang Gong, 2005. *Airfare, Competition, and Spatial Structure: New Evidence in the US Airline Deregulation*. Doctoral Dissertation, Boston University.

Glaeser, E., Kallal, H., Scheinkman, J., Shleifer, A., 1992. Growth in cities. *Journal of Political Economy,* 100, 1126–1152.

Gordon, R.J., 1992. Productivity in the transportation sector. In Griliches, Z., *Output Measurement in the Service Sectors,* Chicago, MI: University of Chicago Press, pp. 371–427.

Gwilliam, K., 1998. Multimodal transport networks and logistics: the changing role of government. In *Conference Proceedings of Public Policy Issues in Global Freight Logistics*, FHWA, US Department of Transportation.

Hayami, Y., Godo, Y., 2005. *Development Economics: From the Poverty to the Wealth of Nations*, Oxford: Oxford University Press.

Henderson, J.V., Kuncoro, A., Turner, M., 1995. Industrial development of cities. *Journal of Political Economy,* 103, 1067–1090.

Hobsbawm, E.J., 1979. The development of the world economy. *Cambridge Journal of Economics* 3(3), 305–318.

Hoover, E., 1948. *The Location of Economic Activity*, New York: McGraw-Hill.

Hummels, D., 1999. *Have International Transportation Costs Declined?* Working Paper, Chicago: University of Chicago.

Hummels, D., 2007. Transportation costs and international trade in the second era of globalization. *Journal of Economic Perspectives* 21(3), 131–154.

Isard, W., 1956. *Location And Space-Economy: A General Theory Relating to Industrial Location, Market Areas, Land Use, Trade and Urban Structure*, Cambridge, MA: MIT Press.

Jacobs, J., 1969. *The Economy of Cities*, New York: Random House.

Keeler, T.E., Ying, J.S., 1988. Measuring the benefits of a large public investment: the case of the US federal aid highway system. *Journal of Public Economics* 36(1), 69–85.

Kim, S., 1995. Expansion of markets and the geographic distribution of economic activities: the trends in US regional manufacturing structure, 1860–1987. *Quarterly Journal of Economics,* 110(4), 881–908.

Kim, S., 1998. Economic integration and convergence: US regions, 1840–1987. *Journal of Economic History* 58(3), 659–683.

Krugman, P., 1991. *Geography and Trade*, Cambridge, MA: MIT Press.

Lakshmanan, T.R., Anderson, W.P., 2000. *Case Studies in Trade and Transport Integration*, report prepared for the World Bank Infrastructure Group.

Lakshmanan T.R., Anderson, W.P., 2001, *Transport Governance Systems and Trade Expansion*, The Uddevalla Symposium, Gothenburg, Sweden.

Lakshmanan, T.R., Anderson, W.P., Song Y., Li, D., 2009. *Broader Economic Consequences of Transport Infrastructure: The Case of Economic Evolution in Dynamic transport Corridors*, report prepared for FHWA, U.S. Department of Transportation.

Lakshmanan, T.R., Subramanian, U., Anderson, W.P., Lauetier, F.A., 2001. *Integration of Transport and Trade facilitation: Selected Regional Studies*, Washington, D C: The World Bank.

Litan, R.E., Rivlin, A., 2001. Projecting the economic impact of the Internet. *American Economic Review* 91(2), 313–317.

Mamuneas, T.P., Nadiri, M.I., 2003. *Production, Consumption, and Rates of Return to Highway Infrastructure Capital*, US Depatment of Transportation, Federal Highway Administration.

Manole, V., Weiss, R., 2009. *Impact of ICT on Production of Goods and Services: The Impact of ICT on the Geographic Distribution of Employment*, The Linked World: Working Paper Series, The Conference Board.

Marshall, A., 1920. *Principles of Economics*, London: MacMillan.

McKinnon, A.C., 1995.The distribution systems of supermarket chains. In Akehurst, G., Alexander, N. (eds) *Retail Structure*, London: Frank Cass, pp. 226–238.

Murakami, J., Cervero, R., 2012. *High-speed Rail and Economic Development: Business Agglomerations and Policy Implications*. Final Report UCTC-FR-2012-10, University of California Transportation Center.

Nadiri, I.M., Mamuneas, T.P., 1996. *Contribution of Highway Capital to Industry and National Productivity,* report prepared for US Department of Transportation, FHWA. Office of Policy Development, Washington, DC.

Quigley, J.M., 1998. Urban diversity and economic growth. *The Journal of Economic Perspectives* 12(2), 127–138.

Rosenberg, N., Trajtenberg, M., 2004. A general-purpose technology at work: the Corliss steam engine in the late-nineteenth-century United States. *The Journal of Economic History* 64(1), 61–99.

Schumpeter, J., 1934. *The Theory of Economic Development*, Cambridge, MA: Harvard University Press.

Shapiro, R.J., Mathur, A., 2011. *The Contributions of Information and Communication Technologies to American Growth, Productivity, Jobs and Prosperity.* Washington DC: Sonecon.

Tapscott, D., 1995. *Digital Economy: Promise and Peril in the Age of Networked Intelligence.* New York: McGraw-Hill.

Taylor, P.J., Lang, R.E., 2005. *US Cities in the World City Network.* Washington DC: The Brookings Institutions.

Van Ark, B., 2011. University of Groningen, The Conference Board Presentation, June 6.

Vernon, R., 1960. *Metropolis 1985*, Cambridge, MA: Harvard University Press.

4 Structural Change and the Rise of the Knowledge Economy
Underlying Technologies and Processes

1. Introduction and Overview

As noted earlier, several metropolitan areas in the Megalopolis region have experienced economic decline in the quarter century after 1960, as their manufacturing sectors lost their competitive edge. However, many of these urban regions in the Megalopolis have, in the most recent quarter century, reinvented themselves as hubs of creativity and socioeconomic development, creating jobs utilizing knowledge in technical, economic, social, and cultural fields. The old industrial metropolitan areas of Boston and New York, as well as Washington DC (with large public, health, and scientific sectors), are well advanced in this transition to Knowledge Economy. Baltimore and Philadelphia are following suit as creative regions. These and other metros in the region are the "creative regions" or the "Knowledge Economies"—yielding jointly a Mega Knowledge Region of Megalopolis.

What sorts of economic, social, and spatial processes have been at play in this transition, and how do they interact in the birth of this Megalopolis Knowledge Region and its continuing evolution? How did these metropolitan areas transition in the last three decades or so, from a trajectory of decline to "creative regions"? What sets of innovations underlie such a structural change? To make such a transition successfully, key economic, political, and social actors in a metropolitan region have had to unravel the complexity of change and put in motion strategies of structural change. Such actors have been able to shift mindsets and change behavior of various urban and metropolitan private, public, and social sector agents, in evolving and sustaining innovation, and in maintaining the dynamics of change.

Clearly, several types of structural change and evolution are implied in such a multidimensional transition of the Megalopolis and its component metropolitan areas in the last three decades or more. *First, economic structural change and evolution*: the Megalopolis (that accounts for a fifth of the US economy) and its component metro areas have made the transition from a declining industrial economy to a vibrant Knowledge Economy. What innovations and processes have governed such an economic structural change, yielding new knowledge and its embodiment in new goods and services?

A second evolution, namely, *a global spatial organization* of socioeconomic activities has emerged in the Megalopolis with a global division of labor and the integration of the domestic and international markets. What recent technologies and processes have enabled these globally organized activities in the metropolitan areas of the Megalopolis? As elaborated below, such enabling technologies are the general purpose technologies of transport and ICT.

Third, the emerging increasingly knowledge intensive economy of the Megalopolis is centered on the metropolitan areas which serve functional regions of intense interaction within which firms, public institutions, and social sector change agents create new knowledge, transform it into commercial opportunities, and plug into worldwide business and non-business networks of the global economy. In these urban clusters, creative environments emerge, characterized by 1) the occurrence of knowledge spillovers from one group to another, promoting innovation and growth, and 2) flexible interactive networks—interpersonal, inter-enterprise, and inter-organizational—stimulating innovation. The emergence of these networks, as elaborated below, constitutes a key *economic institutional innovation*. Further, the economic, public (and social) sector actors in such urban areas—engaged in intercity competition for globally mobile economic activities—must not only acquire *new* (but also shed some older) economic and political policies and instruments and innovate *novel structures of urban governance* appropriate to the creation and operation of a new urban physical and spatial structure of land uses and infrastructures which are supportive of the Knowledge Economy. The acquisition of such new capacities is possible only when urban public and social sector change agents complement the work of private sector agents as elaborated below with more inclusive rules of engagement and decision-making among urban public, private, and social sector actors in the form of new models of urban governance. These new governance models facilitate the decisions and implementation of the new physical layouts and the efficient functioning of the new knowledge-rich metropolitan regions.

Much of the available literature on the rise of the Knowledge Economy focuses primarily on the first of the three types of structural change noted here—namely the processes and mechanisms governing economic structural change and evolution. The literature on the other types of structural change and the (socio-political) evolution identified above in emerging Knowledge Economies and regions is, however, limited, spotty and scattered.

This chapter proposes a rich conceptual framework which captures the multiple mechanisms and processes which underlie the multidimensional structural change and evolution embodied in the transition of the Megalopolis to a Knowledge Economy, as noted above. It brings together, builds on, and expands the extant literature on the rise of the Knowledge Economy and formulates a much broader analytical framework and a richer model of the rise and evolution of the Knowledge Economy in the Megalopolis mega region. It does so by formulating an analytical framework that goes beyond the above noted processes of new knowledge creation and their embodiment in the economy. This chapter argues that extant formulations of the rise of the Knowledge Economy tell only part of the story of the rise of the Megalopolis Knowledge Economy.

The argument made in this book is that the rise of the Knowledge Economy in the Megalopolis represents a *convergence and interactions, in recent decades, among four broad types of technologies* (Figure 4.1).

1 & 2. *Two GPTs of transport and ICT*—which promote not only the globalized division of labor and the integration of domestic and international markets in the Megalopolis economy, but also facilitate the creation of new technologies of goods production and knowledge intensive services.

3. *New technologies of production of knowledge intensive goods and services.* Technologies and associated mechanisms underlying the production of knowledge-rich goods have been described in an extensive multidisciplinary literature and will be reviewed below. In addition, this chapter will highlight the technical and organizational innovations that have made possible the ICT-enabled KIBS (comprising of financial, legal, accounting, information and other professional services). Such services enable global corporations in the Megalopolis to develop and support management innovations that make possible the productive and smooth operation of global supply chains and the integration of global corporate operations, and enhance the productivity of many service sectors.

4. *New institutional and organizational technologies,* which promote a) knowledge creation via the new *institution of economic networks* and b) the development of new governance models which make possible *the spatial restructuring of the land uses and infrastructures* emerging in the large metropolitan areas of the Megalopolis. While these institutional and urban governance innovations promote critical urban spatial reorganizations in the large Megalopolis metro areas, which in turn offer increased efficiencies for the GNCs attracted to the region, they generate a variety of costs for low income metropolitan households. This aspect will be addressed in the governance mode. However, it is widely recognized that knowledge-rich production and associated increases of productivity occur only when novel technologies are married to *new and complementary institutional and organizational technologies.* ICT, which promotes the distribution and interactivity of knowledge, does not function optimally in the hierarchical systems of control prevalent in corporate institutions inherited from Industrial America. New institutions needed in knowledge-based society should allow for both discretion and control associated with knowledge creation and incorporation in the new economy. The argument advanced in this chapter is that the institution of economic networks—an addition to the earlier economic institutions (of markets, private hierarchies (firms), and the state)—offers such a capacity and needs to be formally incorporated in the analytical framework of the rise of the Knowledge Economy. Further, this chapter will argue that a viable model of urban and regional regeneration as a Knowledge Economy must provide explanations not only for the capacity to generate flexibility,

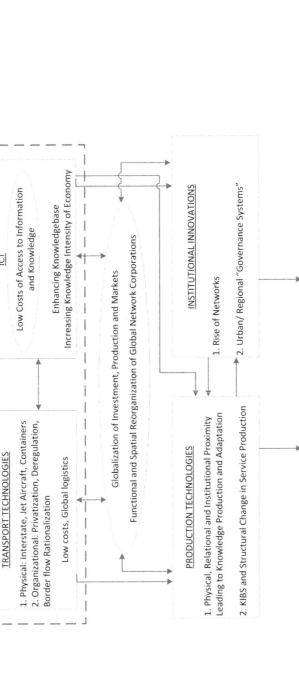

Figure 4.1 Rise and Evolution of Knowledge Economy in the Megalopolis

and tolerance as noted above, but also social and organizational capital in the form of new urban/regional governance models—which are all necessary for the effective functioning and collaboration of the economic, social, and political sectors in their joint creation of effective functioning, spatially reorganized socioeconomic activities of the Knowledge Economies in the large Megalopolis metropolitan regions. In resurgent Megalopolis, metropolitan knowledge regions (e.g. Boston and New York), *governance activities* involved in such *urban spatial restructuring* of the Knowledge Metropolis have been created.

Figure 4.1 lays out the resulting four innovations—*Transport, ICT, Production and Services,* and *Institutions*—which (this book argues) account—jointly and interactively—for the origin and evolution of the Knowledge Economy in the Megalopolis. The rest of this chapter advances, elaborates, and substantiates this argument.

2. GPTs of Transport and ICT: Enabling the Global Division of the Megalopolis

GPTs, as noted in Chapter 3, are a set of technologies that appear to drive important eras of technical progress and economic growth in a region (Breshnehan and Trajtenberg 1992; David and Wright 1999). These GPTs become important in the economy in some eras, as they provide inputs to a large number of downstream sectors with considerable potential for technical improvements and innovation. Thus, as GPTs improve, they spread throughout the economy, bringing about structural change and generalized productivity gains.

The GPTs of transport and ICT help create the broader spatial context in which the Megalopolis economy operates, namely *the global division of labor and the integration of domestic and international markets* in the Megalopolis—as elaborated in Chapter 3. As noted there, the space-shrinking technologies of transport and ICT provide high levels and progressively lower cost *physical connectivity and access, operational linkages and interactions* among globally distributed economic and social actors. In the same period, new institutions governing highly open trade regimes for trans-border investment, production, and sales have also emerged. The global network corporations in the Megalopolis efficiently implement this new spatially and functionally distributed Knowledge Economy.

Recent Transport and ICT Innovations

There have been, in the last three to four decades of the twentieth century, transformational changes in US transportation, driven by a combination of new transport technologies—both *physical* and *institutional*. As elaborated in Chapter 3, the key physical transport technologies in this period were: the Interstate Highway system, containers, and jet aircraft. The new institutional innovations have appeared in the form of new governance technologies of *deregulation, privatization, and the reinvented system of border inspection of goods.*

Containers, first introduced for international service in 1966 in a Megalopolis port by US lines, have greatly enhanced shipping efficiency—substantially reducing port labor costs, lowering ship's port dwell time, increasing cargo holding capacity per ship ton and ship speed, and promoting intermodal international and inland transport of freight (UNCTAD 1970). The introduction of the high speed, divided highways of the Interstate System and their network expansion in the country have made, as analyzed by a number of econometric studies, significant contributions to the productivity of the American economy (Lakshmanan and Anderson 2001). The jet aircraft and the technical evolution in the aviation sector have led to the sharp drops in air passenger and freight prices domestically and internationally. The transport institutional innovations of deregulation and privatization have influenced the scope of freight services powerfully; first, deregulation and liberalization policies have enabled and motivated a broad range of transport service and process innovations and logistical improvements; second, the changes in transport physical flow rules—less restrictions on vehicle size/weight attributes and improved ports/customs rules, etc.—have influenced the capacities on transport routes and terminals and logistical potential (Lakshmanan et al. 2001). The variety of service innovations and process innovations in freight services, enabled by a combination of transport and IT and public policy reforms, have promoted in turn a new set of freight service attributes, the restructuring of business logistics, and affordable transport provision nationally and globally.

ICT pertains to technologies and tools, which individuals and enterprises use to collect information and to communicate with one another (one on one or in groups)—distributing, sharing, and processing that information. While it is frequently used as an expanded synonym for IT, ICT emphasizes the aspect of *unified communications*—among economic and social actors.

A variety of new developments in ICT in the last quarter century have made possible a large scale expansion of IT use (personal computers, phones, and tablets) and the broad range of benefits, which vast numbers of individuals and economic and social enterprises derive from such use. As elaborated in Chapter 3, these developments provide novel capabilities in the form of significantly new and greater flexibility in organizing both production activities and the delivery of services.

Such joint benefits offered by transport and ICT—sharply lower costs, time savings, flexible time-definite more frequent delivery etc.—transform the space–time relationships of enterprises in the Megalopolis, US, and the world. Enterprises gain the capacity to lower overall costs of search and delivery of materials production components. Further benefits accrue from this consequent increasing division of labor.

Further, public policies initiated in recent decades by the US and other countries have promoted freer trade regimes (GATT, NAFTA, WTO, etc.) in the Megalopolis' firms—vastly expanding trade and capital flows. The resulting enhanced interactions among these globally distributed economies are centered in some major metropolitan areas of the Megalopolis enjoying high levels of *global connectivity*. According to Taylor and Lang (2005), who track the global distribution of 100 leading advanced services firms to arrive at measures of global connectivity (an important aspect of cities' economic connectedness to other world cities and the patterns of these linkages around the globe) the Megalopolis metros of New York, Washington DC and Boston occupy the first, seventh, and eighth ranks in the US.

Such high levels of global connectivity facilitates the GNCs located in these large Megalopolis metro areas in their organization of production in multiple countries (Dunning 1993; Dicken 2000; Castells 2000; Andersson et al. 2004). Further, the GNCs implement the *functional integration* of such production activities distributed around the globe. Such effective functional integration of the globalized economic activities by GNCs is facilitated (as elaborated next) by a new and evolving international financial system and a variety of knowledge intensive professional and business services (Sassen 2000).

3. Production Technologies: Knowledge-Embodied Goods and KIBS and Structural Change in Service Production

A variety of disciplines, concerned with urban/regional evolutionary economic and spatial changes, have been harnessed in the last quarter century to provide explanations of the rise of the new vibrant urban/regional Knowledge Economies: Economic Geography, Urban and Regional Economics, Regional Science, Business Economics, Management Studies, and Urban and Regional Planning. The highlights of this extensive new literature—on the rise of the Knowledge Economy and the processes underlying the creation of new knowledge and its embodiment in new products and services in some large urban agglomerations—have been presented widely (e.g. Jacobs 1969; Brusco 1982; Piore and Sabel 1984; Porter 1990; Krugman 1991; Storper 1995; Markusen 1996; Quigley 1998; Scott 1998; Fujita et al. 1999; Feldman 2000; Sassen 2000; Malecki 2000; Camagni 2004; Bathelt et al. 2004; Bryson and Daniels 2007; Capello 2011; Cooke et al. 2011).

Rise of Knowledge-Embodied Goods

It would be a fool's errand to attempt here a fair synopsis of this vast interdisciplinary literature and the rich concepts underlying the rise of new knowledge and its incorporation in new economic goods and services in urban/regional clusters. However, it may be useful to highlight *three central themes*, which animate this theoretical literature. In this vein, it is reasonable to argue that the creation of new knowledge and the rise of the regional Knowledge Economy derive from three complementary schools of thought that inform our understanding of regional innovation and economic development. These three approaches highlight *three kinds of proximity—physical, relational, and institutional*—among the various regional social/economic/political actors— as underlying the creation of the Knowledge Economy.

Physical Proximity

There is an extensive literature developed over many decades—from intellectual traditions in location economics and economic geography—about *increasing returns* in the form of dynamic location advantages enjoyed by some urban/regional agglomerations, enabling innovation and dynamic competitiveness in some regions. According to Marshall (1920), economic enterprises are able to take advantage of *increasing returns* by locating in large urban agglomerations. Such increasing returns flow from their ability to promote innovation and capture agglomeration economies from three sources: first, in large urban areas enterprises share production inputs (e.g. labor, materials, etc.). The input supplier markets in a large urban areas can offer a broader range of inputs at lower costs. Second, in large agglomerations, workers with a broad range of skills are able to match more easily their skills with the broader range of skills demanded by employers. Third, in such dense locations, there is greater probability of *knowledge spillovers*, with workers serving as vehicles of such transfer.[1]

While Marshall emphasized the contributions of external economies for a particular industry, Jane Jacobs (1969) focused her attention on the physical proximity and interactions among diverse ideas in a urban region as underlying innovation and subsequent economic performance. Like historians such as Braudel (1992), Jacobs argues that the multiplicity and cross-fertilization of different "ideas" in variegated environments of a large population and economic cluster stimulate creativity and innovation.[2]

Krugman (1991) reinterpreted Marshall's theoretical results on economic and structural changes in large agglomerations, under the assumption of increasing returns to scale. That has yielded Krugman's "New Economic Geography Model."[3] This model, while accounting for the rise of agglomerations, sheds little light on the processes of knowledge creation and innovation-led growth in urban agglomerations.

Another analytical tradition pertaining to the importance of physical proximity among economic actors engaged in innovation and economic growth in urban agglomerations has to do with problems in the transfer of *tacit knowledge* (Polyanyi 1944; Granovetter 1985). Research findings that can be codified and expressed through text and formulations can be communicated over long distance via a variety of media. But more complex and nuanced information, which can range from scientific discoveries with great commercial potential to methods of trading and marketing, may only be effectively communicated by means of frequent face-to-face contact. In many cases of new knowledge with great commercial potential (e.g. bio-sciences or the creation of KIBS), much knowledge is tacit and embodied in the intellectual capital of the knowledge creators. The absorption and use of that knowledge for new applications would be difficult without frequent face-to-face contact or other interactions with the creators of this knowledge. Physical proximity among various economic actors in such an urban region facilitates interactions, enabling access to, appropriation and sharing of tacit knowledge, and taking advantage of "untraded interdependencies" (Von Hippel 1988; Storper 1995; Gertler 2003).

Relational Proximity

A second broad approach developed in the 1980s—in response to the *collectively created and managed innovation in products and processes and services*, and the success of the small and medium-sized enterprises in both mass and specialized markets—initially in Italy (Brusco 1982, and the "Flexible Specialization" of Piore and Sabel 1984). In this approach, knowledge is created at the regional or local level through *cooperative learning processes* that require spatial proximity. Small firms may be in existence for too short a time to develop a solid stock of firm-specific knowledge. This handicap is overcome by the regional milieu and the relations within it, which assure a continuity of knowledge through labor market stability, high intra-regional mobility, and intense innovative interactions among customers and suppliers and by firm spinoffs (Capello 2011). The resulting extensive interactions, creativity, and recombination capacities pave the way to a rich learning process. In this process, *relatedness* between economic activities in terms of shared competences is an effective knowledge transfer process (Capello 2011).[4]

Institutional Proximity

There is a third modality of learning for firms, which stands in between the two above noted approaches of internal learning and collective learning. The firm engages in learning through "network cooperation," where the firm complements its capabilities by externally purchased inputs. Further, the firms become concerned with the reduction of a *new class of costs* they confront in this Knowledge Economy. These are the *adaptive costs* incurred by the firm as it monitors the environment for changes in technology and products, identifies competitive strategies, and implements such strategies quickly enough to retain or improve market share (Lakshmanan and Button 2009). These linkages and interactions allow firms and other economic agents to complement their core competencies with requisite knowledge and capacities (from complementary sources) creatively, speedily, and flexibly. Such knowledge linkages are really "embedded in the social network." Firms (often small and medium-sized) in such regions develop flexible and interdependent relationships with suppliers and competitors and increasingly depend on intangibles, like know-how, synergies, and untraded knowledge (Von Hippel 1988; Storper 1995).

Knowledge Intensive Business Services

Historically, the service sector has been viewed as unproductive. The notion that service sectors do not add value goes back to Adam Smith (1776)[5] and other classical economists. Since services could not be stored, they had no exchange value and could not, unlike agriculture and industry, add to the wealth of nations.

In the US where the transition to the service economy is advanced, the share of service employment has progressed from a little over 50 percent in 1950 to over 75 percent by the year 2000. A less observed characteristic, over the past two to three decades of the US transition to a service economy, is that the share in the economy of business services has grown monotonically, as the share of the manufacturing sector has been dropping.

Several decades ago, the idea emerged that the fast-growing service sectors evidence lower productivity gains and thus will dampen overall growth processes—as elaborated in Baumol's (1967) model of "unbalanced growth." Recent research suggests, however, that model is somewhat blunt to account for the many changes in the scope of many service sectors and their evolving multidimensional roles in last three decades in contemporary economies in the US and other OECD countries (Sapprasert 2007; Pilat 2001; Triplett and Bosworth 2003).

Firms in the service industries that are "information intensive" focus on *communicative and transactional operations*, which in turn create an "ICT-friendly" atmosphere. Since innovation in service industries adopt ICT to facilitate interactions involved in service operations/activities, such an atmosphere is essential. Given the central role of communication and information transfer in services, the use of ICT plays a vital role in service firms' innovation activities, and in boosting their performance. The extensive use of ICT by service sectors—coupled with organizational innovations—has led to rapid growth in both productivity and output levels (Brynjolfsson and Hitt 2000, 2003; Brynjolfsson et al. 2002).

Due to the important role of user-producer interaction (e.g. in service "co-production") and customization in service firms, in contrast to that of standardization in manufacturing firms (Drejer 2004), ICT facilitates real time and placeless monitoring of customers' demands, replacing the old physical information systems. For instance, ICT reduces the need for front-office staff to interact with customers as in e-shopping, e-learning, and e-booking.

Although computers are utilized in most sectors, the use of ICT is largely concentrated in service industries (McGuckin and Stiroh 2001). Pilat and Wolfl (2004) suggest that in the US manufacturing is indeed much less ICT-intensive than services. This is largely due to the nature of services that process and diffuse information in abundance (for example, financial services and telecommunications).

The evidence from many studies suggests that turning investment in ICT on to higher productivity is not straightforward. Often it requires complementary investments and changes, e.g. in new or retrained human capital, changes in enterprise organizational forms, and innovation. ICT-related improvements are not automatic, but rather arise out a process of search and experimentation that can lead to the failure of some firms and the rapid growth of others. A lot depends on the region's business environment and its institutional adaptability (Pilat 2001).

Business services are third party offerings that may complement or substitute for services provided in-house. KIBS are a subset of business services that employ ICT or other advanced technologies and can promote innovation, structural change, and productivity growth in the firms that they serve.

Miles et al. (1995) identified three principal characteristics of KIBS:

- They rely heavily upon professional knowledge.
- They are themselves primary sources of information and knowledge or they use knowledge to produce intermediate services for the production activities of clients.
- They are of competitive importance and supplied primarily to businesses.

Employment and output statistics in most countries over the past 20 years show a persistent growth in commercial services that appears to come at the expense of manufacturing. The structural shift reflects a changing and increasingly complex social division of labor between economic sectors. Increased specialization by firms in KIBS makes it possible for them to achieve scale economies and to attract and develop specialized human capital. This leads to increased benefits to outsourcing of services that were previously in-house and the growing encapsulation of manufacturing products in a "service jacket" (Kox and Rubalcaba 2007).

The argument advanced here is that in recent decades business services (particularly KIBS) have played a major role in economic growth and innovation in the US and Megalopolis. They contribute both directly through their own rapid growth and indirectly through the technological spillovers they confer on other firms. The spillovers take the forms of a) original innovations, b) speeding up knowledge diffusion, and c) the reduction of human capital indivisibilities at the firm level. The external supply of knowledge and skill inputs by KIBS sectors confers the cost benefits of scale economies along with a higher quality of service arising from technological innovation.

Further, the KIBS sector includes the major corporate central organizational services, such as financial, legal, accounting, and many professional services. Such services permit corporations with headquarters in New York or Boston to coordinate their various value adding production chains spread across the globe (Sassen 2000, 2002). Thus KIBS sectors play a crucial role in the operation of the global economy and in the facilitation of the American economy's structural evolution.

The levels of employment and average wages in KIBS sectors in 1997 and 2007 in the nation, Megalopolis, and its five major metros are presented in Table 4.1. While the Megalopolis had 17 percent of the national employment in 1997 and 2005, it was over-represented in the employment in those years in the KIBS sectors, garnering respectively 26.7 percent and 25.3 percent of the national totals (Chapter 2). Further, the average wage per worker is higher in the Megalopolis and component metros in 1997—with this gap widening from 1997 to 2007. As noted earlier, these KIBS sectors support the arrival and increasing productivity of many services.

4. Institutional and Organizational Technologies and Structural Change in the Megalopolis

Institutional Innovation of Economic Networks

Institutions comprise of a set of formal and informal rules, including the conditions of their enforcement. By defining and delimiting the set of options available to individuals, institutions can reduce uncertainty, simplify action choices, and offer an incentive structure for activities and interactions among economic agents. Institutions have long been recognized as important in shaping economic development.

Three major economic coordinating mechanisms or institutions—*markets, firms or private hierarchies,* and *the state*—have emerged in modern

Table 4.1 KIBS in the Megalopolis and the US, 1997 and 2007

	1997		2007	
	Number of Employees (%*)	*Average Wage (2007 US Dollars)*	*Number of Employees (%*)*	*Average Wage (2007 US Dollars)*
New York	381,722 (4.06)	70,141	478,409 (4.37)	82,363
Philadelphia	137,730 (4.50)	66,167	142,742 (4.11)	71,689
Boston	106,292 (3.78)	74,977	163,071 (4.60)	87,860
DC	241,800 (7.85)	69,414	374,383 (9.73)	84,319
Baltimore	49,021 (3.41)	57,911	80,521 (4.75)	76,012
Megalopolis	1,091,625 (4.15)	67,921	1,441,850 (4.73)	80,641
US	4,092,136 (2.65)	57,436	5,696,838 (3.17)	64,675

* % of Regional/national employees in the KIBS sector.

Source: 1997 and 2007 Economic Census, US Census Bureau.

economies. The emergence of these various institutional types depends on the circumstances prevailing in a particular economy. For example, in the Megalopolis in the industrial era (late nineteenth century and the first half of the twentieth century and beyond) when the product demand was stable and undifferentiated, and the technology standardized and changing infrequently, firms in the region organized production in large vertically integrated units (private hierarchies or firms) that exploited economies of scale and density by using single-purpose machines and low to moderate skilled workers in fashioning standardized products (Chandler 1977; Williamson 1985). The automobile and textile industrial districts exemplify this type of system.

The context of economic development has been changing in recent decades with the rise of the Knowledge Economy. Are new economic institutions likely to emerge to facilitate the rise of the new economy? From an economic perspective, institutional change is mainly triggered by changes in relative prices or in individual preferences (North 1990, 1994). Changing prices reflect transaction costs, the costs of acquiring new knowledge technologies or competences, and relative factor prices. Thus price changes are in large part driven by innovators and entrepreneurs. Adaptations by economic actors to these changes stimulate the mechanisms of institutional change. Thus historical and emerging changes in technology, markets, and the evolving nature of economic interactions help reshape contemporary institutions. Such emerging changes in economic interaction lead to experiments, trial and error processes, and learning among economic agents at the micro level and potentially at the macro institutional level (Nelson and Winter 1982; Groenewegen et al. 1995).

Other social scientists have suggested that economic institutions are constrained by the social context in which they are embedded (Polanyi 1944; Granovetter 1985; Sabel 1997). The rise of the Knowledge Economy in recent years, and its predominant spatial location in a number of dynamic metropolitan economies in North America, Europe and Asia, offers such a context of major technical and market evolution and the consequent modification in the nature and structure of incentives for economic actors—a fertile ground for the reform and evolution of new economic institutions. New institutions needed in this context should allow for both *discretion and control* associated with knowledge creation and incorporation in the new economy. Unless the older centralized production organizational arrangements of Industrial America are modified and more organizational autonomy and flexibility required by the new knowledge technologies developed in a co-evolutionary process, the rise of and the transition to the Knowledge Economy will experience delay (Lakshmanan and Button 2009; Hollingsworth and Boyer 1997).

The argument advanced in this section is that the institutional innovation of *economic networks*—an addition to the earlier economic institutions (*of markets, private hierarchies (firms)*, and *the state*)—offers such a capacity and needs to be formally incorporated in the analytical frameworks which address the rise of the Knowledge Economy.

As the emerging Knowledge Economies are increasingly character-ized by differentiated product demand, volatile markets, and rapid technical change, firms choose innovative and flexible production strate-gies—knowledge intensive, cooperative-competitive hybrid approaches, flexible machines, skilled labor, etc. With the maturation of the Knowledge Economy, knowledge-rich technologies arrive in various aspects of produc-tion—design, fabrication, input and output logistics, marketing, after-sales services, etc. In this increasingly knowledge intensive context, value derives from knowledge, and enterprises seek to add value to their core competen-cies by taking advantage of complementary assets and capabilities of other enterprises. In this highly interactive and somewhat codependent ambience among innovative economic actors and enterprises, economic networks become crucial institutions.

This development introduces new competitive factors and alters the incen-tive structures in regional economies typically populated by dynamic small and medium enterprises (Hage and Alter 1997). First, innovation becomes a more pivotal competitive factor than cost reduction and productivity enhancement emphasized by NIE (New Institutional Economists) such as Williamson (1985) and Chandler (1977). Second, the firms become concerned with the reduction of a *new class of costs* they confront in this Knowledge Economy. These are *adaptive costs* incurred by the firm as it monitors the environment for changes in technology and products, identifies competi-tive strategies, and implements such strategies quickly enough to retain or improve market share (Hage and Alter 1997). In such dynamic or creative and cooperative regions innovation and lowering of the consequent adaptive costs becomes the critical competitive factors for firms.

This combination of the criticality of innovator/entrepreneur and adaptive cost reduction shapes the nature and structure of incentives for regional eco-nomic actors in the new economy. It requires new competences on the part of economic actors, and new patterns of interactions among them to support the creation and maintenance of new knowledge and its commercial applica-tion (Cook and Brown 1999; Amin and Cohendet 2004).

Spurred by the need to be innovative and to lower adaptive costs, firms form alliances and joint ventures to access competences, share R&D costs, and to be agile in the face of competition. Participants can remain small (or become small through downsizing) in this cooperative framework, and real-ize the benefits from the joint products, while lowering the adaptive costs. In other words, the network participants are functionally interdependent but autonomous. Clusters become important (Enright 1998). Further, small firms staying in these networks learn over time the tacit knowledge of the net-work partners and build trust (Polyani 1983). As tacit knowledge gained from this cooperation among partners grows, the firm's most valuable asset—its human capital—also increases. The growth in tacit knowledge can pave the way for more innovative products and services. Further, other developments are steering firms away from autonomy. For example, small high tech firms sensing new or niche markets and lacking capacities for large-scale production and distribution may form joint ventures to access such expertise.

The institutional mechanism that coordinates such complex cooperative relationships among economic actors is the *network* (Table 4.2). Networks exhibit some features of self-interest and some of social obligation, but they are not a halfway point between a firm (a private hierarchy) and a market (Hage and Alter 1997). Networks represent forms developed in response to the changing context of desired interactions among economic agents in innovative regions. Networks differ from the hierarchical coordination of the firm since each participant has autonomy because networks have "visible hands" in the form of complex decision-making groups at multiple levels. Networks comprise sometimes of only firms, at other times of firms, public sector actors, and social sector actors.

A regional economy of networks becomes increasingly a system of cooperative interactions among economic actors or a web of links between individuals, firms, and organizations with links based on knowledge assets and evolving through cooperative learning processes.[6]

Entrepreneurial City and New Models of Urban Governance

In recent decades, as a globally organized knowledge production system has been evolving, there has been a reversal of relative roles of national and city

Table 4.2 Essential Characteristics of Networks

Characteristic	Description
1. Organizational Attribute	Voluntary interchanges over time periods Multilateral Exchange Semiformal Membership
2. Compliance Mechanism	Resource Interdependence Contractual Bonds Trust developed among agents outside economic arena
3. Institutional Failures	
* Enforcement	Need for an external enforcement authority
* Public Good & Externality	Strong in the provision of enhanced quality of goods and training
* Efficiency	Efficiency in industry with complex and rapidly changing technology
* Equity	When widely developed into industrial districts, networks can promote greater equality, if weakly developed, networks can enhance social inequality

Source: Lakshmanan and Button (2008, p. 454).

governments—in terms of economic tasks, roles, and activities. In the recent decades of growing neo-liberal ideologies, the national government is hiving off its economic policy roles through "privatization of the public sphere" in the form of *deregulation, liberalization, muted macroeconomic policy roles, and the emphasis of free markets and voluntarism.* On the other hand, urban governments assume increasing economic policy roles, as explicit spatial policies are needed to help the globalized Knowledge Economy function effectively in the keen economic competition among cities worldwide.

As the Knowledge Economy is dominantly located in large urban areas, urban governments assume increasing economic policy roles. In the late industrial era (preceding the rise of the Knowledge Economy) urban regions in the US used "beggar thy neighbor" policies of grants and capital subsidies, which were ineffective in attracting new economic activities to a specific region. In the emerging Knowledge Economy, however, explicit urban spatial policies are needed. In the context of these challenges to growth and economic sustainability, many urban areas reinvent themselves as entrepreneurial cities, modifying their identities and functions (Lakshmanan and Chatterjee 2005). *Urban policy actors are increasing their economic policy roles and attenuating their urban public goods functions.* In the process, urban actors have developed new policies for sustainable intercity competition, as well as new institutions and organizations for implementation.[7] Urban policy is no longer the exclusive domain of the public sector. Partnerships between public, private, and civil society actors in many cities creatively assemble relevant physical infrastructures by securing land, physical, and human capital. Urban transaction costs for global network firms are lowered in this process in a variety of ways, thereby promoting growth in relevant cities. Thus, the entrepreneurial city (Lakshmanan and Chatterjee 2005) appears to be adapting to the urban economic growth challenge and the transition to the Knowledge Economy.

Such urban areas or "entrepreneurial cities" seek to assist private actors in commercial activities that also serve the urban area's growth objectives. The city government becomes a risk-taker and a promoter of global competitiveness for businesses in the city (Clarke and Gaile 1998). It also enables discovery of new markets and catalyzes the formation of private-public partnerships in testing and developing new technology. It innovates by developing new policies and institutional forms which permit cities like New York and Boston to help local industries reap competitive advantages in external markets, by increasing sales of their goods and services. This requires addressing problems (inherited from the industrial era) resulting from unbalanced demand and supply of goods and services, such as decaying transportation infrastructure, insufficient or inappropriate industrial space, inadequate housing quality, lack of critical skills, crime, etc. These cities, such as New York, are thus creative actors essentially endogenizing their own growth. Utilizing their own resources, they adapt old areas to new uses in numerous permutations and combinations, and pyramid one asset onto another as part of continuous reinvention (Savitch 1988; UNCHR 2002; Lakshmanan and Chatterjee 2005;

Lakshmanan et al. 2000). Urban transaction costs for global network firms are thus lowered, thereby promoting growth in relevant cities.[8]

Innovations in Urban Governance

Typically, the literature on urban locational issues and entrepreneurial decision-making has focused on the behavior of market actors, and on the impacts of such activity on the regional economy (e.g. Acs et al. 2002; Malecki 1994; Stohr 1989). This chapter extends the discussion of urban entrepreneurship to the roles of non-market—social sector and public sector—entrepreneurs and the manner in which all three types of actors influence each other in their entrepreneurial decisions in Knowledge Economy urban space. The creation of new physical and non-physical urban infrastructures, and restructured urban economic and physical space appropriate to the requirements of the emerging Knowledge Economy is possible only when the urban public and social sector agents complement the work of private sector agents (traditionally associated with economic growth). This process of *joint action* by urban private/public/social actors (with their complex interdependencies) produces urban *public value* (Moore 1996).

This emerging, inclusive urban decision context comprises diverse economic actors adjusting to ongoing global structural change. Governance institutions—defined as new modes of governing economic interactions among such actors—emerge where political, social, and private sector actors participate in different kinds of networks. The purpose of engagement in these networks is twofold: (i) the reduction of uncertainty in a volatile economic environment, and (ii) the ex-ante coordination of actors from various urban sectors who collectively produce new capacities and the consequent structural competitiveness for that city in the Knowledge Economy (Jessop 1997).

5. Processes of Structural Change and the Passage to a Knowledge Economy in the Megalopolis: Highlights

The central argument of this chapter is that the rise and evolution of the Knowledge Economy in the Megalopolis represents a *multidimensional structural change and transition* from an older dysfunctional industrial economy to a vibrant increasingly knowledge intensive economy. The first dimension is *economic structural change and evolution*. What processes and mechanisms govern such an economic structural change yielding new knowledge and its embodiment in new goods and services?

The second dimension pertains to the *global spatial organization* of metropolitan socioeconomic activities, which has emerged in the Megalopolis with a global division of labor and the integration of the domestic and international markets. What recent technologies and processes have enabled these globally organized activities in the metropolitan areas of the Megalopolis?

The third dimension of structural change towards the Knowledge Economy of the Megalopolis is centered on the metropolitan areas, which serve as socioeconomic and urban platforms for private, public, and social sector change agents who create and commercialize new knowledge and operate the global economy and its worldwide business and non-business networks—which both direct and adapt to structural change. These networks constitute a key economic institutional innovation. Further, the public sector actors in such urban areas—engaged in intercity competition for globally mobile economic activities—must not only acquire *new* economic and political policies and instruments and innovate *novel structures of urban governance* appropriate to the creation and operation of a *new urban physical and spatial structure of land uses and infrastructures* which are supportive of the Knowledge Economy. The acquisition of such new capacities is possible only when urban public and social sector change agents complement the work of private sector agents with more inclusive rules of engagement and decision-making among urban public, private, and social sector actor—in the form of *new models of urban governance*. These new governance models facilitate the decisions and implementation of the new physical layouts and the efficient functioning of the new knowledge-rich metropolitan regions.

This chapter has proposed a rich conceptual framework which captures the multiple mechanisms and processes which underlie the multidimensional structural change and evolution embodied in the transition of the Megalopolis to a Knowledge Economy. The argument made in this chapter is that the rise of the Knowledge Economy in the Megalopolis represents a convergence and interactions, in recent decades, among four broad types of technologies.

1 & 2. *Two GPTs of transport and ICT*, which *promote* a) the globalized division of labor and the integration of domestic and international markets in the Megalopolis economy, and b) facilitate the creation of new technologies of goods production and knowledge intensive services. Contemporary space-shrinking transport technologies (Interstate Highway system, aviation, containers, and recent high speed railroads) and ICT (e.g. the Internet) have facilitated the rise of global systems of investment, production, markets, and the organization of enterprises. Further, the enhanced and low price connectivity offered by ICT among economic and social actors and ideas in global space increases the potential for new *combinations of goods and services, input sources, markets*, and organizations—in other words, *technical change*, in the Schumpeterian sense.

3. *New technologies of production of knowledge intensive goods and services*: a) technologies and associated mechanisms underlying the production of knowledge-rich goods, and b) the technical and organizational innovations which have made possible the ICT-enabled KIBS, which enable global corporations in the Megalopolis to develop and support management innovations that make possible the productive and smooth operation of global supply chains and the integration of global corporate operations, and enhance the productivity of many service sectors and,

4. *New institutional and organizational technologies*, which promote a) knowledge creation via the new *institution of economic networks* and b) the development of *new governance models and the interactive engagement of*

political, social, and economic entrepreneurs and change agents, which make possible *the spatial restructuring of the land uses and infrastructures* emerging in the large metropolitan areas of the Megalopolis.

Spatial Distributional Effects of the Rise of the Urban Knowledge Economy

The narrative of this chapter is a multidimensional structural change and a transition to a Knowledge Economy as a result of convergence and interactions of four broad classes of technologies. It is in this context, in the last three decades to the present day, a remarkable *reversal* of regional economic decline and indeed a notable economic resurgence has occurred in the metropolitan areas of the Megalopolis. A variety of knowledge intensive production and service sector enterprises have arrived and continue to grow in the several metropolitan areas of the Megalopolis. These metropolises, representing large concentrations of high quality human, cultural, and organizational capital, are the vibrant contemporary "knowledge regions," which jointly make up the mega region of the Megalopolis.

Lest this picture exudes triumphalism, one must draw attention to *two sets of adverse distributional consequences associated with this transition to the Knowledge Economy in the Megalopolis metropolises* and experienced by the population in lower income strata. One set of such adverse effects has been noted earlier in this chapter and derives from the spatial structuring and land use reorganization in response to the requirements of GNCs. In view of the powerful forces underlying intercity competition, it is likely that such consequences—in terms of adverse opportunities and amenity access—will compound in the future, creating worsening livelihood chances for a significant group of lower income knowledge era urban residents. The current focus on growth and the neglect of issues of income distribution and urban quality of life is not, however, sustainable too long in the age of globalization. It is likely that urban social entrepreneurs (SEs) will formulate and address forcefully such distributional issues—generating in the near future an agenda for future policy initiatives for addressing these growing quality of life disparities and tackling these equity issues (Lakshmanan and Chatterjee 2005).

A second class of considerable adverse effects of the rise of the Knowledge Economy derive from the increasing globalization of the Megalopolis metropolitan economies and the hollowing out of the low and increasingly moderate value adding components of sectors in their economies and moving such activities to low wage countries worldwide. The consequence has been employment losses, and wage declines among the low and the medium income levels of the Megalopolis labor force. This process of *globalization and the consequent rapid rise of income inequality* in the US, in the Megalopolis, and in the component major metropolitan areas are analyzed in detail in Chapter 7.

Box 4.1 Urban Resilience and the Passage to the Knowledge Economy: Role of Social and Political Entrepreneurs

Urban Resilience refers to the ability of the urban system to build the capacity to deal with change towards a Knowledge Economy and continue to develop.

The contemporary literature on entrepreneurial decision-making and the rise of the urban Knowledge Economy has focused largely on the behavior of market actors, and on the impacts of such activity on the regional economy (e.g. Acs et al. 2002; Malecki 2000; Stohr 1989). The discussion here extends the scope of urban entrepreneurship additionally to the roles of non-market actors—*social* (civil society) and *public* sector entrepreneurs—*and how all three classes of actors influence one other and jointly promote the entrepreneurial decisions in shaping urban space in the emerging Knowledge Economy.*

Urban SEs respond to existing urban conditions and use innovative strategies to change social realities, and the urban environmental context broadly defined, for the collective good. First, SEs take a strategic view—visualizing and judging the potential of urban localities and aiming to bring about urban transformation. SEs try to alter perceptions that members of civil society, the public sector, and the business community have of development potentials of certain urban localities. Second, they focus on improved service delivery in specific localities and of the role that improved service delivery plays in promoting development potentials of those localities. Thus, SEs recognize an urban social need and relevant innovative solutions, promote and market their ideas changing the perceptions and attitudes among public, private, and social sector actors, and marshal personal and community resources through institutional innovation, risk taking, and performance-oriented implementation.

SEs have raised, in the industrial era in this manner, social and political consciousness about urban "market failures" and "government failures," and demanded solutions for welfare improvements in specific urban locations. They have also provided a variety of innovative solutions (that have improved the life chances and mobility of urban residents and fostered social change in urban areas) and have been primarily viewed as social reformers. Examples of such SEs include late nineteenth and early twentieth century social innovators such as: Jane Addams (Settlement House, housing in Chicago), Horace Mann (promotion of public education), Chamberlin (first public provision of urban water, sewer, and power in Birmingham, UK), Olmstead (urban parks and environment), and Patrick Geddes (English New Towns).

The translation of innovative ideas of a few SEs or visionaries about socioeconomic change in urban space is, however, contingent. Their ideas about new urban development directions and supportive institutions need to be promoted and marketed in an ambience where agents of change confront defenders of the status quo. When the "time for an idea has come," what is implied is that there is some individual or a collective which has successfully implemented a radical idea—promoting an idea, overcoming social resistance, taking risks, investing monetary and non-monetary resources, and other elements of entrepreneurial behavior (Lakshmanan 1993) Thus, SEs change the behavior of other decision makers in society, by building on the ideas and accomplishments of those before them, and by their own truly original ideas. They make societal change possible through their innovative solutions and persistent strategies. Their ideas and solutions spread through the body politic, moving new initiatives from the desirable to the doable. A major impact that SEs have is in creative institution building, consciousness-raising, marshalling support, and new service provision.

The success of SEs depends on their possessing two critical and related attributes—namely their capacity to network and to understand the social milieu in which their innovative actions have to be embedded. Networks are interconnected dyadic relationships where the nodes may be roles, individuals or organizations. Networking remains crucial since entrepreneurship is a continuous process of innovative activity requiring information on new opportunities and constraints. While entrepreneurship is a continuous process, entrepreneurs are not continuously entrepreneurial. They act in the entrepreneurial role when new opportunities for intervention are identified. Networking provides information about risks, uncertainties, peer evaluation for successful venture creation and growth (see Table 4.3). It allows successful entrepreneurs to mobilize social resources and increase their stock of social capital. Networks are socially embedded relationships and network ties can be of three types—information networks, exchange networks, and networks of influence. All three types of networks are common to entrepreneurs in general, though the relative weighting of these network ties varies by the type of entrepreneurial activity. Information networks are critical for SEs since they lack monetary resources (relative to business and public entrepreneurs) to implement their ideas. They need to convince a larger citizenry of the benefit and feasibility of their innovative solutions to alter existing urban realities. Their networks primarily work through informal channels of mentoring and social contact and their ability to effect change is based on *people* power rather than on *monetary* power even though access to monetary resources are facilitative. One of the many constraints faced by SEs is funding for innovative projects. Networks of influence and exchange with public and business entrepreneurs are also critical for the success of SEs and their networks extend to entrepreneurs of the other two sectors.

Table 4.3 Urban, Political, Social, and Economic Entrepreneurs: A Comparative Profile

	Political Entrepreneurs (PEs)	Social Entrepreneurs (SEs)	Economic Entrepreneurs (EEs)
Attributes and Motivations	Seek political payoffs, risk takers with strategic vison, detecting potentials in localities; flexible and patient in order to change attitudes of different types of people; PEs can influence generative allocations of urban entrepreneurial resources; PEs can cause rent-seeking activities.	Aim is social value creation to improve quality of life; combine innovations, resourcefulness and opportunity to transform attributes of urban space to improve social efficiency and equality; focus on accountability to urban constituencies.	Profit bottom-line; bring to market new products and processes; reconfigure special competitiveness.
Activities	Change reward structures (e.g. rules for entrepreneurial activities); leverage social, public funds from private and civil society sectors; allocate revenues for innovative solutions; knowledge transfer; various partnerships with SEs and EEs; co-production of urban development with economic and social sectors. Fosters opportunities and removes barriers for SEs and EEs.	Problem identification, consciousness raising; large input of vison, determination, community support but limited money; demanders of new policies; focus on risk reduction and on (change of urban location values); providers of targeted services; consensus building; communicate to an gain support from clients.	Spatial arbitrage; risk taking and new locations and ventures; production of negative externalities.
Composition	Political and elected leaders, administrators, special commissions, etc.	Not-for-profit, non-profit, private voluntary sector.	Global corporations, SMEs, real-estate interests, financial institutions.

	Political Entrepreneurs (PEs)	*Social Entrepreneurs (SEs)*	*Economic Entrepreneurs (EEs)*
Networks	Node in the flow of knowledge linking SEs and EEs; node for resource transfer through grants, loans loan guarantees, fostering SE and EE networks and their cooperation.	Networks and connectivity within and between communities. Networks based on 'trust'; with PEs and EEs; leverage community and market power for locality improvement.	Inter-enterprise networks. University/firm networks. Town/government networks. Untraded interdependences among sectors.

Source: Lakshmanan and Chatterjee (2012).

SEs focus on institutional development, primarily through establishing innovative start-ups or radical modification of existing "not-for-profit" institutions. The activities of SEs are implemented through non-governmental organizations (NGOs) that start small and are community based. However, these start-ups have the potential to grow in their original location and, through processes of diffusion, spread to other cities in the nation and internationally. Institution building is the major instrument in their efforts to bring about change in perceptions of *the what and how of social innovations.*

Table 4.3 identifies the variety of functions and the variety of coordination issues to be confronted in the entrepreneurial urban area hosting the emerging Knowledge Economy. They include attributes and motivations, activities, composition, and network characteristics of the urban private, public, and social sector actors, as the latter jointly generate urban "public value."

Box 4.2 Policy and Institutional Evolution of Knowledge Metropolises: Illustrative Experience from Boston

Institutional innovations and governance models have been developed in Boston (as well as in other regions) to facilitate the translation of new economic growth of the Knowledge Economy into inherited industrial urban space, and avoid market failure of spatially produced goods. Such capacity to generate new urban/regional land uses and

infrastructures is created from within the urban region through collaborative innovation embracing many private, public, and social sector
actors (as well as individuals and firms).

Table 4.4 selectively provides the variety of institutional forms found
in one entrepreneurial city—Boston. Moreover, the success or failure of
these institutions depends on how consistent they are with the individual city's socio-political climate and economic context—all of which are
highly dynamic in the entrepreneurial cities. The discussion here provides only a framework for elucidating the characteristics and variety of
institutions. For each institutional form, the table identifies *objectives
sought, types of policy instruments (financial and the underlying fiscal),
and physical and administrative infrastructures used to promote urban
policy objectives.*

In areas adjacent to universities (e.g. MIT, Harvard, Boston
University) in Cambridge and Boston (Massachusetts) the focus is
on combining university R&D activities with those of local development councils, and adopting a business incubator model, involving the
participation of entrepreneurial firms tapping into public and venture
capital seed funds. Towards this end, infrastructure investments were
made in industrial parks on greenfield and brownfield sites by both the
public, not-for-profit, and for-profit private sector institutions to spon-
sor flexible and sophisticated human capital creation. The financial
instruments for the development of this infrastructure capital could be
drawn from the issuance of debt instruments such as revenue bonds and
tax increment financing by the public sector and capital development
loans by the universities. These are complicated processes not only in
the variety of institutions involved, but also in the diversity of the vested
interests of each institution. The public sector is increasingly adopting
a catalytic and enabling role in protecting public interest while reducing
its own service delivery responsibilities.

Table 4.4 does not provide an exhaustive list because the variations
in time and space are numerous and specific institutional forms derive
from the geographical and historical context of the city. Since globalization affects cities differentially, responses vary according to local
considerations, local resource capacities, and local abilities to mobilize social and political capital and institutional history. The objective
here has been to provide a flavor of the great diversity of institutions
involved in the American entrepreneurial city of Boston and to show
the complexity involved in co-production strategies growing out of the
continuing experiment of fostering partnerships between the numerous
public and private sector stakeholders. Policies are most effective when
the public sector can induce private and social institutions with diverse
instruments to work together for the common urban welfare.

Table 4.4 Entrepreneurial City's Objectives, Institutions, Instruments, and Infrastructures in Boston

Institutional Forms	Types of Instruments*		Infrastructure		Objectives
	Financial	Fiscal	Physical	Administrative	
Community Development Corporation (CDC)	Community bloc development grants, other project grants, venture capital pools	Tax abatement for city	Capital improvement in streets & neighborhoods	Streamlining licensing & permitting	Downtown revitalization
Local development councils and business incubators	Use of various debt instruments such as revenue bonds, venture capital pools	Tax increment financing	Industrial parks on greenfield & brownfield sites	Skilling, networking	Startup companies
Public-private partnerships for employment creation	Loan guarantees	Special assessment districts	Historic & landmark preservation	Regional economic development groups	Advertisement & tourism development
Empowerment zones & enterprise communities. EZ/ EC (Partnership but Fed/ State) city gov't & private	Federal grants for financing capita	Property improvement tax abatement; income assistance for commuting; sales tax credit; tax exemptions	Transportation assistance for commuting; worker training	Creation of business technology center; market associations	Retain existing industry; attract new investment; foster local entrepreneurship
Rebuild Boston Energy Initiative [Partnership of city gov't, power companies, community organizations and energy consultation)	Funding for energy companies	—	Retrofitting buildings; consulting new construction	Linkage to business owners via Boston Office of Business Development	Upgrade energy efficiency of new and retrofitted facilities; reduce factor costs, attract new investment

* A selected & illustrative list. Not all instruments were used by all cities. The package varied between cities and in time within a city.

Source: Lakshmanan and Chatterjee (2005, 2009).

Notes

1 Agglomeration economies have been further characterized in the work of Hoover (1948) and Isard (1956) as a) localization economies (being proximate to other producers of the same good or service), which embrace factors that reduce the average cost of producing outputs in that location, and b) urbanization economies (being proximate to producers of a broad range of goods and services) which are external economies accruing to enterprises because of savings from large-scale operation in a large agglomeration (and thus independent of industry) in the form of knowledge gains from diversity (Jacobs, 1969). Research by Vernon (1960) and Chinitz (1961) on the causes and consequences of spatial clustering of economic activities in a metropolis like New York focused on issues linking growth and agglomeration.

2 Further, such diversity fosters specialization in inputs and outputs, yielding higher returns (Quigley, 1998). Glaeser et al.'s (1992) analysis of a large number of US cities suggests that industrial diversity in a region is important to subsequent economic performance. Henderson et al. (1995) suggest that the extent of diversity in manufacturing industries at the start of the period was not important in determining employment and subsequent performance of mature industries, but did matter in attracting new industries such as scientific instruments and electronic components.

3 This is the spatial version of the Dixit-Stiglitz monopolistic competition model (1977).

4 Camagni (2004) emphasizes the "physical" and "social" proximity of persons working in the enterprises within the urban clusters. He suggests that the physical and social proximity leads to what he calls "relational capital," by which people are able to connect with one another, to develop notions of trust, exchange knowledge and innovate.

5 "They perish in the instant of their performance" ... "The labor of the servant seldom leaves any trace or value behind them."

6 The resulting learning, knowledge accumulation and economic evolution are helped in such regions by two kinds of proximities: geographical—leading to reduction of production and transaction costs—and socio-cultural–shared behavioral, cognitive and moral codes (Camagni 2004). This combination of geographic and socio-cultural proximities leads to a greater intensity of interactions, limited opportunistic behavior, greater division of labor, and cooperation among the enterprises.

7 Government intervention has thus taken on a spatial role. It faces the need to adjust spatial imbalances between demand and supply at the city level. Private entrepreneurs at the urban level cannot solve the basic production problem of securing capital and land at the right place, time, and cost, so fixed and operating costs might be lowered to maintain profitability. Consequently, public-private cooperation in the form of partnerships (public acquisition of land, partial public ownership of facilities, concessions, leases, etc.) bring major competitiveness-enhancing developments, such as Times Square in New York and the Docklands in London. The entrepreneurial city is the newest manifestation of active public intervention to ensure that the market for spatially determined goods acts in an orderly way (Lakshmanan and Chatterjee 2005).

8 The transformation of a variety of spaces and structures—urban manufacturing zones and production facilities left redundant by industrial decline, public and privately owned spaces and structures—into productive land uses is a case in point. The conversion of waterfront zones into "new landscapes of consumption" had the dual objective of attracting tourists and high wage white collar firms. While American cities lost their older industrial base, the entrepreneurial cities became centers of production for higher-order goods and services, thereby, increasing their competitive edge in international markets. Urban public and private sector decision makers began to recognize the global economy as both a source of competition as well as a marketing opportunity for locally produced goods and services.

References

Acs, Z.J., FitzRoy, F.R., Smith, I., 2002. High-technology employment and R&D in cities: heterogeneity vs specialization. *The Annals of Regional Science* 36(3), 373–386.

Amin, A., Cohendet, P., 2004. *Architectures of Knowledge. Firms, Communities and Competencies*, Oxford: Oxford University Press.

Andersson, A., Chatterjee, L.R., Lakshmanan, T.R., 2004. Urban policy in a global economy. In Capello, R., Nijkamp, P. (eds) *Urban Dynamics and Growth*, Amsterdam: Elsevier, pp. 837–863.

Bathelt, H., Malmberg, A., Maskell, P., 2004. Clusters and knowledge: local buzz and global pipelines and the process of knowledge creation. *Progress in Human Geography* 28(1), 1–56.

Baumol, W., 1967. Macroeconomics of unbalanced growth: the anatomy of urban crisis. *The American Economic Review* 57(3), 415–426.

Braudel, F., 1992. *The Perspective of the World: Civilization and Capitalism 15th–18th Century*, Berkeley, CA: University of California Press.

Breshnehan, T.F., Trajtenberg, M., 1992. *General Purpose Technologies: Engines of Growth?* NBER Working Paper 4148.

Brusco, S., 1982. The Emilian model: productive decentralization and social integration. *Cambridge Journal of Economics* 6(2), 167–184.

Brynjolfsson, E., Hitt, L.M., 2000. Beyond computation: information technology, organizational transformation and business performance. *Journal of Economic Perspectives* 14(4), 23–48.

Brynjolfsson, E., Hitt, L.M., 2003. Computing productivity: firm-level evidence. *The Review of Economics and Statistics* 85(4), 793–808.

Brynjolfsson, E., Hitt, L.M., Yang, S., 2002. Intangible assets: computers and organizational capital. *Brookings Papers on Economic Activity* 1, 137–198.

Bryson, J.R., Daniels, P.W., 2007. *The Handbook of Service Industries,* Northampton, MA: Edward Elgar.

Camagni, R., 2004. Uncertainty, social capital, and community governance: the city as a Milieu. In Capello, R., Nijkamp, P. (eds) *Urban Dynamics and Growth: Advances in Urban Economics,* Amsterdam: Elsevier, pp. 121–149.

Capello, R., 2011. Innovation and productivity: local competitiveness and the role of space. In Cooke, P., Asheim, B., Boschama, R., Martin, R., Schwartz, D., Tödtling, F. (eds) *Handbook of Regional Innovation and Growth*, Northampton, MA: Edward Elgar, pp. 107–119.

Castells, M., 2000. *The Information Age: Economy, Society and Culture*, Oxford: Blackwell.

Chandler, A.D. Jr., 1977. *The Visible Hand: The Managerial Revolution in American Business*, Cambridge, MA: Harvard University Press.

Chinitz, B.J. 1961. Contrasts in agglomeration: New York and Pittsburgh. *American Economic Review* 51(2), 279–289.

Clarke, S.E., Gaile, G.L., 1998. *The Work of Cities*, Minneapolis, MN: The University of Minneapolis Press.

Cook, S.D.N., Brown, J.S., 1999. Bridging epistemologies: the generative dance between organizational knowledge and organizational knowing. *Organization Science* 10(4), 381–400.

Cooke, P., Asheim, B., Boschama, R., Martin, R., Schwartz, D., Tödtling, F., 2011. *Handbook of Regional Innovation and Growth*, Northampton, MA: Edward Elgar.

David, P.A., Wright, G., 1999. General purpose technologies and surges in productivity: historical reflections on the future of the ICT Revolution. Presented at the symposium on *Economic Challenges of the 21st Century in Historical Perspective*, Oxford, 2–4 July.

Dicken, P., 2000. A new geo-economy. In Held, D., McGrew, A. (eds) *The Global Transformations Reader: An Introduction To The Globalization Debate,* Cambridge: Polity Press, pp. 251–258.

Dixit, A.K., Stiglitz, J.E., 1977. Monopolistic competition and optimum product diversity: reply. *American Economic Review* 69(5), 961–963.

Drejer, I., 2004. Identifying innovation in surveys of services: a Schumpeterian perspective. *Research Policy* 33(3), 551–562.

Dunning, J.H., 1993. *The Globalization of Business,* London and New York.: Routledge.

Enright, M., 1998. *Regional Clusters and Firm Strategy*, Oxford: Oxford University Press.

Feldman, M.P., 2000. Location and innovation: the new economy geography of innovation, spillovers, and agglomeration. In Clark, G., Feldman, M., Gerler, M. (eds) *The Oxford Handbook of Economic Geography*, Oxford: Oxford University Press, pp. 373–394.

Fujita, M., Krugman, P., Venables, A.J., 1999. *The Spatial Economy*, Cambridge, MA: MIT Press.

Gertler, M.S., 2003. Tacit knowledge and the economic geography of context, or the undefinable tacitness of being (there). *Journal of Economic Geography* 3(1), 75–99.

Glaeser, E., Kallal, H., Scheinkman, J., Shleifer, A., 1992. Growth in cities. *Journal of Political Economy,* 100, 1126–1152.

Granovetter, M., 1985. Economic action and social structure: the problem of embeddedness. *American Journal of Sociology* 91(3), 481–510.

Groenewegen, J., Pitelis, C., Sjostrand, S.-E., 1995. *On Economic Institutions: Theory and Applications*, European Association for Evolutionary Political Economy, Brookefield: Edward Elgar.

Hage, J., Alter, C., 1997. A typology of interorganizational relationships and networks. In Hollingsworth, J.R., Boyer, R. (eds) *Contemporary Capitalism: The Embeddedness of Institutions,* New York, NY, Cambridge, UK: Cambridge University Press, pp. 94–126.

Henderson, J.V., Kuncoro, A., Turner, M., 1995. Industrial development of cities. *Journal of Political Economy,* 103, 1067–1090.

Hollingsworth, J.R., Boyer, R. (eds), 1997. *Contemporary Capitalism: The Embeddedness of Institutions*, Cambridge, UK: Cambridge University Press.

Hoover, E., 1948. *The Location of Economic Activity*, New York: McGraw-Hill.

Isard, W., 1956. *Location and Space-Economy: A General Theory Relating to Industrial Location, Market Areas, Land Use, Trade and Urban Structure*, Cambridge, MA: MIT Press.

Jacobs, J., 1969. *The Economy of Cities*, New York: Random House.

Jessop, B., 1997. The entrepreneurial city: re-imaging localities, redesigning economic governance. In Jewson, N., MacGregor S. (eds) *Realizing Cities: New Spatial Divisions and Social Transformation*, London: Routledge, pp. 28–41.

Kox, H.L.M., Rubalcaba, L., 2007. *Business Services and the Changing Structure of European Economic Growth*, CPB Memorandum 183, CPB Netherlands Bureau for Economic Policy Analysis.

Krugman, P., 1991. *Geography and Trade*, Cambridge, MA: MIT Press.

Lakshmanan, T.R., 1993. Social change induced by technology: promotion and resistance. In Ackerman, N. (ed.), *The Necessity of Friction*, Heidelberg: Physica Verlag, pp. 135–158.

Lakshmanan T.R., Anderson, W.P., 2001, *Transport Governance Systems and Trade Expansion*, The Uddevalla Symposium, Gothenburg, Sweden.

Lakshmanan, T.R., Andersson, D.E., Chatterjee, L.R., Sasaki, K., 2000. Three global cities: New York, London and Tokyo. In Åke, E., Andersson, D.E. (eds) *Gateways to Global Economy*, Cheltenham: Edward Elgar, pp. 48–80.

Lakshmanan, T.R., Button, K.J., 2009. Institutions and regional economic development. In Cappello, R., Nijkamp, P. (eds) *Advances in Regional Economics*, Cheltenham: Edward Elgar, pp. 443–460.

Lakshmanan, T.R., Chatterjee, L.R., 2005. Economic consequences of transport improvements. *Access* (Spring), 28–33.

Lakshmanan, T.R., Chatterjee, L.R., 2009. New governance institutions in the entrepreneurial urban region. *Innovation: The European Journal of Social Science Research* 22(3), 371–391.

Lakshmanan, T.R., Chatterjee, L.R., 2012. Entrepreneurial creative clusters in the global economy. In Girard, L.F., Levent, F., Nijkamp, P. (eds) *Sustainable Cities and Creativity*, Aldershot: Ashgate, Chapter 5.

Lakshmanan, T.R., Subramanian, U., Anderson, W.P., Lauetier, F.A., 2001. *Integration of Transport and Trade Facilitation: Selected Regional Studies.* Washington DC: The World Bank.

Malecki, E.J., 1994. Entrepreneurship in regional and local development. *International Regional Science Review* 16, 119–153.

Malecki, E.J., 2000. Knowledge and regional competitiveness. *Erdkunde* 54, 331–334.

Markusen, A., 1996. Sticky places in slippery space. *Economic Geography* 72(3), 293–313.

Marshall, A., 1920. *Principles of Economics*, London: MacMillan.

McGuckin, R., Stiroh, K., 2001. Do computers make output harder to measure? *Journal of Technology Transfer* 26(4), 295–321.

Miles, I., Kastrinos, N., Flanagan, K., Bilderbeek, R., den Hertog, P., Huntink, W., Bouman, M., 1995. *Knowledge-Intensive Business Services: Users, Carriers and Sources of Innovation,* EC, Luxembourg (DG13 SPRINT-EIMS).

Moore, H., 1996. *Creating Public Value and Strategic Management in Government*, Cambridge, MA: Harvard University Press.

Nelson, R.R., Winter, S.G., 1982. *An Evolutionary Theory of Economic Change*, Cambridge, MA: Harvard University Press.

North, D.C., 1990. *Institutions, Institutional Change and Economic Performance*, Cambridge, U.K.: Cambridge University Press.

North, D.C., 1994. Economic performance through time. *American Economic Review* 84(3), 359–368.

Pilat, D., 2001. Innovation and productivity in services: state of the art. In OECD (ed.) *Innovation and Productivity of Services,* OECD: Paris, pp. 17–54.

Pilat, D., Wolfl, A., 2004. ICT production and ICT use: what role in aggregate productivity growth? In OECD (ed.) *The Economic Impact of ICT—Measurement, Evidence, and Implications,* OECD: Paris, pp. 85–104.

Piore, M., Sabel, C., 1984. *The Second Industrial Divide,* New York: Basic Books.

Polyani, M., 1983. *The Tacit Dimension,* Gloucester, MA: Peter Smith.

Polyanyi, K., 1944. *The Great Transformation: Political and Economic Origins of Our Time,* New York: Beacon Press.

Porter, M., 1990. *The Competitive Advantage of Nations,* New York: Free Press.

Quigley, J.M., 1998. Urban diversity and economic growth. *The Journal of Economic Perspectives* 12(2), 127–138.

Sabel, C.F., 1997. Constitutional orders: trust building and response to change. In Hollingsworth, J.R., Boyer, R. (eds) *Contemporary Capitalism: The Embeddedness of Institutions,* Cambridge, England and New York: Cambridge University Press, pp. 101–149.

Sapprasert, K., 2007. *The Impact of ICT on the Growth of Service Industries,* Center for Technology, Innovation and Culture, University of Oslo, Working Paper 20070531.

Sassen, S., 2000. *Cities in a World Economy,* Thousand Oak, CA: Pine Forge Press.

Sassen, S., 2002. Introduction: locating cities in global circuits. In Sassen, S. (ed.) *Global Networks, Linked Cities,* New York: Routledge, pp. 1–36.

Savitch, H.V., 1988. *Post-industrial Cities: Politics and Planning in New York, Paris, and London,* Princeton, NJ: Princeton University Press.

Scott, A.J., 1998. *Regions and the World Economy: The Coming Shape of Global Production, Competition and Political Order,* Oxford: Oxford University Press.

Smith, A., 1776. *The Wealth of Nations,* London: Strahan and Cadell.

Stohr, W.B., 1989. Regional policy at the crossroads: an overview. In Albrechts, L., Moulaert, F., Roberts, P., Swyngedouw, E. (eds) *Regional Policy at the Crossroads,* London: Jessica Kingsley Publishers.

Storper, M., 1995. The resurgence of regional economies, ten years later: the region as a nexus of untraded interdependencies. *European Urban and Regional Studies* 2(3), 191–221.

Taylor, P.J., Lang, R.E., 2005. *US Cities in the World City Network,* Washington DC: The Brookings Institutions.

Triplett, J.E., Bosworth, B.P., 2003. Productivity measurement issues in service industries: Baumol's Disease has been cured. *Federal Reserve Bank of New York* 2014 (September), 23–33.

UNCTAD, 1970. *Unitization of Cargo,* Geneva, Switzerland: United Nations.

United Nations Centre for Human Settlements (UNCHS), 2002. *Cities in a Globalizing World,* London: Earthscan.

Vernon, R., 1960. *Metropolis 1985,* Cambridge, MA: Harvard University Press.

Von Hippel, E., 1988. *The Sources of Innovation,* Oxford: Oxford University Press.

Williamson, O.E., 1985. *The Economic Institutions of Capitalism,* New York: Free Press.

5 Passage of the Megalopolis to the Knowledge Economy

The Empirical Record

1. Introduction and Overview

The aim of this chapter is to review a) the observed structural change patterns and the socioeconomic evolution in the last three decades in the Megalopolis and its five major metropolitan areas (Boston, New York, Philadelphia, Baltimore, and Washington DC) and b) assess the degree of coherence between those observed patterns and the predictions of our Model of Economic Structural Change and the region's passage to the Knowledge Economy, presented in Chapter 4.

The opening part of this chapter describes the recent transition of the Megalopolis from the mature industrial economy to the beginnings of the Knowledge Economy and its subsequent evolution, highlighting in the process its key attributes. It proceeds then to a statistical portrait of the Knowledge Economy identifying its scale, composition, and growth patterns in the Megalopolis and in the US in a recent ten-year period. Finally, it situates the dominant Knowledge Economy sectors in the Megalopolis in the national context.

The latter part of this chapter offers a more detailed portrait of the ongoing economic structural evolution in the major metropolitan areas of the Megalopolis. These metro areas are the epicenters of the Megalopolis Knowledge Economy. Four of these metropolitan areas (Boston, New York, Philadelphia, and Baltimore) began as ports two to three centuries ago, and have successfully evolved and reinvented themselves repeatedly, initially from commercial economies to vibrant industrial economies and currently reinventing themselves as Knowledge Economies.[1] Indeed, the case study in this chapter of Boston metropolitan area—with its near four century run of different innovations—lays out the history of *economic growth, decline, resilience, and reinvention* at various times, to highlight the factors and processes undergirding Boston's historical record of repeated regional resilience evocative of the contemporary era of its regional reinvention as a Knowledge Economy.

2. Knowledge Economy in the Megalopolis

Rise of the Knowledge Economy

The contemporary discussions of the Knowledge Economy draw a lot from the ideas and speculations in the late 1960s and early 1970s of some intellectuals with backgrounds in economics (Machlup 1962), futurology (Drucker 1969), and sociology (Bell 1973). These scholars believed that the mature industrial societies of their times would transition into a post-industrial era where knowledge would become a new factor of production. This new economy would depend on ideas rather than physical abilities and on the utilization of ideas rather than of physical effort and on the application of knowledge and technology rather than the conversion of physical materials with the use of cheap labor. The nature of work would transition, they argued, from being muscle-based to mind-based.

However, these notions of a likely transition to a mind-based economy did not attract much attention among social scientists, urbanists, or planners and lay unelaborated and dormant till the early 1990s, when a variety of scholars in many fields discovered and elaborated in quick order the attributes of and the processes underlying the growth and evolution of the Knowledge Economy in North America, Europe, Japan, and elsewhere. A flood of literature from various social sciences, urban studies, and the management and business literature has followed since. A noteworthy early example is Manuel Castells' (1996) work *The Rise of the Network Society,* which suggested that information now drove the new economy, and that information also characterized the new mode of production. However, Castells went beyond *just* information and knowledge to their application to generate further knowledge and use of information processing/communication devices, in a cumulative feedback loop between innovation and the uses of innovation in the creation of value and wealth. While Castells pays considerable attention to technology, he noted that "minds" were now the most important asset. For him, the human mind has always been, but more than ever in the current era, the source of wealth and power.

Using the number of patents registered in the 1963–2001 period with the US Patent Office as one measure of knowledge growth activity, one observes that the number of patents issued to US inventors in 1979 was lower than in 1963. However, in the subsequent period 1983–2001 (when the increasing embodiment of knowledge in goods and services has been widely noted) the number of patents issued to US inventors lot more than doubled—from 47,642 to 168,040—suggesting a clear acceleration of the generation of new knowledge in that period (Powell and Snellman 2004).

Further, in the last two decades, many national statistical agencies around the world and international bodies such as OECD and the World Bank have attempted to develop statistical portraits of the size and composition of the Knowledge Economies in North America, Europe, OECD Asia, and other parts of the world. Such a statistical portrait becomes possible and valuable, if we understand the processes governing the emerging economy—where knowledge intangibles are important, where ICT enables networked systems to augment information flows and introduce process and organizational innovations, and how all of these developments are reshaping emerging economies in the Megalopolis and elsewhere.

Three dimensions of this recent transformation toward the Knowledge Economy are worthy of note. First, with the rapid advances in ICT, a variety of electronic devices lower the need for routine skills and capabilities, while the demand for analytical, cognitive, and integrative skills increases in the economy over time. An empirical exploration of such changes over time of the skill content of economic activities has been carried out by Autor and colleagues (2003). These economists constructed trends in routine and non-routine tasks using the *Dictionary of Occupational Titles* (Department of Labor 1977) using task measures by gender and occupation, paired to employment and population data for 1960–1998. Non-routine analytical and non-routine interactive tasks have grown more rapidly in recent years as the share of knowledge-rich activities has grown. Shares of the labor force employed in routine occupations have dropped in the same period of the advent of the Knowledge Economy (Figure 5.1).

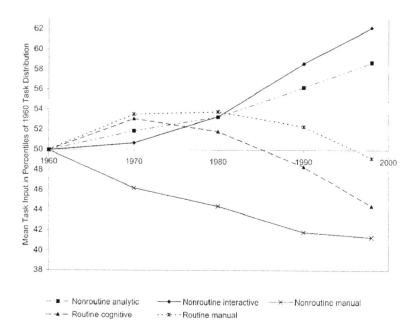

Figure 5.1 Trends in Routine and Non-Routine Task Input, 1960–1998

Source: Autor et al. (2003).

The second aspect of the emerging economy is the growth of the world trade particularly in higher value added goods. As noted in Chapters 3 and 4, the advent of the two GPT technologies of transport and ICT and the technical innovations in production and services delivery has promoted globalization trends and the rise of worldwide production and markets. The emerging aspects of the Knowledge Economy are driven by the growing demand for higher value added goods and services emanating from better educated and more discerning consumers and supplied by global network corporations (Lakshmanan and Chatterjee 2005; Brinkley 2008). In 1970, trade accounted for 27 percent of the World GDP, but by 2000, world trade rose to 47 percent of world GDP. Most of this growth in world trade in manufacturing was in high technology manufacturing and to a lesser extent in medium-high technology (World Bank 2007).

A third dimension of the transformation to a Knowledge Economy is the shift in business investment behavior in the US from the 1980s onwards. A Federal Reserve Bank of San Francisco study (Basu and Fernald 2006) found that US enterprises were investing heavily, not in assets such as machines and buildings (characteristics of the industrial era) but in *intangibles or knowledge-based assets—such as R&D, design and development, new process innovation, investments in human and organizational capital and brand equity.* Figure 5.2 shows the manner in which the composition of business investment has been changing in the United States between the 1950s and 2000s. In the decades of the 1980s to 2000s—characterized by the rise and growth of the Knowledge Economy in the US—there has been a significant shift in favor of intangible assets in American investment behavior. In the industrial economy of the US in the 1950s to the early 1980s, intangible assets lagged

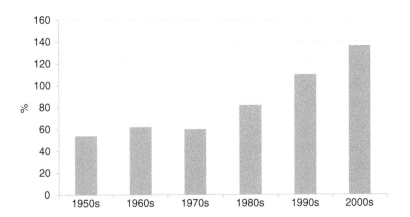

Figure 5.2 Ratio Between Investments in Intangible and Tangible Assets in the US, 1950s to 2000s

Source: Corrado et al. (2009), table 1, line 9.

behind tangible asset investments characteristic of the industrial era. In the 1990s and 2000s, as the Knowledge Economy was picking up steam in the Megalopolis and the United States, investments in intangible assets (R&D, investment in human and institutional capital and design and new product development, etc.) increasingly exceeded investments in tangible assets.

Key Attributes of the Knowledge Economy

The key attributes of the emerging Knowledge Economy are:

- a high and intense use of ICT in enterprises operated by highly educated and trained workers;
- Knowledge Economy enterprises introduce new management procedures in order to handle, store, and share information and create new knowledge across the organization;
- a rapidly growing share of capital investment is in intangible assets (R&D, investment in human and institutional capital and design and new product development, etc.) as compared to physical capital (buildings and machinery);
- the new enterprises consist of innovative organizations which introduce new technologies and which create process and organizational innovations;
- the Knowledge Economy is not only present in knowledge intensive sectors but increasingly penetrating all sectors of the economy.

Scale and Composition of the Knowledge Economy in the Megalopolis

How does one size the Knowledge Economy in the US and in the Megalopolis and map its evolution in recent times? Two approaches to identify this size are possible—one based on the number of *knowledge workers* in the economy, and the other based on the workforce in sectors defined as technology and *knowledge-based industries*.

The two most frequently used proxies for knowledge workers are: *an educational qualification and occupational class*. The proportion of workers aged 25 and above with an educational attainment of a bachelor's degree or above is widely used as a measure of a knowledge worker (Table 5.1). By this measure, the labor force in the Megalopolis in 2011 has a higher proportion (36 percent higher) of this level of educational attainment than the national labor force. This higher proportion of workers with a college degree and additional college preparation climbs to over 50 percent in the case of one Megalopolis metropolitan region (Boston)—as compared to the nation.

The second measure of a knowledge worker pertains to *membership in a knowledge intensive occupational class*. The occupational class comprising of workers in Management, Business, Science, and Arts (Table 5.1) is often

Table 5.1 Educational Attainment and Occupation by Class of Workers in the US, Megalopolis, and Five Component Metro Areas in 2011 (%)

		New York	Philadelphia	Boston	DC	Baltimore	Megalopolis	US
Educational attainment (aged 25 or above)	Less than high school	15.2	11.3	9.4	11.1	11.1	12.7	14.1
	High school graduate	26.5	31.1	24.5	28.3	26.6	27.1	28.4
	Some college/associate	22	24.7	23	27.3	26.6	23.8	29
	Bachelor's degree or higher	36.3	32.9	43.1	33.4	35.8	36.4	28.5
Occupational classes of workers	Management, business, science, arts	39.6	40.9	46.4	50.7	44.6	41.4	36
	Service	19.7	16.9	16.3	16.2	16.1	18.1	18.3
	Sales and office	24.7	25.4	22.9	20.8	23.8	24.1	24.5
	Natural resources, construction, maintenance	6.9	7.3	6.4	6.8	7.5	7.3	9.1
	Production, transportation, material moving	9	9.6	8	5.5	8	9.2	12.1

Source: 2011 American Community Survey, US Census Bureau.

identified as a knowledge worker group. Again, the Megalopolis and its component five large metro areas display a higher level of knowledge intensity in its workforce than the nation, with Washington DC and Boston metro areas topping the list.

As noted earlier, certain agencies such as OECD and EUROSTAT have attempted statistical definitions of knowledge-based industries and thereby estimate the growing size of the Knowledge Economies in Europe, USA, and OECD Asia. Though no agreed upon definitions of knowledge industries have arrived, many studies recognize high tech manufacturing (NACE categories 24.4, 353, 30, 32, 33), medium tech manufacturing (NACE 29, 31, 34, 35) and a variety of knowledge services (professional and business services, finance and insurance, education and health—NACE 71–74, 65–67, 80, 85). However, the NACE system is not followed in the US.

Given the nature of the data available in US statistical agencies, this study has utilized the following definitions of knowledge service and manufacturing sectors:[2]

Knowledge Services
* Business Services (NAICS 54)
* Finance & Insurance (NAICS 52)
* Information Services (NAICS 51)
* Health Services (NAICS 62 except 624)

Knowledge Manufacturing
* Chemicals (NAICS 325)
* Machinery (NAICS 333)
* Transport (NAICS 336)
* Computers and Electronics (NAICS 334)
* Medical Equipment and Supplies (NAICS 3391)

This is a narrower definition of the Knowledge Economy sectors as compared to some other studies and may therefore understate the size of the Knowledge Economy in the Megalopolis and the US.

Tables 5.2 and 5.3 describe the scale and composition of the Knowledge Economy—in terms of employment and payroll—over the years 2003–2012 in the Megalopolis and in the US.[3]

Over the ten-year period (2003–2012), employment in the Knowledge Economy of the Megalopolis and the USA declined while payroll (in constant dollars) increased substantially. The employment grew in knowledge service sectors—1 percent in the Megalopolis and 6 percent in the US—but declined in Knowledge Manufacturing sectors (–25 percent and –16 percent respectively in the Megalopolis and in the US). The total payroll of the knowledge service sector *rose* 10 percent and 7 percent respectively in the Megalopolis and in the US. The average per capita payroll in the knowledge service sector rose in this period from $54,021 to $59,549 in the Megalopolis,

Table 5.2 Knowledge Economy in the Megalopolis

			2003	2008	2012
Employment	Services	Information	882,706	733,620	673,626
		Finance & Insurance	1,588,772	1,496,251	1,320,558
		Business Services	1,842,470	1,997,323	1,996,151
		Health Services	2,623,230	2,828,396	3,019,482
		Total	6,937,178	7,055,590	7,009,817
	Manufacturing	Chemicals	169,303	146,149	120,214
		Machinery	121,764	102,493	87,248
		Transport	106,290	95,008	90,664
		Electronics	220,209	190,326	159,630
		Scientific Instruments	57,519	52,243	46,791
		Total	675,085	586,219	504,547
Payroll	Services	Information	44,844	45,641	45,203
		Finance & Insurance	126,747	152,735	132,997
		Business Services	108,913	124,120	127,746
		Health Services	94,247	104,412	111,481
		Total	374,751	426,908	417,427
	Manufacturing	Chemicals	9,935	7,856	6,847
		Machinery	5,374	4,535	4,007
		Transport	5,172	4,607	4,521
		Electronics	12,047	10,770	9,442
		Scientific Instruments	2,511	2,467	2,302
		Total	25,114	30,235	27,119

(Units: employment—number of employees, payroll—millions of 1998 US $).

Source: County Business Patterns, US Census Bureau.

and from $43,033 to $46,246 (1998 dollars) in the country. While the manufacturing sector declined in this period in employment and payroll, the average payroll/capita in the Knowledge Manufacturing sector increased in the Megalopolis by 44 percent from $37,201 in 2003 to $53,749. Over the

Table 5.3 Knowledge Economy in the US

			2003	2008	2012
Employment	Services	Information	3,599,902	3,434,234	3,136,025
		Finance & Insurance	6,463,706	6,511,616	5,979,661
		Business Services	7,340,246	8,032,847	8,016,181
		Health Services	13,283,513	14,600,914	15,536,802
		Total	30,687,367	32,579,611	32,668,669
	Manufacturing	Chemicals	841,375	810,788	738,641
		Machinery	1,129,140	1,149,654	1,044,231
		Transport	1,606,713	1,526,879	1,315,478
		Electronics	1,189,485	1,014,545	850,295
		Scientific Instruments	305,850	309,940	293,501
		Total	5,072,563	4,811,806	4,242,146
Payroll	Services	Information	181,727	176,883	181,252
		Finance & Insurance	349,936	395,418	370,420
		Business Services	354,637	408,113	422,401
		Health Services	434,264	495,912	536,707
		Total	1,320,564	1,476,326	1,510,780
	Manufacturing	Chemicals	43,228	40,100	38,934
		Machinery	43,639	44,774	42,914
		Transport	71,227	63,271	58,858
		Electronics	59,307	52,753	45,864
		Scientific Instruments	12,100	12,756	12,599
		Total	229,501	213,654	199,169

(Units: employment—number of employees, payroll—millions of 1998 US $).

Source: County Business Patterns, US Census Bureau.

same period in the US it rose by only 4 percent from $45,244 to $46,950 (see Table 5.4 for more details).

This would suggest that as globalization proceeded and quickened in this decade, the less skilled and lower wage manufacturing subsectors in the

Table 5.4 Highlights of the Knowledge Economy in the Megalopolis and the US, 2003–2012

		Megalopolis			US		
		2003	*2012*	*% change*	*2003*	*2012*	*% change*
Service	Emp.	6,937,178	7,009,817	1.0	30,687,367	32,668,669	6
	Payroll	$374,751	$417,427	11.4	$1,320,564	$1,510,780	14
	Payroll/ Emp.	$54,021	$59,549	10.2	$43,033	$46,246	7
Manufact- uring	Emp.	675,085	504,547	–25.3	5,072,563	4,242,146	–16
	Payroll	$25,114	$27,119	8.0	$229,501	$199,169	–13
	Payroll/ Emp.	$37,201	$53,749	44.5	$45,244	$46,950	4

(Units: employment—number of employees, payroll—millions of 1998 US $ entries here computed from Tables 5.2 and 5.3).

Source: County Business Patterns, US Census Bureau.

Megalopolis and in the US economies are being increasingly outsourced to low wage newly industrializing countries—yielding the losses in employment and payroll in the Megalopolis and US manufacturing sectors. This combination of loss of lower wage jobs and the relative retention of medium to high wage jobs explains the *increase in average payroll/capita* in the *declining* manufacturing sector in the Megalopolis and in the country.

The Knowledge Economy appears to be proportionately larger and more established in the Megalopolis than in the USA. While growth in employment performance is lower than in the US, the higher levels and faster growth in earnings indicate a concentration on high skilled, technically oriented work in the Megalopolis.

The Knowledge sector employment in the Megalopolis stood at 7,612,263 in 2003, forming 21.3 percent of the national employment in that category. By 2012, this sector employment in the Megalopolis (at 7,514,364) declined slightly to 20.4 percent of the national total. Despite this, total the share of total payroll in the US total actually increased from 25.8 percent to 26 percent over the same period. This reflects the fact that payroll per employee grew much faster in the Megalopolis that in the US. The inference here is that while knowledge jobs have been growing more rapidly in the rest of the US, the highest order jobs, commanding the highest salaries, are more concentrated in the Megalopolis in 2012 than they were in 2003.

The Megalopolis, representing less than 2 percent of the national land surface area and 17 percent of the population of the nation, accounts for 20.4 percent of the Knowledge Economy employment and 26 percent of Knowledge Economy payroll in the nation.[4] Further—as noted in Table 2.7 in Chapter 2—*8 of the top 10* US states identified as top Knowledge Economies by the Kauffman Foundation are part of the Megalopolis. One could venture a view that the Megalopolis region is the US Knowledge Economy *par excellence!*

Dominant Knowledge Economy Sectors in the Megalopolis

The major knowledge intensive services in the Megalopolis are:

- financial services;
- professional and business services;
- health care services;
- educational services.

Table 5.5 provides a profile of the top five Megalopolis metropolitan areas in terms of employment in the financial services sector and their national

Table 5.5 Financial Services Employment in the Megalopolis Metropolitan Areas, 2004

Metropolitan Area (National Rank in Employment)	Total Employment	Share of National Employment	CAGR of Employment 1990–2004	Average Wages	CAGR of Average Wages 1990–2004
New York-Northern New Jersey-Long Island (1)	427,296	13.0	0.44	$168,802	7.66
Boston-Cambridge-Quincy (4)	133,342	4.0	3.48	$114,696	7.83
Philadelphia-Camden-Wilmington (5)	113,112	3.4	2.21	$73,158	6.12
Hartford-West Hartford-East Hartford (9)	65,219	2.0	1.38	$86,851	6.52
Washington DC (12)	58,098	1.8	1.99	$76,880	5.64

Source: Cluster Mapping Project, Institute for Strategy and Competitiveness, Harvard Business School.

employment ranks. This high wage sector utilizing highly skilled person-nel and offering a vigorous wage growth rate has New York, Boston, and Philadelphia metros taking the first, fourth, and fifth ranks, and Hartford and Washington following with the ninth and twelfth ranks in the nation. This sector has recently recovered from the 2006 Great Recession and the Megalopolis continues to be a major national and international player.

Table 5.6 displays the earnings in the broader category of producer ser-vices in the six metropolitan areas of the Megalopolis in 1988 and 2000. The six metropolitan areas of the Megalopolis are again dominant accounting for 26.6 percent of the national earnings in this sector. In one subsector—Security—Megalopolis accounts for 56 percent of the national earnings.

As noted earlier in Chapter 3, these producer services are key to the organ-ization of the global economy in the Megalopolis. These services are key to the organization of production in multiple countries by global network corporations (Dicken 2000; Dunning 1993; Castells 2000). In the context of the space-shrinking technologies of transport and ICT, the value adding components of production in the OECD economies are divided up increas-ingly finely and distributed to production locations across the globe by the GNCs—in order to maximize the comparative advantage of locations in terms of value added and lower factor costs. Thus, the GNCs implement the *functional integration* of such production activities distributed around the globe. Thus these producer and business services play a significant role in the major Megalopolis metro areas engaged in such restructuring of the global economy (e.g. New York, Boston).

The employment in health services in the Megalopolis metropolitan areas in the country is presented in Table 5.7. Three of the top five metros in the country—New York, Philadelphia, and Boston—appear among the top ten in the nation in terms of health services employment, recording over an aver-age 3 percent annual wage growth rate. Washington DC takes the ninth rank.

Another knowledge intensive service sector with a large concentration in the Megalopolis is a subsector of the health and educational services sector, termed "Colleges and Universities." They act as a powerful job generator (McSweeney and Marshall 2009). They have a powerful economic impact by improving the quality of the labor force. The highly educated labor force in the Megalopolis and its major metropolitan areas (Table 5.8) tends to attract knowledge-rich sectors such as finance, business services, IT, biotechnology, etc. McSweeney and Marshall (2009) have carried out a location quotient analysis of the colleges and universities sector of the top 13 metropolitan areas in the country. The result is presented in Figure 5.3. The Megalopolis metro areas of Boston, Philadelphia, Washington DC, and New York take the first, second, fourth, and fifth ranks in the nation in this measure of concentration of this knowledge sector. The Boston area location quotient indicates that college and university employment was approximately three-and-a-half times more concentrated, compared with the US average, and even significantly higher than the other Megalopolis cities.

Table 5.6 Producer Services Earnings by Industry in Six Metropolitan Areas, 1988 and 2000 (2000 Billion Dollars)

Industry	US 1988	US 2000	Six MSAs 1988	Six MSAs 2000	New York 1988	New York 2000	Boston 1988	Boston 2000	Washington 1988	Washington 2000	Baltimore 1988	Baltimore 2000	Philadelphia 1988	Philadelphia 2000	New Haven 1988	New Haven 2000
Banking	75.2	148.5	16.8	30.5	12.2	19.8	NA	4.2	1.5	NA	0.8	1.2	2.0	4.9	0.2	0.3
Security	41.1	174.8	22.6	98.3	19.8	83.2	1.6	8.8	NA	1.8	0.3	1.6	0.8	2.8	0.1	0.1
Insurance carriers	47.6	96.9	10.0	18.5	5.8	11.3	1.4	2.4	NA	NA	0.6	1.0	2.0	3.5	0.2	0.3
Insurance agents, brokers, and services	30.1	49.2	5.9	9.2	3.4	5.7	0.8	1.1	0.5	NA	0.3	0.5	0.8	1.7	0.1	0.2
Holding and other investment offices	16.2	49.3	4.2	15.4	3.5	12.2	NA	2.1	0.2	0.9	0.1	0.2	0.4	NA	0.1	0.1
Business services	136.8	490.9	36.1	105.9	18.9	46.0	5.1	18.9	6.3	23.7	1.4	4.4	4.0	11.6	0.4	1.3
Motion pictures	12.9	34.0	2.4	6.4	2.1	5.4	0.2	0.3	NA	0.3	NA	0.1	0.1	0.3	0.0	0.0
Legal services	70.5	127.6	19.7	34.4	11.1	16.9	2.0	3.9	3.3	7.4	0.8	1.3	2.3	4.5	0.2	0.4

continued

Table 5.6 Continued. Producer Services Earnings by Industry in Six Metropolitan Areas, 1988 and 2000 (2000 Billion Dollars)

Industry	US		Six MSAs		New York		Boston		Washington		Baltimore		Philadelphia		New Haven	
	1988	2000	1988	2000	1988	2000	1988	2000	1988	2000	1988	2000	1988	2000	1988	2000
Engineering and management services	103.2	253.6	28.8	64.4	13.5	26.3	4.5	11.9	6.5	15.2	1.3	3.4	2.7	6.9	0.3	0.6
Miscellaneous services	9.9	23.1	2.4	1.8	1.6	1.7	0.2	NA	0.2	NA	0.1	NA	0.2	NA	0.0	0.1
All producer services	543.3	1447.9	148.9	385.0	92.0	228.6	15.8	53.7	18.4	49.4	5.7	13.7	15.2	36.2	1.7	3.4
% of US total producer services	100.0	100.0	27.4	26.6	16.9	15.8	2.9	3.7	3.4	3.4	1.1	0.9	2.8	2.5	0.3	0.2

Source: Bureau of Labor Statistics, US Department of Labor.

Table 5.7 Local Health Services Employment in the Megalopolis Metropolitan Areas, 2004

Metropolitan Area (National Rank in Employment)	Total Employment	Share of National Employment	CAGR of Employment 1990–2004	Average Wages	CAGR of Average Wages 1990–2004
New York-Northern New Jersey-Long Island (1)	1,113,374	7.6	1.91	$42,631	3.64
Philadelphia-Camden-Wilmington (4)	373,167	2.5	1.71	$38,436	3.17
Boston-Cambridge-Quincy (5)	310,759	2.1	1.45	$42,180	3.95
Washington-Arlington-Alexandria (9)	221,485	1.5	2.29	$43,770	3.35
Baltimore-Towson (16)	150,055	1.0	1.86	$40,832	3.90

Source: Cluster Mapping Project, Institute for Strategy and Competitiveness, Harvard Business School.

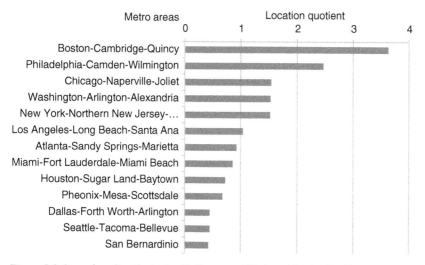

Figure 5.3 Location Quotients for Colleges and Universities in the 13 Largest Metro Areas in the US, 2006

Note: US Location quotients for colleges and universities = 1.00.

Source: McSweeney and Marshall (2009).

Table 5.8 Colleges, Universities, and Professional Schools (NAICS 6113): Employment and Payroll, The Megalopolis Major Metropolitan Regions, 2003–2012

	Number of Employees			Annual Payroll (Thousands of 2003 Dollars)		
	2003	2008	2012	2003	2008	2012
Baltimore	24,382	31,622	36,406	972,241	1,236,872	1,492,373
Boston	108,767	106,458	111,592	3,478,293	3,825,808	4,121,816
New York	122,002	144,852	154,832	4,441,902	5,344,262	5,860,679
Philadelphia	63,696	73,280	83,940	2,116,052	2,918,923	3,272,650
Washington	36,052	38,326	47,668	1,211,785	1,441,193	1,569,230
US	1,435,661	1,622,296	1,805,199	41,837,719	48,500,086	54,458,660

Source: Bureau of Labor Statistics, US Department of Labor.

Venture Capital and the Knowledge Transition in the Megalopolis

The Megalopolis region was the nation's original source of venture capital. In the ongoing transition to the Knowledge Economy, as in much of the nation's economic evolutionary history, a great proportion of the initial capital mobilized by new entrepreneurs was not made available by established providers of investment finance, but by new actors who are able to address the financial and management risks associated with new industries churning with innovations. As early as 1911, the Boston Chamber of Commerce generated a pool of risk capital which was offered to new industries. In the 1930s, Edward Filene and other New England industrialists launched the New England Industrial Corporation offering organized assistance to new industries. Further, the growing realization after World War II of the commercial potential of government investments in Science and Technology—especially as they were developing in the Boston region along Route 128, and the Silicon Valley, California—stimulated great interest in investing and supporting critical early investments in incipient innovative industries with some potential for non-marginal change.

The American Research Fund (ARF) Corporation appeared in 1946 in Boston as the nation's first formal venture capital fund. Other significant early venture capital investments were made by private individuals and wealthy families from New York and Boston. This was followed by a large number of venture capital funds generated in major financial centers such as New York, Chicago, Boston, and San Francisco. The modern venture capital industry emerged with the rise of high technology industries in the Silicon Valley, the Boston region, and many other knowledge centers around the nation.

The contemporary venture capital system has evolved in recent decades into an organized national system for mobilizing capital and providing managerial and strategic assistance to firms engaged in innovative activities. Figure 5.4 displays the national distribution of venture capital activity in 2012, indicating high levels and the densest spatial concentration of such activities in the Megalopolis.

3. Boston Metropolitan Area's Transition into a Knowledge Economy

Recent Regional Turnaround after Economic Distress, and Decline (1980s to the Present)

As noted in Chapter 2, the Boston region was a pioneer of the American Industrial Revolution in the first half of the nineteenth century, and remained a major industrial center in the country for over a century, before a significant portion of its manufacturing capacity and employment moved away in the post-World War II era to low labor cost locations, first in the American South and later globally to newly industrializing countries—enduring thereby a multiple-decade economic decline. The resulting job losses of manufacturing and trade have led to an economic restructuring in Boston and a pronounced shift toward a service-oriented economy (Table 5.9).

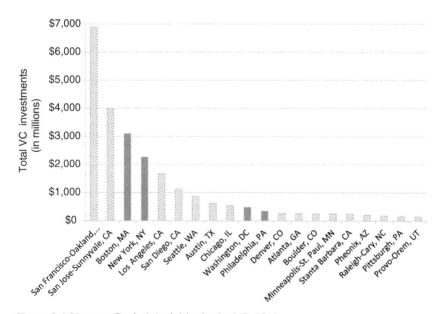

Figure 5.4 Venture Capital Activities in the US, 2012

Source: Florida (2013).

Table 5.9 Shift to Service Economy in the Megalopolis Metropolitan Areas, 1980

	Cities (Central City County)	Service Employment as % of Total Employment	National Rank
1	Boston	53.9	1
2	New York	49.5	3
3	Philadelphia	43.9	5
4	Baltimore	40.1	10
5	Washington DC	39.6	11

Source: Brown (1982).

A large study by the Brookings Institution (Bradbury et al. 1982) offered a detailedportrait of the economic conditions and the dimensions of the ongoing industrial decline and economic structural changes in the 154 largest cities in the country, including the City of Boston and its suburbs. This review of the demographic and economic indicators of (in early 1970s) Boston and its metropolitan area is a bleak portrait—suggesting that the City of Boston was among the most *distressed,* and the Boston metropolitan region had some of the greatest *disparities*in the nation.[5]

However, two large studies of demographic and economic evolution of US metropolitan areas implemented just *a decade later in the 1990s* offer a starkly different picture of *an economic recovery and resurgence*—"the Great Turnaround" in the metropolitan economies of Boston and some other large metro areas in the Megalopolis (Glickman et al. 1996; Bluestone and Stevenson 2000). The Glickman et al. study found that though the City of Boston ranked seventeenth in median family income in the country in 1989, it had the fastest growing median family income in the nation during the 1980s. The towns and suburbs of Boston improved their economies in the 1990s. In 1989, suburban Boston achieved *second rank in the nation* in family income growth reflecting both rising wages and dropping dependency rates. Further, these income improvements were shared by black households (Bluestone and Stevenson 2000).[6] Clearly the Boston region, which experienced serious distress and decline in the 1970s, had halted this downward spiral and has experienced an economic revival and resurgence by the 1990s.

Such sharp improvements in the economic position of the households in the Boston region in the last three decades reflect the advent of a *new economic base* that began to replace the earlier mature and declining manufacturing activities. In this period, the Boston region began to undergo structural change, attenuating further the industrial era manufacturing activities and beginning to create and expand the production and delivery of knowledge-laden goods and services—in other words, a transition from *a mill-based to a brain (or mind)-based economy.*

This passage in recent decades of the Boston economy from decline and distress to a vibrant contemporary Knowledge Economy is another example of several such episodes in the near four century history of Boston. Box 5.1 describes three of the four such episodes in Boston's history of *Growth, Decline, Resilience, and Reinvention.* The key ingredients of this recurring economic resilience in Boston appear to be: a diverse economy, large stocks of human capital, knowledge networks, and institutional innovations.

Box 5.1 Boston's Recurring History of Growth, Decline, and Reinvention

There are newer urban regions in the US (Silicon Valley, Seattle, Austin Texas, Raleigh-Durham Research Triangle, North Carolina, etc.), which have ridden the innovation wave in recent decades and made the transition to Knowledge Economies. Boston, with its near four century run of impressive innovations (technological, financial, human capital, social and institutional capital), has a long history of *economic growth, decline, resilience, and reinvention* at various times.[7] We review here briefly such key episodes of Boston's history of growth, evolution, decline, and reinvention so as to highlight the factors and processes undergirding *Boston's historical record of repeated regional resilience* evocative of the contemporary era of its regional reinvention.

The four episodes of rise, decline, and reinvention in Boston are:

- 1630–1790: Farm Economy to Seafaring Economy.
- 1790–1830s: Transition from Seafaring to Mercantile Economy.
- 1830s–1980s: Mercantile to Manufacturing boom and decline.
- 1980–present: The ongoing transition to contemporary Knowledge Economy.

Farm Economy to Seafaring Economy

Founded in 1630 as a Puritan colony, Boston region's belief systems were akin to those emphasized by the great German sociologist Max Weber—rational, hard work, moral uprightness, education, and accumulation. This Calvinistic ethic (Lakshmanan 1993) emphasized:

- *Educational achievement of the population*—creating in Boston the first school (Latin school in 1635) and the first college (Harvard College in 1636 with a large dose of public funds) in the US. At the beginning of the nineteenth century, the states in New England began to require minimum years of public schooling, so that New England reported in the late nineteenth century highest levels of education anywhere.[8] This emphasis on education from the early days and the continuing investments since, account for the high contemporary stocks of Boston's human capital.

- *The Church and social networks*, which helped mold a stable and well-structured society, also creating a variety of community organizations. The resulting dense social networks, and the more egalitarian political networks in New England towns yielded the participatory, exchange-intensive town meetings and home rule, and a version of the "rule of law" (Kim and Margo 2003).
- *Business orientation and push for accumulation.* Lacking a locally generated valuable export commodity for Europe, Boston forged a complex multi-country trading system, using its sheltered harbor, producing food in Massachusetts, and shipping it to the American South and the Caribbean. The "triangular trade," connected to slave trade, involved in addition an English port. In addition, the lumber resources of New England combined with the seafaring experience of the region promoted the ship building industry and associated production and services—employing a third of Boston's workforce in these shipping trades (Glaeser 2003). Boston's ship-building industry supplied most of the American and British ships. The stable government laws and a judicial process allowing laws to adapt to new problems offered a supportive business environment (Temin 1999).

Boston's economic fortunes based on seafaring, shipbuilding, fishing, and trading, began to decline, overtaken by the mid-eighteenth century by Philadelphia and New York, with better ports and larger hinterlands and closer to the American South and Caribbean. Boston's population barely grew in the latter half of the eighteenth century.

Transition from Seafaring to Mercantile Economy

Boston began to recover from the decline that set in its farming, shipping, and trading system in the 1790s. The trade restrictions—imperial tariffs, restrictions on trade with England's enemies—that disappeared since the US became independent helped. The value of US imports and exports increased sharply.

At the beginning of the nineteenth century, Boston took advantage of these various strengths in sailing ship seafaring—financial capital, human capital, trading experience, entrepreneurship and financial innovations such as maritime insurance, and the increasing globalization in the early nineteenth century—and created the Pacific-China trade, whale hunting in the Pacific, and manufacturing whale products. It was the first major example of the Boston region building on its past strengths and reinventing itself as a mercantile economy with supporting institutions and engaging in global operations. The resulting growth phase continued in Boston till the steam boat arrived and indigenous sailing ship skills began depreciating. The resulting decline was managed when the Boston region pioneered the industrial age in the US. The huge profits earned in the China trade were later directed to the financing of the pioneering industrial revolution in the Boston region and the development of railroads in New England and the nation in the nineteenth century.

Industrialization and Urbanization in the Boston Region

The Boston region pioneered the American industrial revolution in the textile sector built around a factory system using water power. Since the Charles River in Boston was too small, the factory system based on modified English technology was located in the 1820s by Boston capital on a larger existing dam in Lowell, MA (Temin 1999). New England's superior educational system provided good education to women, who dominated the labor force in this sector.[9] Wages of women relative to men were lower in the Northern US, leading to their greater utilization, and their real wages rose 1 percent a year (Temin 1999).[10] Skilled labor force, cheap transport, and water power allowed Massachusetts to lead other states in the nation textile production in 1850. This industry began with a large educated female labor force, which was replaced after a couple of decades by Irish immigrants accepting lower wages.[11]

While the initial manufacturing centers were in smaller towns (where water power was available) in Massachusetts, Boston and its immediate environs became the dominant manufacturing center of New England toward the latter part of the nineteenth century, fabricating a wide range of products, particularly foundries and high quality machinery, with power provided by the stationary steam engine. Technical innovations such as lathes and sewing machines allowed the shift to smaller factory buildings in Boston and take advantage of the benefits of proximity to a larger city workforce. As Kim (1995) has documented, manufacturing activities became increasingly concentrated in the larger urban areas. Thus increasing industrialization led to large scale urban growth in Boston and elsewhere. Boston city's population rose from 177,840 in 1860 to 748,060 by 1920, making it the fifth largest American city. As often observed, this urbanization process was driven by new manufacturing technologies, climbing agricultural productivity, the transport revolution, and the flood of immigrants.

Several key factors underlie this pioneering industrialization and the economic/demographic reinvention of the Boston region in the nineteenth century:

1. *Education and large human capital stocks.* The regional emphasis on education and public schools and the high standards established by SEs such as Horace Mann (creating the Mass. Board of Education) provided a skilled labor force. A worker who can read the bible can also read blueprints and operate several lathes, improving operations.[12] Indeed, New England led the nation in the patents per capita by the first half of the nineteenth century.

2. *The innovation of the American System of Manufactures in New England.* The American system was a major New England generated productivity-enhancing innovation comprising of volume production of identical interchangeable parts and fast assembly, reducing unit production time. First developed in small arms manufacturing,[13] this *skill-enhancing innovation* spread in the nineteenth century and early twentieth century to other industries such as sewing machines, clocks, reapers, and bicycles. It is important to note that this innovation was different in kind and scope from the succeeding era of mass production ("Fordism"), which involved extreme Taylorist methods and *deskilling* of labor.

3. *Innovator networks and knowledge creation in nineteenth century New England.* There has been a tradition in New England from the early days to set up venues where information about work techniques can be exchanged among farm workers[14] in the eighteenth century and later among industrial workers improving the technologies of the American System of Manufactures. Various firms (e.g. Pratt and Whitney, Browne and Sharpe) created a fellowship and networks of skilled machinists, who visited one another and engaged in technical talks and demonstrations (Temin 1999). Such networks were a potent force in creating and disseminating new knowledge—*not unlike the much celebrated knowledge-generating high technology networks in contemporary creative regions such as Boston and the Silicon Valley.*

4. *Financial innovations and infrastructures in Boston region.* The initial capital for the cotton textile industry came, in the first third of the eighteenth century, from the Caribbean-England-China trade profits made in Boston and Salem. The steady stream of profits soon attracted capital from professionals, financial institutions, and many women.[15] Boston capital also financed construction of railroads in New England and the Midwest.

5. Apart from playing a major role of organizing the capital forma-
    tion in textile and railroad industries, Boston's financial community
    generated two key *financial innovations* which created a smoothly
    functioning investment market.

a. One was the "Suffolk system" developed by the Suffolk Bank
    before the Civil War (by the investors who founded the textile
    industry). This bank issued its own notes which were redeemable at
    par (along with those issued by any NE bank, provided those banks
    maintained deposits at the Suffolk Bank) thus rapidly expanding
    industrial capital in New England.
b. The creation of the "Trust bank."

Maturing Industrial Economy and Boston's Decline, 1920–1970s

The manufacturing economy of the Boston region started declining
after a vibrant century of growth and expansion. This decline derives
from two broad sets of socioeconomic factors:

1. The *spatial shift* of mature production technologies from older
    industrialized regions such as Boston (dominated by lower wage
    industries such as textiles, shoes and leather) to the American
    Sunbelt locations, which have benefited from post WWII trans-
    portation (divided highways, containers, and jet aircraft) and other
    technical developments.
2. The recent long term *evolutionary economic shift toward* a *service
    economy*.

Three factors *account for* Boston region's decline (running through several decades) resulting from the spatial shift noted above—*when people*
and economic activities shifted massively away from the Northeast to
the Sunbelt.

•   The automobile and the Interstate Highway system greatly
    improved the relative accessibility of the American South and the
    West and the urban fringes in the Megalopolis, offering cheaper
    well serviced land for industrial activities. Manufacturing fled the
    Northeast—from the urban regions of Boston and elsewhere in the
    Northeast to the Sunbelt, and from metro areas to the suburbs and
    exurbs.
•   Southern states offered low wages and a compliant labor force
    (with right to work laws).

- The advent of *air conditioning and public health improvements* in the American South leveled the playing field in terms of living environments and promoted a great shift of manufacturing to the Sunbelt.

By the mid-1970s, the Boston region experienced serious decline in economic activities and population, with the consequent unemployment, poverty, and dropping real estate values. However, there has been a reversal of these economic and demographic trends and resurgence in the last three decades or more.

The fourth era of the Boston region's resilience and reinvention, in the form of the ongoing transition to the Knowledge Economy (from the 1980s to the present) is the story of recovery from industrial decline to a vibrant Knowledge Economy.

Source: Lakshmanan and Chatterjee (2011).

Boston Region's Passage to the Contemporary Knowledge Economy

As noted earlier, by the1960s, growth of service sectors in the Boston region exceeded the growth of manufacturing sectors. In the industrial sector, the manufacturing firms were shifting from *non-durable goods* (textiles and shoes) to *durable goods* (aircraft engines, missiles, general machinery, high technology office, lab, and factory equipment) (Bluestone and Stevenson 2000). The high concentration of universities, research labs, knowledge networks, and the prevalence and the long history of venture capital activity in the Boston region have all contributed to the large and rising regional knowledge capital and the flourishing manufacturing and service enterprises built around that capital.

Further, the four-lane circumferential divided highway, Route 128, completed in 1951, offered rapid access to low priced land located in attractive suburbs (accessible to MIT and Harvard in 20 minutes) and played a key role in attracting new technology firms and fashion the transformation of Boston region[16] from a mature industrial economy to an entrepreneurial Knowledge Economy. The outer beltway (Route 495), completed more recently, has extended spatially (into New Hampshire) the Boston region's knowledge intensive production and service sector activities. Such activities—biotechnology, scientific instruments, software, medical and educational services, financial, business and professional services—have initiated a remarkable economic renaissance, employing a high proportion of knowledge workers.

Finally, in resurgent cities and regions such as Boston, we offer (later in this section) evidence of *urban governance innovations* which bring together multiple urban/regional economic, social, and political sector actors and stakeholders. Such urban and regional stakeholders in the Boston region share aims, have hazy boundaries, possess interdependent resources, and engage in joint actions. We describe below the institutional innovations and urban/regional *governance models* developed in this context in Boston to facilitate the translation of new economic growth of the Knowledge Economy—as expressed in new land uses and infrastructures into inherited industrial urban/regional space—and avoid market failure of spatially produced goods and services.

The transition of the Boston region to a vibrant Knowledge Economy has two key components:

1. new production sectors based on innovative regional technologies (e.g. instruments, biotechnology industry, microelectronics, minicomputer etc.);
2. the rise of innovative technologies which add high value in the much larger service sector economy.

The Boston metropolitan region's assets—*in the form of a highly educated labor force, a remarkable constellation of leading universities and a broad range of research institutions, knowledge intensive business services, dense networks of human and social capital, and an illustrious history of venture capital investments*—have enabled the rise of new innovation sectors.[17] The scale of the resultant innovation industry clusters is evident in Table 5.10 which displays the employment levels in such innovative sectors in 2010 in the state of Massachusetts.[18]

Table 5.10 Massachusetts Innovation Industry Cluster Employment, 2010: Q1

Rank	Sector	Employment
1	Health Care Delivery	337,000
2	Financial Services	159,000
3	Postsecondary Education	141,000
4	Business Services	139,000
5	Software & Communications Services	131,000
6	Bio-Pharma & Medical Devices	73,000
7	Scientific, Technical and Management Services	62,000
8	Diversified Industrial Manufacturing	40,000
9	Defense Manufacturing & Instrumentation	38,000
10	Computer & Communications Hardware	35,000
11	Advanced Materials	31,000
Total		1,186,000

Source: annual index of the Massachusetts Innovation Economy, The Innovation Institute, Massachusetts Technology Collaborative.

Figure 5.5 shows the relative importance of various production and service super sectors (based on a location quotient analysis by the US Bureau of Labor Statistics) in the Boston metropolitan region in 2006 (McSweeney and Marshall 2009). The service sectors—all *the knowledge intensive ones* such as colleges and universities, education and health services, finance, professional and business services, and information—have location quotients *in excess of one,* while the manufacturing and construction sectors display location quotients of less than one.

The origin and evolution of knowledge production sectors are related largely to what may be described as innovation networks which nurture and commercialize innovation and industrial adaptation in various regions (Bathelt 2001; Scott 1998; Saxenian 1996; Best 2000). The key idea here is that innovation or the creation and commercialization of new knowledge in a dynamic region is based on interactions among autonomous but interdependent economic agents. In such economic regions there are very many linkages and interconnections between various (large and small) regional economic agents.

The initial boom in high technology industries in the Boston region was punctured in the late 1980s by the decline of the minicomputer industry and the fall-off in military research budgets. High technology industries in the Boston region have been, however, able to readjust and rejuvenate their product and process structures in order to sustain further innovation and growth, through a network model of complementary, vertically disintegrated, open system firms

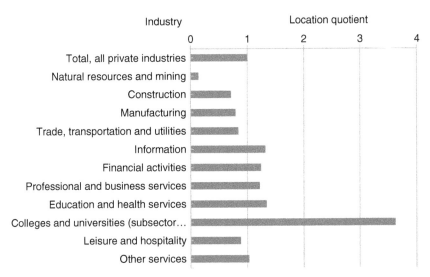

Figure 5.5 Location Quotients by Major Industry Sector in the Boston Metropolitan Area, 2006

Note: US concentration for industry super sector = 1.00.

Source: McSweeney and Marshall (2009).

(Bathelt 1999; Best 2000). Further, Boston's revitalization is based on its technological diversification rather than in an existing trajectory (Best 2000), given its rich and diverse human capital and its dynamic labor markets.[19]

The majority of the studies of resurgent regions such as Boston often limit themselves to a discussion of the performance of mostly fabrication sectors, such as military electronics, microcomputer industry, electronic components, instruments, and the biotechnology industry (Bathelt 2001), ignoring the larger knowledge intensive services. As Tables 5.11 and 5.12 indicate, from

Table 5.11 Progression of Knowledge Services and Manufacturing Employment and Payroll in the Boston Metropolitan Region, 2003–2012

			2003	*2008*	*2012*
Employment	Services	Information	94,396	91,343	91,632
		Finance & Insurance	177,617	193,053	172,438
		Business Services	210,444	229,414	225,649
		Health Services	282,232	313,068	337,021
		Total	764,689	826,878	826,740
	Manufacturing	Chemicals	17,749	14,112	13,751
		Machinery	16,885	15,283	12,719
		Transport	7,456	5,502	7,590
		Electronics	62,433	45,395	41,346
		Scientific Instruments	7,883	8,042	6,204
		Total	112,406	88,334	81,610
Payroll	Services	Information	5,798	6,039	6,467
		Finance & Insurance	12,520	15,869	15,059
		Business Services	13,602	15,936	16,612
		Health Services	10,634	12,577	13,793
		Total	42,554	50,421	51,931
	Manufacturing	Chemicals	1,078	787	858
		Machinery	873	799	731
		Transport	363	280	473
		Electronics	3,744	2,704	2,553
		Scientific Instruments	394	523	385
		Total	6,452	5,093	5,000

(Units: employment—number of employees, payroll—millions of 1998 US $).

Source: County Business Patterns, US Census Bureau.

Table 5.12 Highlights of the Knowledge Economy in Boston and the US, 1998–2012

		Boston			US		
		2003	2012	% change	2003	2012	% change
Service	Emp.	764,689	826,740	8.1	30,687,367	32,668,669	6
	Payroll	$42,554	$51,931	22.0	$1,320,564	$1,510,780	14
	Payroll/ Emp.	$55,649	$62,814	12.9	$43,033	$46,246	7
Manufacturing	Emp.	112,406	81,610	−27.4	5,072,563	4,242,146	−16
	Payroll	$6,452	$5,000	−22.5	$229,501	$199,169	−13
	Payroll/ Emp.	$57,399	$61,267	6.7	$45,244	$46,950	4

(Units: employment—number of employees, payroll—millions of 1998 US $).

Source: County Business Patterns, US Census Bureau.

2003 to 2012 the knowledge intensive service sector grew more rapidly in Boston than in its national counterpart in terms of employment, payroll, and payroll per employees. Boston's superior performance in the payroll measures is especially noteworthy. In knowledge intensive manufacturing, by contrast, the Boston region underperformed the nation, except in payroll/ employee, which is consistent with a pattern of decline in all but the highest value added manufacturing activities.

Key knowledge intensive services in the Boston region are: financial services, professional services, health care services, and educational services. The financial services sector is a large sector that is growing in the region, utilizing highly skilled personnel and offering high wages. The Boston metro area has the fourth largest employment, third highest average wage, and the second highest wage growth rate (1990–2004) among the top 15 metros in the financial sector in 2004 (Table 5.5). In Massachusetts, this sector accounts for 10.8 percent of the state GSP, 5.5 percent of employment, with 65 percent of the workers with a post-secondary degree, and has a significant multiplier effect on professional and technical services. The magnitude and importance of the financial services sector in the Boston region are not surprising given its past history of merchant and industrial capital in earlier times and the many recent and past financial innovations in the region (merchant banking, marine insurance, "Suffolk Bank" notes, venture capital, mutual funds, etc.).

Two Quintessential Knowledge Economy Sectors of the Boston Metro Region

Two quintessential Knowledge Economy sectors are discussed next to high-light the general and specific attributes of the Boston metropolitan region as it has evolved in the last three decades into a vibrant national and international Knowledge Economy. The key supportive regional attributes include: *a highly educated labor force, a remarkable constellation of leading universities and a broad range of public and private research institutions, and highly interactive dense networks of human and social capital lodged in these universities, hospital research centers, and private enterprises within the Boston metropolitan geography.* These two sectors are:

- the research infrastructure of leading universities, research hospitals and public research institutes;
- the biotech industry.

Leading Universities, Research Institutes and Hospitals and Economic Contributions

As noted earlier, the Boston metro region exhibits the highest location quotient in the "colleges and universities" economic sector both in 2006 and historically back to 1990 (McSweeney and Marshall 2009). Over this 16-year period, this sector has had a positive regional economic impact, acting as a powerful job generator, with job growth roughly twice the rate for total private industry in the region.

Higher education plays a major role in the Boston region than in most metropolitan areas. In 2000, Boston metro ranked first in college and university enrollment, first in degrees granted, and first in per capita spending per 100,000 people. Further, the numerous colleges and universities improve the quality of the labor force, and the region's highly educated labor force continues to attract knowledge-based industries such as IT, nanotechnology, biotechnology, and business and finance services—sectors that offer also high wages.[20]

A useful way to frame the broad range of economic effects of the universities on the Boston region is in two parts:

- The *first* approach is *the traditional economic impact analysis* in terms of growth impacts of major university activities in the region.
- The *second* approach pertains to the more diffuse but vital economic development and evolution impacts which flow from the research and innovative outputs of the faculty and research associates and advanced graduate students of the region's universities and their associated research institutes and research hospitals—which jointly make up the regional "innovation infrastructure."

Economic Growth Impacts of Major Research Universities in the Boston Region

A 2003 study of traditional economic impacts of eight research universities in the Boston metro region—Boston College, Boston University, Brandeis University, Harvard University, the Massachusetts Institute of Technology, Northeastern University, Tufts University, and the University of Massachusetts Boston—highlighted the following economic growth impacts (Appleseed, Inc. 2003):

- These eight research universities and their affiliated institutes and hospitals attracted in the year 2000 research funding of $2.5 billion (97 percent from federal and non-local sources).
- They employed 50,500 persons, spent $1.3 billion in local purchases, and engaged in local construction expenses of $850 million, with a total regionalmultiplier effect of 37,000 fulltime jobs in the year 2002.
- These universities were granted 264 patents, signed 250 commercial licensing agreements, and helped form 400 start-up companies.
- Approximately 310,000 of the eight universities' alumni live in the Boston metro region.
- They account for 30 percent of all residents of the region who have four-year college or higher degrees.

Before one can proceed to a discussion of the broader economic development and evolution impacts which flow from the innovative outputs of the research universities, it would be useful to clarify the size, scope, and some attributes of the hospitals and the public and independent research institutes which jointly make up the infrastructure for the innovations in health services and biotechnology.

The health services sector, as noted earlier, is a large sector in the Boston region, about 2.5 times as large as the financial sector in employment. The Milken Institute has created a comprehensive *Health Pole Index* to measure how important the health care industry is in a given MSA compared with the nation as a whole (DeVol and Koepp 2003). The Health Pole concept measures both the spatial density and diversity of health care sectors in a metropolitan economy in a way that may be compared with the US as a whole.[21] This index displayed in Table 5.13 is a more comprehensive descriptor of the diversity and depth of health services sector activities than the employment measure offered in Table 5.7. The MSAs of Boston, New York, and Philadelphia take the top three health pole ranks in the nation, and Washington and Baltimore metro areas follow close behind. Clearly, the top Megalopolis metropolitan areas offer a broad array of top quality health services available in the nation.

Table 5.14 offers an overview of the research and innovation record of the research university/hospital/institutes of the Boston region—as indicated by the level of annual research funding received from the National Institutes of

Table 5.13 Megalopolis Metropolitan Areas Ranked by the Health Pole Index

National Rank	Metropolitan Area	Health Pole
1	Boston, MA-NH	100.00
2	New York, NY	99.85
3	Philadelphia, PA-NJ	97.53
6	Washington, DC-MD-VA-WV	48.18
12	Baltimore, MD	33.55

Source: DeVol and Koepp (2003, p. 6).

Table 5.14 Principle NIH-Funded Research Institutions in the Boston Metropolitan Region, 2000

National Rank	Institution	Total National Institutes Health Support (Millions)
7	Harvard University	$250.4
17	Massachusetts General Hospital	$180.5
22	Brigham & Women's Hospital	$162.5
38	Boston University	$108.2
47	Dana-Farber Cancer Institute	$87.2
53	Beth Israel Deaconess Medical Center	$82.1
54	Whitehead Institute for Biomedical Research	$81.3
58	Massachusetts Institute of Technology	$75.0
60	University of Massachusetts Medical School	$73.9
74	Children's Hospital	$52.9

Source: Biotech Statistics Report.

Health in the year 2000. The top ten recipients of these highly competitive health research grants received from the National Institutes of Health in the Boston metro region include not only *research universities* such as Harvard University, Boston University, MIT, Tufts, and University of Massachusetts but also *research hospitals* such as Mass. General Hospital, Brigham and Women's hospital, Beth Israel Medical center and Children's hospital, and *top research institutes such as* Dana Farber Cancer Institute and Whitehead Institute for Biomedical Research.

The geographic colocation of these and other knowledge intensive institutions in the Boston metropolitan region, with their impressive array of intellectual capital, research experience, and innovative knowledge outputs—embodied in faculty, research associates, postdoctoral and doctoral associates—supports this region's prospects for further scientific and technical advances in health care services and the related biotechnology industry.

The biotech industry in Boston region is one of the largest agglomerations of biotechnology research and production in the world. This highly spatially clustered industry appears, besides Boston, in two other US metro areas of San Francisco and San Diego. Breznitz and Anderson (2005) view the Boston biotech industry as an "industrial cluster" and bring to bear the extensive recent literature on the origin and development of industrial clusters to interpret the growth and development of the Boston biotech industrial cluster (Porter 1990; Markusen 1996; Maskell and Malmberg 1999; Saxenian 1994). They advance the view in their concluding comments that "the most interesting characteristic of the Boston biotech cluster is the central role of the universities.

This notion is elaborated and further developed, in what follows here, in the broader definition of the region's large and diverse knowledge infrastructure (which includes the broader research community of universities, research hospitals, public and private research institutes, and science-driven companies) and the associated highly interactive multiple networks of human and social capital, geographically co-located in the Boston metropolitan region in a two-step process.

First, the faculty and researchers in the university-research hospital-institute complex in the Boston region generate *novel science and cutting edge biotech knowledge*. If one applies the concepts of new knowledge generation in Chapter 4, one can argue that the generation of new knowledge by researchers in life sciences embedded in the Boston region occurs as a result of two types of learning processes: one, called "buzz," by *being there*, active in the various interlocking regional knowledge networks and the other from the knowledge attained by investing in building network connections—called *pipelines*—to selected researchers located outside the region (Storper 1995; Scott 2002; Bathlet et al. 2004). Indeed, Porter et al. (2005) provide several mappings of the multiplicity of such knowledge generation linkages and networks—a) inside the Boston region and b) between the universities, hospitals, and research institutes in the Boston region and "pipelines" to other American and globally distributed health and biotech research locations.

Second, how does such new knowledge generated by the university-hospital-institute complex lead to *economic development effects* in the Boston region—indeed, a biotech cluster began in the 1970s and 1980s, local venture capital came in the 1990s, and major pharmaceutical firms have located in the Boston region in the first decade of the current century (Table 5.15).

With well over half of its biotech jobs engaged in the development of new drugs and treatments, this sector's growth and development in the Boston region are closely tied to university research, and strong ongoing affiliations among universities, research hospitals, public research centers, and small and large pharma firms, and reciprocal flows of ideas and personnel among these

Table 5.15 Selected Indicators of Biotechnology Commercialization in the Boston CMSA

1. Venture capital investment (1995–2001)	$1.916 billion
2. Value of research alliances between pharmaceutical companies and local biotech companies (1996–2001)	$3.924 billion
3. Market capitalization of local biotech companies (year 2001)	$52.756 billion
4. Local biotech firms (with >100 employees) in year 2001	33
5. Employment in pharmaceuticals (NAICS 3254) in year 2001	6945
6. Employment in life sciences R&D (NAICS 5413) in year 2001	11,249

Source: Biotech Statistics Report.

different groups—in order to develop scientific advances in support of new medicines and therapies (Owen-Smith and Powell 2004; Powell 1996; Porter et al. 2005).

This is clearly a case of new knowledge created by basic university research generating significant local economic impacts. The capability to generate regional commercial development relates in part to the ability to transfer *tacit knowledge*. Information that can be codified and expressed clearly in a written or electronic form may be transferred over long distances with very little interpersonal contact. But much of the information that is relevant to research and commercialization of science, as in the bio-sciences (e.g. recombinant DNA), is tacit and transfers most effectively by the kind of face-to-face contact that occurs in a lab setting. Private firms hoping to capitalize on such knowledge must be in close and frequent contact with the scientists who develop it. The presence of world class university departments in key sciences such as molecular biology may therefore be the most important locational factor for biotech industries. This, and the fact that many university scientists are patent holders, makes certain lines of biotechnology business spatially "sticky" in the Boston region, where about one-half of the university scientists who have affiliations with Boston area biotech firms have local university appointments (Hill 2006). Further, university faculty members who start biotech firms contribute not only quality human capital but also *social capital* networks embodied in a broad range of laboratory networks and their wider, cosmopolitan affiliations with co-authors and colleagues (Murray 2004). Thus interactions among multiple interlocking networks of the human and social capital embodied in researchers in universities, hospitals, and institutes generate the basic and applied knowledge stock that supports the biotech industry.[22]

The Boston region has also a highly educated labor force, rich stocks of scientific knowledge, senior research fellows, doctoral scholars and college students drawn from around the world—who can provide the quality labor force for the regional biotech firms. Industry scientists work intensely with university scientists, producing joint publications, participating in conferences, hiring top grad students from university labs, etc., creating a university/private sector scientific community. While significant knowledge breakthroughs occur in a university or a corporate lab, the subsequent development of a drug or treatment (first to the world medicines and therapies) is separate from the initial discovery and may need a protracted period of 5–10 years (Owen-Smith and Powell 2004).

Porter et al. (2005) further note that a variety of institutions have risen in the Boston region to address the multiplicity of skills demanded—scientific, clinical, manufacturing, legal, financial, regulatory, sales and distribution, etc. This skill heterogeneity is not easily assembled in one organization, but in the constellation of institutions involved in the biotech sector in Boston. They argue that:

> Without a single dominant actor, there is no fixed recipe, instead multiple bets are placed in a milieu that becomes competitive and forward-looking, that the dense networks that connect these diverse organizations afford multiple, independent pathways through which new ideas and resources can flow, facilitating research progress.

4. Passage of the New York Region into the Knowledge Era[23]

> What is barely hinted in other cities is condensed and enlarged in New York.
> Saul Bellow

New York is the gateway city *par excellence*. Since around 1810, New York has been America's gateway, playing an increasingly important role in national economic growth, and social and cultural evolution. By 1850, it was leading the nation in every major economic activity save agriculture and mining (Lichtenberg 1960). Thanks to the natural advantages of the port, and the strategic actions and social innovations of its business and political communities (and a little luck), the city in the nineteenth century was dominant nationally in foreign trade, wholesaling, and in financial and related services. In the century after the Civil War, the New York Metropolitan Region emerged as the dominant force in many of the nation's national market activities—relating to strategic positioning, management, control, and financing—in the form of central offices, of money market specialists, of manufactured goods sold to the nation, and some highly specialized services. Again in the last three decades to the present day, the New York region has reinvented itself in the emerging era of "Knowledge Societies," characterized by complex economic, political, and cultural dimensions of globalization. Engaging in social learning, adaptation, and strategic activities, New York has emerged at the head of a set of major international financial and business centers or "global cities." These global cities form a new geography of centrality and agglomeration in today's distributed global economy and culture (Sassen 1997, 1998; Crahan and Vourvoulias-Bush 1997; Castells 1996).

This recurrent ability of New York to remain an economic leader over two centuries reflects both its capacity to exploit technological advances and its "social intelligence," comprising of its capacity to create the institutions, the policymaking, and the incentives that promote continual learning and adaptation in a rapidly evolving context. Such a combination of technical "know-how" and institutional knowledge and creativity (as noted in Chapter 4) has enabled New York in the contemporary era as the region develops and uses the diverse networks through which the world economy is constituted. Such networks of economic globalization pertain to a) the internationalization of capital, b) the organization of command and control centers able to innovate, manage, and coordinate the linked activities of global network firms, c) the innovation and production of urban activities, which not only promote the emerging dynamic sectors (of finance, IT, and advanced business services) but also *facilitate* social learning and adaptation in the city, and d) the acquisition and maintenance of the diverse urban human capital equal to the tasks at hand in such a global city. New York has indeed developed these dense multi-faceted networks which underlie its current dynamism and its strategic role in the global economy and the international social and cultural realms (Mallenkoff and Castells 1991; Sassen 1998; Drennen 1991; Castells 1996).

While this section surveys briefly the recent transformation of New York into a strategic pole of the international economic system and its resurgence as an economic powerhouse in the knowledge era, it also draws attention to one less noted aspect of the many rich networks mentioned above, namely the diversified labor force networks of New York. The City's rich and varied labor force has facilitated the ongoing structural change in New York—from its status a few decades ago as a declining metropolitan center managing national economic production to its current booming presence in managing international production. The argument here is that the diverse migrants (domestic and foreign) attracted to the city in the last quarter century or more have endowed it with not only the economic flexibility and rapid adaptation to the "flexible mode of production" characteristic of Knowledge Economies (Piore and Sabel 1984), but also the human capital resources to continue to operate as a "learning environment" for the creation of technical and social innovations that facilitate New York's command and control of the world economy.[24]

This account of New York's passage to a major center of the Knowledge Economy opens with a brief description of a) the spatially distributed global economic system, and the technical infrastructure and the "social infrastructure" which knit this system, and b) the radical concentration of financial, management, and strategic resources in a set of cities such as New York, that act as centers of coordination and control for the global system. It proceeds to a discussion of the new immigrants and how their diverse knowledge, competencies, and organizational capacities have facilitated new economic activities and cultural production, and adaptation to changing circumstances. Then the following discussion outlines the operation of social and economic networks which help and sustain the immigrant labor force in New York in its production of goods, and of cultural goods and services—in the context of New York's historical cultural hegemony and the more recent brisk cultural exchange between the mainstream city and the new immigrants. Finally, this account of New York's passage to the Knowledge Economy and society explores the role of New York institutions in determining the quality and experience of the new immigrant social and economic networks, which underlie a significant part of the dynamism of New York's economic and cultural realms.

The notion of a strategic place as central to a global market system and spatial division of labor is not new. It is a critical part of the historian Braudel's (1973) conception of the three facets to a world economy: a) a given geographic space with limits to mark it off, b) a pole or a center represented by one dominant city … and c) every world economy is divided into successive zones. The contemporary *variation* of the Braudel view is that not one central place (e.g. Amsterdam or London or New York, as in the past) but a small number of gateway cities around the world jointly play the strategic pole role in today's world economy.

However, there are different theoretical conceptions of how and why these cities function as geographical foci of global economic activity at a time when the constraints of what Braudel called the "tyranny of distance" seems to be attenuating. One view holds the global cities as agglomerations of internationally oriented financial and business services which are critical to the governance of the global economy (Sassen 1998). These cities a) concentrate command functions in the global economy; b) are production sites for leading financial and business service firms; and c) are transnational market places where firms and governments can buy financial instruments and specialized services (Sassen 1997). A second idea is that in an economy where most activities can be reduced to knowledge generation and information flows regarding ever-changing linkages, these cities are the poles of the "Informational Economy" (Castells 1989). A third approach is to think of these cities as locales offering a flexible pool of labor and industries in an era when the focus is more toward to economies of scope and away from economies of scale, and achieving this flexibility through agglomeration (Scott 1988).[25]

While these alternative explanations account for many observed activities of global gateway cities, they do not offer any clues to the urban processes underlying global economic governance. Our view of these processes and their dynamics, as noted above, derives from the notion of urban learning environments that incubate continually the innovative activities which enable a city like New York to continue to serve as a strategic pole of global economic governance. A dynamic social entity such as New York not only acquires and deploys the knowledge necessary for its development but also the social capacity to monitor, analyze and guide the efficient performance of various dimensions of the global economy. These activities constitute social learning and require the creation of institutions, policy-making, and incentives for continual learning and adaptation to changing circumstances. The delineation of the social learning activities is clearly a large project, far beyond the scope of this section. The aim here is limit the discussion to explore one critical aspect of New York's ability in this regard. The focus here is on the new migrants in New York—outlining the multiplicities of the economies and work cultures they represent, the flexibility and adaptability they provide to a restructuring of the metropolitan economy, the endogenous urban growth generated by the application of their physical and human capital, and the multiple networks and institutions they develop and adapt in New York. We begin with a brief profile of New York and its recent economic evolution.

Economic Profile of New York

While the service sectors dominate the region's economy and the manufacturing sectors have declined in employment in recent years, it is worth noting that New York Metropolitan area has currently dropped to second rank among the US metropolitan areas in terms of merchandise exports to the World (Table 5.16). Philadelphia and Boston SMAs from the Megalopolis appear in this list of the top 15 major goods exporters in the United States.

The broad growth in service sector jobs in New York has led to both high wage (FIRE [finance, insurance, and real estate], legal, medical, accounting, etc.) and low wage (personal and hotel services) jobs. The FIRE sector provides some of the highest paid work in the city; medical, legal, accounting, and other professional and business services offer other high remuneration; personal services, hotels, and some low end manufacturing provide the low wages. The middle is largely missing.

This restructuring of New York as an "hourglass" labor market is a departure from the city's historical identification as a middle class city, albeit with a considerable working class. The expansion throughout the twentieth century of a large urban middle class was linked to the growth of the manufacturing industry. That expansion went hand in hand with rising wages, strong worker organization, suburban growth, and greater government services. Until recently, this middle class had great capacity for enlargement (facilitating the assimilation of immigrants and fostering social mobility). The last three decades or more have been, however, harsh on the middle income population in New York City. This combination of significant growth in New York of high wage occupations such as Financial Services, Business and Professional Services, the squeeze on middle class incomes, and the large influx of low wage workers has led in recent decades to high levels of income inequality in New York. Figure 5.6 shows the resultant highly disproportionate concentration of incomes at the very high end of income recipients in 2009.

Tables 5.17 and 5.18 offer a more accurate picture of the size and growth of the NY Knowledge Economy in terms of the knowledge intensive services

Table 5.16 Top Metropolitan Areas in Goods Export, 2012 and 2013 (Billion Dollars)

Rank	Metropolitan Area	2012	2013
1	Houston-The Woodlands-Sugar Land, TX	$110.3	$115.0
2	**New York-Newark-Jersey City, NY-NJ-PA**	$102.3	$106.9
3	Los Angeles-Long Beach-Anaheim, CA	$75.0	$76.3
4	Seattle-Tacoma-Bellevue, WA	$50.3	$56.7
5	Detroit-Warrant-Dearborn, MI	$55.4	$53.9
6	Chicago-Naperville-Elgin, IL-IN-WI	$40.6	$44.9
7	Miami-Fort Lauderdale-West Palm Beach, FL	$47.9	$41.8
8	New Orleans-Metairie, LA	$24.4	$30.0
9	Dallas-Fort Worth-Arlington, TX	$27.8	$27.6
10	San Francisco-Oakland-Hayward, CA	$23.0	$25.3
11	**Philadelphia-Camden-Wilmington, PA-NJ-DE-MD**	$23.0	$24.9
12	Minneapolis-St. Paul-Bloomington, MN-WI	$25.2	$23.7
13	San Jose-Sunnyvale-Santa Clara, CA	$26.7	$23.4
14	**Boston-Cambridge-Newton, MA-NH**	$21.2	$22.2
15	Cincinnati, OH-KY-IN	$20.0	$21.0

Source: International Trade Administration, 2014, US Metropolitan Area Exports 2013, Department of Commerce. (Megalopolis MSAs in bold type.)

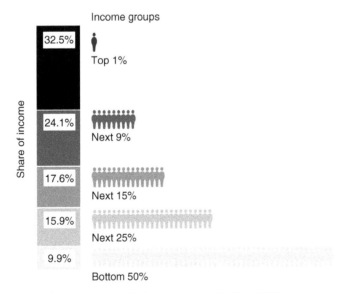

Figure 5.6 New York City's income distribution, 2009

Source: New York City Comptroller's Office analysis based on 2009 New York City income tax files "Income inequality in New York City 2012." Table 1: US percentile shares of total adjusted gross income inequality.

Table 5.17 Progression of Knowledge Services and Manufacturing Employment and Payroll in the New York Metropolitan Region, 2003–2012

			2003	2008	2012
Employment	Service	Information	395,293	320,250	290,926
		Finance & Insurance	654,885	637,118	563,177
		Business Services	647,778	693,350	687,999
		Health Services	1,010,384	1,057,619	1,154,260
		Total	2,708,340	2,708,337	2,696,362
	Manufacturing	Chemicals	81,928	67,048	54,041
		Machinery	26,751	18,626	16,399
		Transport	13,627	10,273	8,597
		Electronics	41,589	31,163	34,067
		Scientific Instruments	17,918	15,576	16,309
		Total	181,813	142,686	129,413
Payroll	Service	Information	20,082	21,753	21,241
		Finance & Insurance	67,888	93,704	78,056
		Business Services	38,806	44,099	43,965
		Health Services	37,131	40,033	43,414
		Total	163,907	199,589	186,676
	Manufacturing	Chemicals	4,808	3,642	3,166
		Machinery	1,181	739	693
		Transport	577	438	414
		Electronics	2,157	1,519	1,882
		Scientific Instruments	782	785	882
		Total	9,505	7,123	7,037

(Units: employment—number of employees, payroll—millions of 1998 US $).

Source: County Business Patterns, US Census Bureau.

Table 5.18 Highlights of the Knowledge Economy in New York and the US, 2003–2012

		New York			US		
		2003	*2012*	*% change*	*2003*	*2012*	*% change*
Service	Emp.	2,708,340	2,696,362	−0.4	30,687,367	32,668,669	6
	Payroll	$163,907	$186,676	13.9	$1,320,564	$1,510,780	14
	Payroll/ Emp.	$60,519	$69,233	14.4	$43,033	$46,246	7
Manufact- uring	Emp.	181,813	129,413	−28.8	5,072,563	4,242,146	−16
	Payroll	$9,505	$7,037	−26.0	$229,501	$199,169	−13
	Payroll/ Emp.	$52,279	$54,376	4.0	$45,244	$46,950	4

(Units: employment—number of employees, payroll—millions of 1998 US $).

Source: County Business Patterns, US Census Bureau.

and manufacturing sectors (relevant NAICS subsectors) in the New York Metropolitan area. The descriptors are employment and payroll in the knowledge intensive subsectors in the 1998–2012 period. This period includes the "Great Recession," which moderated to some degree by 2012.

Table 5.18 indicates that even while employment knowledge intensive service sectors stagnated over the 2003–2012 period, payroll grew by 14 percent. Consequently the growth in payroll/employee in services was twice as rapid in New York as it was in the US over the same period. This suggests that growth in New York is more focused on the highest value added activities. The picture in terms of manufacturing is one of decline, yet even here payroll per employee kept up with the national trend. Again, this suggests that those manufacturing jobs that are surviving are in the highest value categories.

New Immigration: Mirror and Shaper of New York City's Evolution

Demographic Dimensions of the New Immigration

The vast flow of migrants has shaped New York City throughout its history— in terms of its demography, economy, politics, and culture. The geographic sources and the ethnic composition of this migration into New York have changed over time, yielding a diverse demographic and economic mosaic. For much of the city's history, people of European and African origin dominated these immigrant streams. Recently, Third World migration has made the city's population truly global in character, with persons of European background becoming a minority. These migrants are drawn largely from Latin America and Asia. In every era over the last two centuries, new groups of people have brought new competencies and entrepreneurial energy to the city, helping it to reinvent itself economically, socially, and culturally.

The recent immigration flows set in motion by the 1965 Immigration Act have led to a marked increase in the number of immigrants entering the US in general and New York in particular. This increasing immigration has offset considerably the population losses due to suburban out-migration. Fifty-five percent of New Yorkers are now first-or second-generation immigrants. Thirty-nine percent of the 2013 population of New York City is foreign-born, and close to 50 percent of the city's population aged 5 years and over do not speak English at home (Table 5.19).

Table 5.19 Migrant Composition of New York City Population, 2013

Place of Birth	
Total Population	8,405,837
Native (born in US, US Island areas or born abroad to American parent(s))	4,995,048
Foreign born	3,106,661
World Region of Birth of Foreign Born	
Europe	473,940
Asia	863,700
Africa	138,998
Oceania	9,034
Latin America	1,597,321
Northern America	23,668
Language Spoken at Home	
Population 5 years and over	7,850,081
English only	4,000,415
Spanish	1,938,507
Other Indo-European languages	1,042,096
Asian and Pacific Islander languages	670,681
Other languages	198,382

Source: 2013 American Community Survey.

The New Immigrants and New York's Economic Evolution

Today's immigrants into New York City have a comparable role in shaping the city's economy, polity, and culture as their counterparts had a century and a half ago. This role is best described in the context of the emerging patterns of labor demand in the global economy as a whole and in its strategic gateway cities like New York.

The major reason for the continuation in the last quarter century of large inflows of immigrants from Asia and the Caribbean basin into New York City (at a time of sharp losses in manufacturing and goods-handling jobs) lies in the rapid expansion of the supply of low wage jobs and the casualization of the labor market associated with the new growth industries (Sassen 1998). Sassen persuasively argues that the globalization of the economy has contributed to the *initiation* of the labor migration to New York and other cities, while its *continuation* at high and growing levels is traceable to the economic restructuring in the US and other advanced industrial economies.

The growth of low wage jobs in New York and other cities is partly the result of the global organization that has channeled investments and manufacturing jobs to low wage countries. Cities like New York also have a rapidly growing number of low wage service sector jobs (in addition to the well-known high-income jobs in the financial services and management sectors). Sassen (1998) notes that in addition to using such low wage workers the major reason for the continuation in the last quarter century of large inflows of migrants from Asian and the Caribbean basin countries into New York City (at a time of sharp losses in manufacturing and goods-handling jobs) lies in the rapid expansion of the *supply of low wage jobs and the casualization* of the labor market associated with the new growth industries (Sassen 1998).

The traditional manufacturing sector in the US is eroded in this process directly, the service sector indirectly generates demand for workers for servicing the lifestyles and consumption patterns of the growing affluent managerial and financial class in New York (Lakshmanan and Chatterjee 1999). The demand created by this affluent class for residential and commercial gentrification leads to an army of low wage workers in occupations such as building attendants, child care providers, food preparation and restaurant workers. These are the kinds of jobs that immigrants rather than American citizens take and where the informal economy grows. Thus it is at this intersection of the ongoing internationalization of economic processes and a bimodal labor market evolution in advanced industrial economies that immigrants from low wage countries to New York and other cities play a key *economic facilitative role.*

New Immigrants and Cultural Production in New York

New York City has for a long time been dominant in the national production of cultural goods and services. It built its primacy as a cultural center on its position as the most important port linking Europe and North America and as a transshipment point between Europe and the Caribbean. The interaction in a commercial city between diverse people and ideas, and the hybrid ambience were powerful sources of creativity. Kaplan (1997) notes that the ideas, values, and creativity of New York's diverse residents found expression in cultural production for the market as well as for non-commercial channels in clubs, lyceums, and cafes. New York's ideas, popular entertainment, and high culture, reflecting the vibrant connections among its people, led in turn to cultural tourism and a cultural export economy (the vaudeville circuit, theater tours, etc.) (Kaplan 1997). The market position that New York enjoyed in cultural products derived from the strong local relationship between cultural production and consumption.

Recent technologies (e.g. films, audio and video recordings, jet travel) have undermined the geographical and temporal linkages between cultural production and consumption, making possible the assembling, financing, and marketing of performances (the Three Tenors, rock bands, etc.) to global audiences. Kaplan notes that in this era of broad cultural diffusion, New York is reinventing itself so as to retain its cultural hegemony. While New York remains powerful as a cultural producer and a center of consumption, it provides direction to the cultural enterprise in two ways: first, by establishing aesthetic standards, offering criticism and consumer advice, and by launching styles through media, marketing, journalism, and advertising. Second, by the exercise of cultural control by New York persons and institutions that affect cultural market decisions (e.g. which books, plays, and films to back) or what non-profit cultural activities to support (Kaplan 1997).

New York also plays an important role in the cultural dimension of globalization. The frequent observation that New York, with its rich and complex cultural infrastructure, has a central role in directing cultural globalization and that this is *unidirectional* (only center to periphery cultural flows) is only part of the story.

New York's large and only partially assimilated foreign-born residents today have as rich and vibrant interactions and as hybrid an ambience as earlier groups and are creating cultural crossover products. Orlando Patterson (1994) notes that reggae, drawing upon indigenous Jamaican musical traditions, evolved into an original form in response to American rhythm-and-blues, bluegrass, and cowboy music. This musical genre, brought to New York by poor Kingston immigrants, stimulated in turn the development of African-American rap. Patterson's example illustrates the contributions of today's immigrant groups in New York to the cultural life and to the production of cultural goods and services.

Role of Immigrant Institutions and Social Networks in New York

Social networks, and institutions fostering these networks, affect the economic productivity of immigrants in a variety of ways (Lakshmanan and Chatterjee

1999). They play crucial roles in the assimilation process and in immigrants' labor market absorption. They also foster entrepreneurial development, provide access to legal, capital, and other financial services and contribute to their identity formation through cultural production. These institutions and networks have played formative roles in the continual evolution of New York as a gateway city since the seventeenth century. As successive new immigrant groups entered New York's economy, institutions that had their roots in the culture of the originating country were initially transplanted, and eventually transformed, to address the social and economic needs of the new group in the host city.

New York, relative to most other gateway regions in the world, has a long history of fostering institutions that improve the productivity of immigrants. Helped by commercially minded social leaders, New York became a multi-ethnic city because these social networks aided the assimilation of the immigrants and enriched the culture and economic productivity of the city they settled in. For example, the recent resurgence of New York after its fiscal crisis in the 1970s was partly fueled by the attractiveness of an increasingly cosmopolitan city with new immigrants from the various countries of Asia, Africa, the Caribbean, the Mideast, and Latin America (Berrol 1997). The cosmopolitan atmosphere added to the vibrancy of urban life which then attracted the younger, upwardly mobile professional classes to the city. Both groups—the immigrants and the migrants—invested their capital and labor, thereby turning around the fortunes of a declining urban fabric. The ability of the immigrants to contribute to the cultural and economic life of the city depends on a number of institutions, whose cultural forms may vary with the migrant group, which perform these essential socioeconomic functions.

While the importance of social institutions in fostering the economic development of an immigrant community has not declined in the last one hundred years, the character of these institutions appears to be changing. Two types of community institutions that influence immigrant economic welfare can be observed: the traditional and the emergent. The traditional ethnic associations are based on sub-regional identities and are characterized by strong patron-client relations. They provide employment opportunities, business capital, and overall protection in return for political and social loyalty to key members and leaders. The Italian and Irish bosses, the Chinese and Japanese clans, and the more recent Russian associations are examples of this type. While some may have criminal and illegal elements, the majority are legal, socially conscious, and philanthropic entities. A prime example is the Chinese Consolidated Benevolent Association (CCBA). Its pattern of social organization, transplanted from mainland China, is hierarchical and includes district and clan organizations at lower tiers.

While dominant politically in the Chinese community, it is declining in importance relative to the Chinatown Planning Council (CPC), which also runs various programs to help the social and economic assimilation of new Chinese immigrants. In the Korean community the emergent institutions are based in churches and the media. In the Indian community, they are the business and professional institutions. These newer institutions, of which the CCP is but one example, act as bridges between the ethnic enclave culture and the larger society in which the immigrants are embedded. Thus they can be contrasted to the traditional ones that draw their base from segregating the community.

The newer forms provide information on public assistance and help the immigrant community to access public funds and laws, to learn the languages, customs, mores of the host society, and thus to integrate with the host community more efficiently. These two forms reflect, to a large extent, the changing nature of the immigrants and the maturation of the immigration process. In fact, there appears to be competition between the earlier, traditional form and the emergent, modem form.

Both types perform useful roles in assimilating and enhancing the economic productivity of immigrants. Given the foreign sociocultural milieu of the host country, many, if not most, migrants need assistance in being incorporated into the new society. New York, as an important initial entry point into the United States, has had to develop appropriate institutions to address the needs of newcomers.

5. Philadelphia: From a Manufacturing Powerhouse to an Education and Health Center

Philadelphia is the second largest metropolitan area in the Megalopolis region in terms of population, GDP, and exports. Historically, it was the political and economic seat of the large Pennsylvania Colony. Located at the navigable extent of the Delaware River, it passed Boston to become the largest port in the United States by the time of the American Revolution. Along with the nearby Port of Camden NJ, the Port of Philadelphia became a major industrial transshipment point, connecting coastal and oceanic shipping to three Class I railroads.

Philadelphia first emerged as a major urban center whose merchants traded agricultural commodities from its large and fertile hinterland along the coast and into Caribbean and European markets. Along with the merchants, a large class of artisans working in textiles, wood, and metals developed. These production skills, along with a large labor force, access via rail to Pennsylvania's rich coal reserves, and access via the port to industrial materials including wool, cotton, wood, and metal ores, helped Philadelphia become by 1900 one of the largest manufacturing centers on earth. In 1917 the local chamber of commerce bragged of Philadelphia as the "world's greatest workshop." Unlike Detroit, Pittsburgh, and other US industrial cities that specialized in a single production sector, the Philadelphia manufacturing economy was highly diversified, with major facilities ranging from textiles to metals based engineering. It was also a center of industrial innovation. For example, from its founding in 1825, the Franklin Institute promoted technological advancement in water power, steam power, and areas of industry. The diversified production economy, with many small to medium sized firms who developed strong industrial linkages, did not experience the periods of sudden growth or decline seen in more specialized centers, but remained large and resilient through most of the twentieth century (Society for Industrial Archaeology 1990). In particular, it remained vibrant for some time after the New England manufacturing economy went into decline.

Industrial Philadelphia also benefited from industrial expenditure of the US government, especially the Philadelphia Naval Shipyard. Designated as a shipbuilding facility for the US Navy in 1801, it produced ships for all major wars with activity peaking during World War II, when a labor force of 40,000 built numerous battleships.

From about the 1970s on, however, Philadelphia experienced rapid manufacturing decline. Accounting for more than 50 percent of employment as late as the 1950s, manufacturing's share had fallen to 7.5 percent by 2007. From 1990 to 2007, manufacturing employment fell by well over a third from about 365,000 to 228,000.[26] This loss was more than offset by growth in professional and business services and education and health services, both of which grew by more than 40 percent over the same period (Delaware Valley Regional Planning Commission 2009).

Manufacturing remains strong, however, in certain high value, knowledge-based manufacturing industries. In particular the pharmaceutical industry, which has deep roots in Philadelphia, maintains a significant presence. A number of predecessor firms of today's "big pharmas" were founded in Philadelphia. The origins of Smith, Kline and French, Wyeth and Warner Lambert can be traced to nineteenth century Philadelphia firms. Smith, Kline and French eventually became part of the British giant GlaxoSmithKline (GSK), while both Wyeth and Warner Lambert were acquired by New York based Pfizer. Even though the headquarters functions of these firms shifted from Philadelphia, GSK and Pfizer still have important facilities there. In fact, pharmaceutical employment reached its peak at over 22,000 in 2002, before falling steeply to just under 14,000 in 2013 (see Figure 5.7). The most significant remaining cluster of manufacturing activity is in health related sectors: pharmaceuticals, biotechnology, and medical devices (Delaware Valley Regional Planning Commission 2009).

The shift to the service sector has been remarkably focused in Philadelphia. Location quotients calculated for 2006 showed only four out of 24 sectors with values above 1.2 (indicating a fairly high level of specialization): finance and insurance (1.31), professional and technical services (1.32), educational services (2.27), and health care and social services (1.32) (Delaware Valley Regional Planning Commission 2009).

While financial services are a traditional specialization, it is worth noting that employment in finance in the City of Philadelphia actually fell by 20 percent between 2002 and 2012 (Greater Philadelphia Chamber of Commerce 2014). However, rapid growth in financial activity has occurred

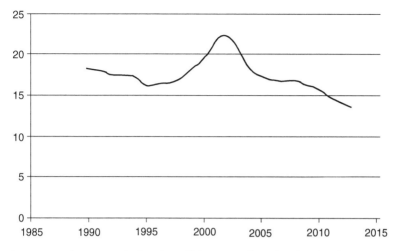

Figure 5.7 Pharmaceutical and Medicine Manufacturing in Philadelphia, PA (MD), Thousands of Persons, Annual, Not Seasonally Adjusted

Source: Federal Reserve Bank of St. Louis and US Bureau of Labor Statistics (2015).

in Wilmington, Delaware, a city with a population of about 70,000, which is included in the Philadelphia MSA. In 1981 the State of Delaware passed legislation eliminating a variety of financial regulations, including usury laws that in most states cap the interest rate that can be charged on credit card balances, in order to attract financial institutions. As a result a number of major credit card issuers and online banking operations have relocated to Wilmington.

The relative durability of health based manufacturing, along with evidence of specialization in health services, points to the emergence of life sciences as a driving force in the Philadelphia economy. In 2005, a Milken Institute ranked Philadelphia third among US cities in terms of the importance of life sciences to the local economy and a 2014 report identified Philadelphia as having the seventh largest life science cluster in the US (JLL 2014).

Philadelphia's very high location quotient for educational services arises from the concentration of 92 colleges and universities in the region. These include two of America's most prestigious institutions: Princeton University in Mercer County, New Jersey and the University of Pennsylvania in the City of Philadelphia, along with others. Philadelphia ranks second to Boston in the number of bachelor and first professional degrees granted per capita.

The education and life science sectors are closely intertwined. A number of the major hospitals are owned by university health services including University of Pennsylvania, Temple, Jefferson, and Drexel. Also university research contributes to innovation in life biotech and medical devices as well as other technology sectors. Philadelphia ranks third among US metropolitan areas in the number of technology transfer licenses issued and fifth in related revenues. But the dependence of the region on these sectors does not necessarily guarantee economic dynamism, as routine health care and educational service provision is noted for relatively low productivity growth (Greater Philadelphia Chamber of Commerce 2014).

Health care and education are especially important in the City of Philadelphia, where about one in three jobs are in those two sectors. In many other respects, however, the City has failed to keep up with the rest of the region. The City's share of regional employment has fallen from over 40 percent in the 1970s to less than 25 percent today. While the region has a higher rate of educational attainment than the US, the City is characterized by a low-skilled labor force.

Tables 5.20 and 5.21 presents data on Philadelphia's knowledge sectors over the 1998 period, which may be compared with the US (Table 5.3) and with the Megalopolis as a whole (Table 5.2).

While knowledge intensive services and manufacturing are well established in Philadelphia, growth in these sectors has not kept pace with the rest of the nation. In 2003 close to a million people were employed, mostly in knowledge intensive services, but by 2012 even the service employment had dropped. Payroll per employment was well above the national level in both service and manufacturing, but it grew more slowly than in the US overall—in fact it declined slightly in knowledge intensive manufacturing. The latter decline may reflect the relative decline in pharmaceuticals. Overall, while knowledge intensive services are a major driver of the Philadelphia economy, they show relatively little dynamism over the 2003 to 2012 period.

6. Baltimore: Rise of Knowledge Industries in a Polarized Economy

Like Philadelphia, Baltimore first emerged as a major economic center due to the strategic location of its port as a link between inland routes and the Atlantic shipping trade. Located where the mouth of the Patapsco River provides a safe harbor leading on to Chesapeake Bay, it eventually became the most important port on that large and centrally located body of water. In the nineteenth century exports of first tobacco and later cotton expanded the port and available waterpower led to its establishment as one of the largest flour milling industries in the US. Much as the Erie Canal expanded the hinterland of New York, the Baltimore and Ohio Railroad (B&O) expanded Baltimore's hinterland. Founded in the 1820s, the B&O was the first eastern railroad to reach all the way to the Ohio River in the 1850s. Other key railroads followed.

Baltimore's labor force, which initially was composed of a number of European immigrant groups, was greatly expanded by the in-migration of freed slaves, both before and after the Civil War. As in Philadelphia, the weight of economic activity shifted from port and trade activities to a

Table 5.20 Progression of Knowledge Services and Manufacturing Employment and Payroll in the Philadelphia Metropolitan Region, 2003–3012

			2003	*2008*	*2012*
Employment	Services	Information	78,874	71,765	68,624
		Finance & Insurance	212,364	187,513	165,248
		Business Services	239,945	204,941	196,529
		Health Services	351,232	358,133	381,037
		Total	882,415	822,352	811,438
	Manufacturing	Chemicals	27,077	28,342	21,905
		Machinery	11,966	12,698	11,552
		Transport	17,302	17,012	12,569
		Electronics	19,436	19,186	17,398
		Scientific Instruments	7,310	6,439	5,410
		Total	83,091	83,677	68,834
Payroll	Services	Information	3,995	4,042	4,456
		Finance & Insurance	11,112	11,409	10,698
		Business Services	14,184	11,853	11,612
		Health Services	12,487	12,663	13,529
		Total	41,778	39,967	40,295
	Manufacturing	Chemicals	1,663	1,730	1,219
		Machinery	490	547	545
		Transport	1,039	892	660
		Electronics	931	1,091	1,022
		Scientific Instruments	319	226	187
		Total	4,442	4,486	3,633

(Units: employment—number of employees, payroll—millions of 1998 US $).

Source: County Business Patterns, US Census Bureau.

Table 5.21 Highlights of Knowledge Economy in the Philadelphia Metropolitan Region and the US, 2003–2012

		Philadelphia			*US*		
		2003	*2012*	*% change*	*2003*	*2012*	*% change*
Service	Emp.	882,415	811,438	–8.0	30,687,367	32,668,669	6
	Payroll	$41,778	$40,295	–3.5	$1,320,564	$1,510,780	14
	Payroll/ Emp.	$47,345	$49,659	4.9	$43,033	$46,246	7
Manufact- uring	Emp.	83,091	68,834	–17.2	5,072,563	4,242,146	–16
	Payroll	$4,442	$3,633	–18.2	$229,501	$199,169	–13
	Payroll/ Emp.	$53,459	$52,779	–1.3	$45,244	$46,950	4

(Units: employment—number of employees, payroll—millions of 1998 US $).

Source: County Business Patterns, US Census Bureau.

diversified set of manufacturing industries toward the end of the nineteenth century. However, the growth of what was to become the largest single steel works in America led to a greater concentration in heavy industry.

Steel production at Sparrows Point in Baltimore County began around 1890 but was greatly expanded after Bethlehem Steel purchased the facility in 1916. This location benefited from two key geographical advantages that emerged from institutional and trade developments in the twentieth century. The first was the end of the "Pittsburgh Plus" steel pricing system, by which all steel producers charged their customers a delivered price based on trans-portation costs from Pittsburgh, even if the steel was produced somewhere else. This anticompetitive arrangement prevented producers located closer to major markets from gaining a competitive edge. When it was abolished, Sparrows Point could deliver steel to huge Megalopolis market more cheaply than Pittsburgh and Great Lakes producers. The second was the growth in international iron ore trade. While a Chesapeake Bay location was not acces-sible to the main source of US iron ore around Lake Superior, it was ideally suited for the importation of ore from Latin America; first Cuba and Chile, followed in the 1950s by Venezuela which became the main source of cheap, high quality ore. The presence of the steel industry supported steel fabrica-tion and other industries such as shipbuilding, which expanded tremendously during World War II (as did aircraft production).

The period of the 1960s, 1970s and 1980s was marked by economic decline and social problems in Baltimore. The steel and shipbuilding industries declined slowly, with steel production ceasing entirely by 2012. Baltimore acquired a reputation for urban decline and racial conflict with African-Americans comprising the majority in the City of Baltimore, while the white population largely shifted to the suburban fringe of the metropolitan area. By the 1990s, however, the region began to show renewed vitality based largely in the emergence of a Knowledge Economy.

The "new" Baltimore economy is characterized by three things: the rehabilitation of the industrial waterfront, the rise of "eds and meds" as leading economic activities, and the advantages of a location close to Washington DC (Vey 2012.)

Baltimore's Inner Harbor is the historic center of the port. Even when other port and industrial activities were still thriving, the Inner Harbor was in decline because it was too shallow for the larger ships that came with the institution of containerization. (These ships continued to call at facilities outside the historic harbor at Fells Point and Canton.) Attempt to re-task the land around the Inner Harbor for recreational and tourist activities date all the way back the 1950s, but accelerated in the 1960s and 1970s with a set of complementary developments including refurbishment of historic buildings on the waterfront, the location of a new convention center, creation on the new National Aquarium, and eventually the nearby location in 1992 of the Camden Yards Sports Complex, including the home stadium of the Baltimore Orioles baseball team. Private enterprise in the form of major hotels, restaurants, and retailers followed and the Inner Harbor is currently one of the leading tourist attractions on the US East Coast. It has been recognized by the Urban Land Institute[27] and others as a model urban redevelopment project. While the Inner Harbor has done much to improve the public perception of Baltimore, television shows such as *Homicide: Life on the Streets* and *The Wire* continue to portray a more gritty and violent image of Baltimore's low income neighborhoods.

Like all the major metropolitan areas of the Megalopolis, Baltimore is home to a large number of post-secondary institutions. There are numerous two-year and four-year institutions in the metropolitan area, several ranking among the best in the nation. Two institutions—the University of Maryland and Johns Hopkins University—are world class research institutions, with the latter consistently ranking at or near the top in terms of total government research funds. A recent study found that in the City of Baltimore alone, colleges and universities directly employ over 22,000 people. When indirect (arising from purchases of goods and services) and induced (arising from the local recycling of employment income) effects are counted, they are estimated to provide almost 38,000 jobs that generate almost $2 billion annually in employment income (Jacob France Institute 2012). Economic impacts of the 13 major hospitals in the City of Baltimore are even larger, with direct employment of over 50,000, total employment of over 80,000 and employment income of over $5 billion annually (Jacob France Institute 2012).

Washington DC has experienced rapid economic growth in recent decades (see below), some of which has spilled over into the nearby Baltimore metropolitan area. There are over 73,000 federal government employees in the region, making it second only to Washington as a hub for federal government activity.[28] This includes headquarters of several major federal institutions, including the National Security Agency and the Social Security Administration. In a variety of ways, Baltimore provides a cheaper and less congested alternative to Washington DC. For example, its airport—which is called "Baltimore–Washington International"—hosts discount carriers that do not serve either of the Washington airports.

Arising from these and other advantages, the Baltimore region by 2010 was performing better than most parts of the national economy and had established a clear advantage in a number of knowledge intensive industries. Post 2000 Baltimore has been among the top ten US metropolitan areas in terms of per capita income, educational attainment and growth in both per capita income and employment.[29] Tables 5.22 and 5.23 indicate that in the recent period from 2003 to 2012, Baltimore was outperforming the nation in terms of both employment and payroll growth for the knowledge intensive service sectors. While the overall change in knowledge intensive employment is strongly positive, knowledge intensive manufacturing employment contracted much faster than in the US, which indicates the pervasive transformation of this once industrial center to a service economy. Baltimore appears to be an example of an industrial economy making a successful transition to a Knowledge Economy led by the KIBS sector.

A recent study by the Brookings Institution Metropolitan Policy Program, however, points out a dark side to this generally positive story (Vey 2012). The observed economic progress has done almost nothing to improve the welfare of the Baltimore region's sizable low income population. In fact, over a period from 2000 to 2010 during which the total metropolitan population rose by 6.2 percent, the low income population rose by 7.2 percent. Thus, rather than lifting people into the middle class, the new economy appears to be adding to the ranks of the disadvantaged. This does not just reflect unemployment and people dropping out of the labor force. In the period from 1980 to 2007, the number of high wage industry jobs grew by less than 10 percent while the number of low wage industry jobs grew by over 60 percent (Vey 2012).

To some extent this reflects the fact that jobs created in industries that are typically associated with the Knowledge Economy—especially in health care and education—are often of the low wage variety. For example, the number of doctors, technicians, and registered nurses employed by a typical hospital may be much lower than then the number of unskilled nurse's assistants, cleaning staff, custodians, and clerical workers.

Table 5.22 Progression of Knowledge Services and Manufacturing Employment and Payroll in the Baltimore Metropolitan Region, 1998–2012

			2003	*2008*	*2012*
Employment	Services	Information	31,526	26,208	23,969
		Finance & Insurance	65,222	62,126	51,877
		Business Services	89,603	104,159	118,626
		Health Services	131,121	153,889	170,585
		Total	317,472	346,382	365,057
	Manufacturing	Chemicals	10,252	7,453	5,551
		Machinery	5,090	4,026	3,286
		Transport	4,432	2,034	4,161
		Electronics	12,376	12,708	9,549
		Scientific Instruments	1,278	776	738
		Total	33,428	26,997	23,285
Payroll	Services	Information	1,357	1,250	1,255
		Finance & Insurance	3,486	3,602	3,248
		Business Services	4,646	5,647	6,871
		Health Services	4,602	5,501	6,048
		Total	14,091	16,000	17,422
	Manufacturing	Chemicals	602	357	249
		Machinery	225	176	140
		Transport	216	76	202
		Electronics	677	817	689
		Scientific Instruments	56	29	23
		Total	1,776	1,455	1,435

(Units: employment—number of employees, payroll—millions of 1998 US $).

Source: County Business Patterns, US Census Bureau.

Table 5.23 Highlights of the Knowledge Economy in the the Baltimore Metropolitan
Region and the US, 1998–2012

		Baltimore			US		
		2003	2012	% change	2003	2012	% change
Service	Emp.	317,472	365,057	15.0	30,687,367	32,668,669	6
	Payroll	$14,091	$17,422	23.6	$1,320,564	$1,510,780	14
	Payroll/ Emp.	$44,385	$47,724	7.5	$43,033	$46,246	7
Manufact-uring	Emp.	33,428	23,285	–30.3	5,072,563	4,242,146	–16
	Payroll	$1,776	$1,303	–26.6	$229,501	$199,169	–13
	Payroll/ Emp.	$53,129	$55,959	5.3	$45,244	$46,950	4

Source: County Business Patterns, US Census Bureau.

The Brookings study also points to other indicators of weakness in the
Baltimore economy. For example, it finds that Baltimore ranks ninety-first
among US metro areas in terms of the proportion of its metropolitan product accounted for by exports. Also, despite the presence of major research
universities, it ranks poorly in measures of technological innovation, such
as the number of patents granted per 1000 workers. (Some of the problems
identified here—especially slow growth in export oriented activities and
increasingly uneven income distributions—are not unique to Baltimore, but
in fact are evident in most of the Megalopolis metro areas, as we will show
in Chapter 7.) This study's prescription is to focus development on industries
that demonstrate *both* good growth potential and the ability to provide good
jobs to people with relatively low skills and educational attainment, including
manufacturing, bio-science, IT, and industries with "green" benefits.

7. Washington DC: Emergence of a Government-Driven Knowledge Economy

The political and economic history of Washington DC is very different from
the histories of the other four major metropolitan areas in the Megalopolis
region. Although the town of Georgetown, Maryland was established as a
port at the highest point on the Potomac River that could be navigated by
ocean-going ships, Washington was never a port of national significance, or

a major trade center. Although it is located on the Fall Line, there was never a time when Washington ranked among significant manufacturing cities in the US. Washington's foundation and growth has always been driven by a single economic entity: the federal government of the United States. Yet the Washington metropolitan area has grown to be the seventh largest urban agglomeration in the US and one of the most important centers for knowledge-based services.

In the years following the American Revolution, both Philadelphia and New York served for some time as the US capital. As political poles emerged around the cash crop oriented and slave-holding economy of the southern states and the more diversified and egalitarian economy of the north, there was pressure to establish a more neutral capital location. The US Constitution of 1787 called for the establishment of an independent capital district, but did not name the location. In 1790, the debt-ridden northern states entered into a compromise with the more financially stable southern states by which the capital would be moved south to the banks of the Potomac River in exchange for the southern state's support for a bill conferring state debts to the new federal government. After some haggling, and eventually the secession of the town of Alexandria, Virginia from the capital district, the District of Columbia was cut out of the state of Maryland to house the capital city named after the hero of the Revolution and first US president, George Washington.

This location is often regarded today as the transition between the US South and North, but at the time it was distinctly southern. It was south of the "Mason-Dixon line" drawn to separate Pennsylvania and Delaware from Maryland, which came to be regarded as the transition from northern to southern culture. Also the state of Maryland did not formally abolish slavery until 1867. However Maryland remained in the Union during the American Civil War, placing Washington on the front line of that conflict. Like Baltimore, Washington's population expanded significantly through migration from the rural south, giving it a large proportion of African-American population.

For the first few decades, the capital had a small population and poor public services, with unpaved roads connecting great public buildings and monument. The expansion of federal government activities during the Civil War, Word War I, and especially World War II led to rapid growth in employment and income. Brinkley (1988) describes how Washington was transformed from a sleepy southern town to a busy metropolis during the war years of the 1940s. The expansion of the federal government into ever more areas of economic activity, first during the Great Depression and then throughout the postwar era, was to be the main impetus to growth. There has been a notable absence of manufacturing activity, however, consistent with a federal system of government that tends to distribute procurement of defense and other hardware to the home states of Senators and Representatives. Today, manufacturing represents only 1.6 percent of total employment in the Washington metro area, which is less than half the manufacturing share of any of the other Megalopolis cities and less than a fifth of the US share.[30] In the twenty-first century, Washington DC is a service economy *par excellence*.

The Washington metro area has been by far the fastest growing component of the Megalopolis region over the past few decades. Between 2000 and 2010, the population of the MSA centered on Washington grew by 16.5 percent, in contrast with the MSAs around Baltimore (6.2 percent), Philadelphia (4.9 percent), New York (3.3 percent), and Boston (3.7 percent).[31] Less than 11 percent of the total Washington MSA population is in the District of Columbia. The city was built at low density so as not to overshadow monuments and public building, so growth quickly spilled over into the abutting states of Maryland and Virginia. The spread into Maryland is so extensive that it is hard to separate the urban field of Washington from that of Baltimore. Northern Virginia has been the location of most of the economic and population growth in recent decades (Fuller 2011a), especially in areas around Dulles Airport and Tysons Corner, one of America's most famous "edge cities."

The relatively rapid population growth is due in large part to generally positive rates of net migration (Sturtevant and Champaign 2012). This has not only expanded the population, but since young people are more prone to move, migration has contributed to an unusually young age structure, especially among the working population. Between 2007 and 2011, the most rapidly growing age cohort of the labor force was aged 25–34. While this cohort grew by less than 5 percent nationally, it grew by well over 20 percent in the Washington MSA (Dani 2013).

Tables 5.24 and 5.25 indicate that knowledge intensive service employment grew by 10.7 percent over the 2003–2012 period. This is 75 percent faster than in the US overall and 32 percent faster that in the entire Megalopolis. Knowledge intensive manufacturing declined during this period but from a small base, so the decline in manufacturing is less than 4 percent of the growth in services.

Consistent with these trends, Dani (2013, Figure 4) has shown that most of the employment growth that has occurred over the period 1990–2011 has been in a single economic sector: professional and business services. Other sectors experiencing steady, but much slower growth include education and health services, state and local government, and hospitality and leisure. Federal government employment, which has been the engine of the Washington economy throughout most of its history, was stagnant.

Does this mean that the region has made a transition from an economy driven by the public sector to one driven by the private sector? The answer is that while more and more employees are working for private firms, the ultimate driver is still the federal government. During the Clinton and Bush presidential administration (1992–2008), there was a relentless trend of contracting out services that had previously been provided by federal employees. The result is that while federal expenditure grew, the number of federal employees stagnated and the workforce of government contractors (mostly attributed to professional and business services) grew by almost 85 percent.

Table 5.24 Progression of Knowledge Services and Manufacturing Employment and Payroll in the Washington DC Metropolitan Region, 1998–2012

			2003	2008	2012
Employment	Services	Information	149,089	107,114	99,544
		Finance & Insurance	129,780	106,603	101,243
		Business Services	379,815	486,560	505,836
		Health Services	190,765	212,628	233,827
		Total	849,449	912,905	940,450
	Manufacturing	Chemicals	3,370	3,287	3,866
		Machinery	2,761	2,979	2,214
		Transport	1,727	1,932	4,666
		Electronics	16,951	12,509	10,737
		Scientific Instruments	1,137	1,342	1,178
		Total	25,946	22,049	22,661
Payroll	Services	Information	7,574	7,438	7,238
		Finance & Insurance	10,353	7,224	7,455
		Business Services	24,237	32,615	34,979
		Health Services	7,570	8,316	9,068
		Total	49,734	55,593	58,740
	Manufacturing	Chemicals	223	190	241
		Machinery	99	119	93
		Transport	117	94	238
		Electronics	1,058	764	683
		Scientific Instruments	40	56	56
		Total	1,537	1,223	1,311

(Units: employment—number of employees, payroll—millions of 1998 US $).

Source: County Business Patterns, US Census Bureau.

Table 5.25 Highlights of the Knowledge Economy in the Washington DC Metropolitan Region and the US, 1998–2012

		Washington			US		
		2003	2012	% change	2003	2012	% change
Service	Emp.	849,449	940,450	10.7	30,687,367	32,668,669	6
	Payroll	$49,734	$58,740	18.1	$1,320,564	$1,510,780	14
	Payroll/ Emp.	$58,549	$62,459	6.7	$43,033	$46,246	7
Manufact- uring	Emp.	25,946	22,661	−12.7	5,072,563	4,242,146	−16
	Payroll	$1,537	$1,311	−14.7	$229,501	$199,169	−13
	Payroll/ Emp.	$59,238	$57,853	−2.3	$45,244	$46,950	4

Source: County Business Patterns, US Census Bureau.

Whether this trend is consistent with the Knowledge Economy depends on the composition of the services in question. Contracted out services could include both computer programming and janitorial services. There is evidence that KIBS play a major role in this employment. For example, Fuller (2011b) shows that the professional, scientific, and technical service sector, which represents almost half of business services, is dominated by technical consulting, computer services, architectural and engineering, and similar high skilled, knowledge intensive sectors. All of these are over-represented in the Washington economy. For example NAICS 5415, Computer System Design and related services employs over 120,000 people and has a location quotient of 7.2.

Further evidence of the Knowledge Economy in the Washington DC metropolitan area is the concentration of colleges and universities. Figure 5.3 shows a location quotient of 1.53, which while lower than Boston and Philadelphia still represents a significant over-representation. A recent study on 2010 data said that Washington's 14 post-secondary institutions serve 155,000 students, 64 percent of whom come from outside the region. Thus this is an exceptionally export oriented educational service. Direct employment is 68,000 and the total over 125,000. The study cannot determine is how much the attraction of out-of-region students contributes to the knowledge base of the regional labor force, but surely the effect is substantial (Fuller 2011c).

The critical question for the future of Washington's Knowledge Economy is this: *is there life after government contracting?* The increasing debt burden of the US federal government, along with a conservative turn in the composition of the Congress, is likely to lead to a significant contraction—or at least a slowdown in growth—for federal expenditures. Unable to reach consensus on the distribution of budget cuts, the Congress has used the blunt mechanism of "sequestration," whereby across the board cuts are mandated if the Congress and the president cannot reach agreement on budgets within preset fiscal guidelines. While sequestration seemed like a temporary expedient when it was introduced in 2011, it came into force in 2013. Thus, for the foreseeable future budgetary austerity is mandated.

How will these cuts affect the Washington regional economy? Early indications are that while Washington was able to bounce back from the recession of 2008–2009 more quickly than most regions, it is starting to underperform the national economy as budget cuts take effect. Federal contracting actually decreased by over 16 percent between 2010 and 2013, causing serious revenue losses for private firms (George Mason University Center for Regional Analysis 2014). To maintain its growth trajectory, therefore, Washington will have to look to private sector investment that is not driven by government contracting. There is ample evidence of the presence of knowledge workers in the labor force, but will that be enough to compete with America's most innovative regions?

A recent study attempted to assess the competitive position of the Washington region by assessing it relative to ten traits of *global fluency* defined as "the level of global understanding, competence, practice, and reach that a metro area exhibits in an increasingly interconnected world economy" as suggested in Clark and Moonen (2013, p. 3). The ten traits, along with ratings for the Washington metro area, are provided in Table 5.26.

While the ratings of the study authors are open to debates, they generally identify the history of global orientation, sensitivity to global change and strong global image as strengths. Weaknesses are identified as arising from a history of dependence on the federal government, a generally introspective attitude in local leadership, and the image of "official Washington" as not indicative of innovation and dynamism.

The picture is mixed, but the indication is that metro Washington will be able to draw on its strengths in the Knowledge Economy, but must also make major adjustments if it is to continue to flourish in the absence of growth in federal government spending.

Notes

1 Washington DC has experienced vigorous economic and demographic growth in the twentieth century due the very great expansion of the national public sector.
2 There is, in addition, another small knowledge service sector (colleges, universities and Professional Schools)—described later in this chapter—in which the Megalopolis and its large metros are dominant.
3 It should be noted that the 2012 data in the Megalopolis and US represent only a partial recovery from the "Great Recession" of 2008.

Table 5.26 Global Fluency Scorecard for Washington DC

Trait	Description	Washington DC rating	Comments
1. Leadership with a World View	Local leaders plugged into global networks	–	Local focus of leadership
2. Legacy of Global Orientation	First mover advantage from long history of global orientation	+	Well established as hub of federal government and tourism
3. Specializations with Global Reach	Distinct local specialization with global appeal	?	Both high tech and low wage jobs present. "All key competitive advantages remain related to the Federal presence."
4. Adaptability to Global Dynamics	Ability to adjust to changes occurring around the world	+	"The region has long been out in front of global change as a result of the strong Federal influence on its economy and workforce."
5. Culture of Knowledge and Innovation	Human capital to generate methods, products and technologies	?	High skills by geared for US federal government
6. Opportunity and Appeal to the World	Open to people and firms from around the world	+	Positive global image, but not a major attractor of global business
7. International Connectivity	Efficient, modern infrastructure to connect to the world	?	Strong position in air cargo and travel, but unlikely to expand freight capability
8. Ability to Secure Investment for Strategic Priorities	Ability to attract investment from international sources	–	Strong traditional reliance on investment from the federal government
9. Government as Global Enabler	Federal, state and local assistant to "go global"	?	State and local governments must rise to the challenge
10. Compelling Global Identity	To portray the city as shaped around a common purpose	–	A strong global image as "official Washington"

Source: George Mason University Center for Regional Analysis, 2014, based on Clark and Moonen (2013).

4 The United States is itself viewed in OECD and other publications as a top tier Knowledge Economy in the world in terms of proportion of national value added, and share of R&D investments by knowledge industries (Brinkley 2008).

5 On a scale of *city decline* ranging –4 to +4, the Brookings Institution study (Bradbury et al. 1982) ranked the city of Boston at –4, in the early 1970s, and –5 in terms of city *distress* scale ranging (from +5 to –5). On a scale of *disparity*, measuring the gap in social indicators between the central city and the surrounding SMSA, Boston scored –5, putting Boston near the bottom of urban America.

6 In 1989 black families in Boston had a median income 22 percent higher than the national median for black families. A decade earlier, Boston's black families had a median income 6 percent *lower* than the national American average.

7 In this respect, Boston is in a small class of such resilient non-national capital cities, like Florence, Venice, and Edinburgh.

8 New England was followed by Meiji, Japan, Scandinavia, Holland, and Prussia in the nineteenth century (Lakshmanan 1993).

9 These were unmarried girls who worked typically for four years, were housed in dormitories fitted with libraries and gardens. These workers regularly wrote and edited the *Lowell Offering*. English visitors (e.g. Charles Dickens) were moved to describing these workers' conditions as "workers' paradise," worthy of emulation elsewhere.

10 One-third of New England workers were women as compared to 20 percent in the US as a whole (Temin 1999).

11 The young female labor force was so outraged by the sharply lower wages (than they received) offered to Irish workers fleeing the potato famine, that they staged the first industrial American labor strikes in Lowell, Massachusetts.

12 The educational system provided civic values and work ethic to a diverse population including migrants.

13 This system was actually perfected for interchangeability standards in the public sector—Springfield Armory (Mass.) and Harpers Ferry Armory—and later customized in various industries (Hounshell 1984).

14 In Connecticut, Massachusetts, and New Hampshire farmers often shared knowledge about farming techniques and household practices in Unitarian and other churches after Sunday Service in the eighteenth and nineteenth centuries.

15 Women and trustees owned on the eve of Civil War ¼ of the equity in the textile mills of Massachusetts (Temin 1999).

16 In 1957, 140 firms located along RT.128; by 1967, these firms numbered 729, and by 1973 grew to 1200—utilizing more than 80,000 workers.

17 The Boston MSA is ranked fourth in the world at 2.5 percent of all patent filings and 7.2 percent of US patent filings, according to the OECD. Boston was ranked sixth among the top 25 most economically powerful cities in the World, based on "gross regional product, the region's banking and financial institutions and its innovation index," or patents generated (Florida, *Atlantic Monthly, Oct.2005*). The Milken Institute has ranked Massachusetts *number one* on its biennial Science & Technology State Index from 2002 to 2010, and Metro Boston tops the life science cluster (Boston Foundation 2012, p. 17).

18 Massachusetts is a leader in 9 of the 11 sectors used to define the innovation economy and has the highest overall concentration of innovation economy employees. Massachusetts is home to a large concentration of research institutions, biotech firms, and software firms. In addition to a diverse array of start-ups, Massachusetts is home to the headquarters or major operations of State Street Bank, EMC, Microsoft, Genzyme, Cisco, and Raytheon. The state is home to many universities, colleges and research institutions including Harvard, Massachusetts Institute of Technology (MIT), Tufts University, Boston University, and the University of Massachusetts system (Massachusetts Technology Collaborative 2014).

19 Heurmann (2009) suggests that human capital externalities accrue predominantly to growing firms, which benefit from sharing, matching and learning externalities arising from a large supply of highly qualified workers in skilled labor markets.

20 In Boston metro region's colleges and universities, this sector's wages as a proportion of total regional private wages were 3.2 percent, compared with only 1.0 percent nationally.

21 The Health Pole rankings are based on combining an MSA's health care industry location quotient (the concentration of health care in an economy) with its share of national health care employment. MSAs then are ranked according to their composite scoring. The metro area with the highest composite score for a given health care industry is assigned a bench mark score of 100. All subsequent ranking metropolitan areas have scores that indicate their placement relative to the benchmark.

22 MIT and Harvard universities in the Boston region have had huge documented effects on the Boston metropolitan regional economy. However, Johns Hopkins University, which is routinely among the largest recipients of federal government research funds, has failed to stimulate significant high tech production in the Baltimore metropolitan region. Since universities with research programs that are similar in scale and quality may have very different local economic impacts, the key role played by the highly interactive multiple networks of knowledge creation and dissemination in the Boston biotech industry as well as the broader Knowledge Economy must be clear. Indeed, this attribute of the Boston region is evident in embryonic form in earlier cases of regional reinvention in Boston.

23 The section on New York is an updated version of Lakshmanan and Chatterjee (2001). With permission from Edward Elgar Publishing. Originally published in Ake E. Andersson and David E. Andersson Gateways to the Global economy, Edward Elgar 2001.

24 New York's financial institutions are dominant globally, offering unparalleled depth, with twice London's number of financial specialists and related business professionals, and dwarfing Tokyo in the expertise in Anglo-Saxon law under which most international transactions are negotiated (Rosen and Murray 1997).

25 Further, as noted in Chapter 4, Krugman's work (1992, 1995) is reviving this emphasis on urban agglomeration economies, which was evident in the much richer and earlier (1950–1970s) analysis of economic role of large cities, in particular New York region's economic governance of the national economy in an earlier time (Lichtenberg 1960; Vernon 1960; Hoover and Vernon 1959; and Allan Pred 1977).

26 Unless otherwise indicated, data are for the Philadelphia-Camden-Wilmington, PA-NJ-DE-MD MSA.

27 Available at http://baltimore.uli.org/initiatives/wavemaker-awards/, accessed March 29, 2015.

28 Available at www.greaterbaltimore.org/UploadedPDFs/government_profile.pdf, accessed March 29, 2015.

29 Economic Alliance of Greater Baltimore, as quoted in Vey 2012. Additional indicators may be found at www.greaterbaltimore.org/research/key-industries.aspx, accessed March 29, 2015.

30 US Bureau of Labor Statistics data, found at www.bls.gov/sae/eetables/sae_annavgl14.pdf, accessed April 3, 2015.

31 US Census data, found at www.census.gov/population/www/cen2010/cph-t/CPH-T-5.pdf, accessed April 3, 2015.

References

Appleseed Inc., 2003. Engines of economic growth, New York: Appleseed.

Autor, D.H., Levy, F., Murnane, R.J., 2003. The skill content of recent technological change: an empirical exploration. *The Quarterly Journal of Economics*, 118(4), 1279–1333.

Basu, S., Fernald, J., 2006. *Information and Communication Technologies as a GPT: Evidence from US Industry Data*, Federal Reserve Bank of San Francisco, Working Paper, 2006-29

Bathelt H., 1999. *Technological Change and Regional Restructuring in Boston's Route 128 Area*, IWSG Working Papers 10-1999.

Bathelt, H., 2001. Regional competence and economic recovery: divergent growth paths in Boston's high technology economy. *Entrepreneurship and Regional Development* 13(4), 287–314.

Bathelt, H., Malmberg, A., Maskell, P., 2004. Clusters and knowledge: local buzz and global pipelines and the process of knowledge creation. *Progress in Human Geography* 28(1), 1–56.

Bell, D., 1973. *The Coming of Post-Industrial Society: A Venture in Social Forecasting*, New York: Basic Books.

Berrol, S., 1997. *The Empire City: New York and Its People: 1624–1996*, Westport, CN: Praeger.

Best, M.H., 2000. Silicon Valley and the resurgence of Route 128: systems integration and regional innovation. In Dunning, J. (ed.) *Regions, Globalization and the Knowledge-based Economy*, Oxford: Oxford University Press, pp. 459–484.

Bluestone, B., Stevenson, M.H., 2000. *The Boston Renaissance: Race, Space and Economic Change in an American Metropolis*, New York: Russell Sage Foundation.

Boston Foundation, 2012. *City of Ideas: Reinventing Boston's Innovation Economy*, The Boston Indicators Report 2012.

Bradbury, K.L., Downs, A., Small, K.A., 1982. *Urban Decline and the Future of American Cities*, Washington DC: Brookings Institution.

Braudel, F., 1973. *Civilization and Capitalism 15–18th Century*, New York: Harper and Row.

Breznitz, S.M., Anderson, W.P., 2005. Boston metropolitan area biotechnology cluster. *Canadian Journal of Regional Science* 28(2), 249–267.

Brinkley, D., 1988. *Washington Goes to War*, New York: Knopf.

Brinkley, I., 2008. *The Knowledge Economy: How Knowledge is Reshaping the Economic Life of Nations*, London: The Work Foundation.

Brown, J.P., 1982. *Boston and 33 Large Cities: Economic Structure and Trends 1969–1980*, Boston, MA: Boston Redevelopment Authority.

Castells, M., 1989. *The Rise of the Network Society*, London: Blackwell.

Castells, M., 1996. *The Rise of the Network Society*, London: Blackwell.

Castells, M., 2000. *The Information Age: Economy, Society and Culture*, Oxford: Blackwell

Clark, G and Moonen, T., 2013. *The 10 Traits of Globally Fluent Metro Areas*, Washington DC: Brookings Institution.

Corrado, C., Hulten, C., Sichel, D., 2009. Intangible capital and U.S. economic growth, *Review of Income and Wealth* 55(3), 661–685.

Crahan, M.E., Vourvoulias-Bush, A. (eds), 1997. *The City and the World*, New York: The Council on Foreign Relations.

Dani, L., 2013, *The Changing Labor Force and Sector Structure of the Washington DC Metropolitan Economy*, George Mason University Center for Regional Analysis, Working Paper 2013-4.

Delaware Valley Regional Planning Commission, 2009. *Greater Philadelphia Economic Development Framework*. Philadelphia, PA: Delaware Valley Regional Planning Commission, Select Greater Philadelphia and Ben Franklin Technology Partners.

Department of Labor, 1977. *Dictionary of Occupational Titles*, Washington DC: Department of Labor.

DeVol, R.C., Koepp, R., 2003. America's health economy. Santa Monica, CA: Milken Institute.

Dicken, P., 2000. A new geo-economy. In Held, D., McGrew, A. (eds) *The Global Transformations Reader: An Introduction to the Globalization Debate*, Cambridge: Polity Press, pp. 251–258.

Drennen, M., 1991. The decline and rise of the New York economy. In Mallenkoff, J., Castells, M. (eds) *Dual City: Restructuring New York*, New York: SAGE, pp. 25–41.

Drucker, P.F., 1969. *The Age of Discontinuity: Guidelines to our Changing Society*, London: Harper and Row.

Dunning, J.H., 1993. *The Globalization of Business*, London and New York: Routledge.

Federal Reserve Bank of St. Louis, US Bureau of Labor Statistics, 2015. *All Employees: Non-Durable Goods: Pharmaceutical and Medicine Manufacturing in Philadelphia, PA (MD)* [SMU42379643232540001A], retrieved from FRED, Federal Reserve Bank of St. Louis https://research.stlouisfed.org/fred2/series/SMU42379643232540001A, March 15.

Florida, R., 2013. The boom towns and ghost towns of the new economy, *Atlantic Monthly*, October.

Fuller, S.S., 2011a. *Northern Virginia's Economic Transformation*, George Mason University Center for Regional Analysis. Available at http://cra.gmu.edu/pdfs/studies_reports_presentations/By_The_Numbers_NoVa_Drives_Area_Growth.pdf accessed on April 3, 2015.

Fuller, S.S., 2011b. *The Future of the Northern Virginia Economy*, George Mason University Center for Regional Analysis. Available at http://cra.gmu.edu/pdfs/researach_reports/recent_reports/Futurepercent20ofpercent20NVA percent20Economy.pdf accessed on April 3, 2015.

Fuller, S.S., 2011c. *The Impact of the Consortium of Universities of the Washington Metropolitan Area on the Economies of theWashington Metropolitan Area and District of Columbia*. George Mason University Center for Regional Analysis, prepared for the Consortium of Universities of the Washington Metropolitan Area. Available at http://cra.gmu.edu/pdfs/researach_reports/recent_reports/Economic_Impacts_of_Washington_Consortium_Universities.pdf accessed on April 3, 2015.

George Mason University Center for Regional Analysis, 2014. *Improving the Washington Region's Global Competitiveness*. Available at http://cra.gmu.edu/global-competitiveness/ accessed on April 3, 2015.

Glaeser, E.L., 2003. *Reinventing Boston: 1640–2003*. NBER Working Paper 10166, Cambridge, MA.

Glickman, N.J., Lahr, M.L., Wyly, E.K., 1996. *State of the nation's Cities: America's Changing Urban Life*, Washington DC: US Department of Housing and Urban Development.

Greater Philadelphia Chamber of Commerce, 2014. *Roadmap for Growth: A Vision for the City of Philadelphia*. Philadelphia, PA: Greater Philadelphia Chamber of Commerce.

Heurmann, D.F., 2009. *Reinventing the Skilled Region: Human Capital Externalities and Industrial Change*, Discussion Paper series No. 02/2009. Institute for Labor Law and Industrial Relations in EC(IAEEG) Trier.

Hill, K. 2006. *University Research and Local Economic Development*, Center for Competitiveness and Prosperity Research, Arizona State University.

Hoover, E., Vernon, R., 1959. *Anatomy of a Metropolis: The Changing Distribution of People and Jobs within New York Metropolitan Region*, Cambridge, MA: Harvard University Press.

Hounshell, D., 1984. *From the American System to Mass Production, 1800–1932: The Development of Manufacturing Technology in the U.S.*, Baltimore, MD, The Johns Hopkins University Press.

Jacob France Institute, 2012. *The Economic Impact of Non-Profit Hospitals, Colleges and Universities on the City of Baltimore*, Baltimore: The University of Baltimore.

JLL, 2014. *Life Sciences Cluster Report*, Chicago, IL: Jones, Lang, LaSalle Brokerage Inc.

Kaplan, J., 1997. Rooting for a logo: culture, identity, and civic experience in the global city. In Crahan, M.E., Vourvoulias-Bush, A. (eds) *The City and the World*, New York: The Council on Foreign Relations, pp. 159–170.

Kim, S., 1995. Expansion of markets and the geographic distribution of economic activities: the trends in U.S. regional manufacturing structure, 1860–1967, *Quarterly Journal of Economics*, 110, 881–908.

Kim, S., Margo, R.A., 2003. Historical perspectives in U.S. economic geography. In Henderson, V., Thisse, J.-F. (eds), *Handbook of Regional and Urban Economics*: Volume 4. *Cities and Geography*, Amsterdam: Elsevier, pp. 2981–3019.

Krugman, P., 1992. *A Dynamic Spatial Model*, NBER Working Papers 4219.

Krugman, P., 1995. Innovation and agglomeration: two parables suggested by city-size distributions. *Japan and the World Economy* 7(4), 371–390.

Lakshmanan, T.R., 1993. Social change induced by technology: promotion and resistance. In Ackerman, N. (ed.). *The Necessity of Friction*, Heidelberg: Physica Velag, pp. 135–158.

Lakshmanan, T.R., Chatterjee, L.R. 1999. *New York: Gateways to the Global Economy*. Boston University Center for Transportation Studies Working Paper.

Lakshmanan, T.R., Chatterjee, L.R., 2001. New York: gateway city to the global economy. In Andersson A.E. and Andersson D.E., *Gateways to the Global Economy*, Northampton, MA: Edward Elgar.

Lakshmanan, T.R., Chatterjee, L.R., 2005. Economic consequences of transport improvements. *Access* (Spring), 28–33.

Lakshmanan, T.R., Chatterjee, L.R. 2011. *Innovation Networks and Regional Reinvention: The Case of the Boston Region*. Paper presented at the Symposium in honor of Professor Folke Snickars at the Royal Institute of Technology, Stockholm, Sweden, May 26–28.

Lichtenberg, R.M., 1960. *One-tenth of a Nation: National Forces in the Economic Growth of the New York Region*, Cambridge, MA: Harvard University Press.

Machlup, F., 1962. *The Production and Distribution of Knowledge*, Princeton, NJ: Princeton University Press.

Mallenkoff, J., Castells, M. (eds), 1991. *Dual City: Restructuring New York*, New York: SAGE.

Markusen, A., 1996. Sticky places in slippery space. *Economic Geography* 72(3), 293–313.

Maskell, P., Malmberg, A., 1999. The competitiveness of firms and region: "ubiquitification" and the importance of localized learning. *European Urban and Regional Studies* 6(1): 9–25.

Massachusetts Technology Collaborative, 2014. FY 2014 Annual Report, Boston. MA.

McSweeney, D.M., Marshall, W.J., 2009. *The Prominence of Colleges and Universities in the Boston Metropolitan Area*, US Bureau of Labor Statistics Report 09-01.

Murray, F., 2004. The role of academic inventors in entrepreneurial firms: sharing the laboratory life. *Research Policy* 33(4), 643–659.

Owen-Smith, J., Powell, W.W., 2004. Knowledge networks as channels and conduits: the effects of spillovers in the Boston biotechnology community. *Organization Science* 15(1), 5–21.

Patterson, O., 1994. Ecumenical America: global culture and American cosmos. *World Policy Journal* 11(2), 103–117.

Piore, M., Sabel, C., 1984. *The Second Industrial Divide*, New York: Basic Books.

Porter, M., 1990. *The Competitive Advantage of Nations*, New York: Free Press.

Porter, K., Whittington, K.B., Powell, W.W., 2005. The institutional embeddedness of high-tech regions: relational foundations of the Boston biotechnology community. In Bresnehan, S., Malerba, F. (eds) *Clusters, Networks, and Innovation*, London: Oxford University Press.

Powell, W.W., 1996. Inter-organizational collaboration in the biotech industry. *Journal of Institutional and Theoretical Economics,* 152(1), 197–215.

Powell, W.W., Snellman, K., 2004. The knowledge economy. *Annual Review of Sociology* 30, 199–220.

Pred, A.R., 1977. *City Systems in Advanced Economies: Past Growth, Present Processes, and Future Development Options*, London: Hutchinson.

Rosen, R.D., Murray, R., 1997. Opening doors: access to the global market for financial services. In Crahan, M.E., Vourvoulias-Bush, A. (eds) *The City and the World: New York's Global Future,* New York: Council on Foreign Relations, pp. 39–50.

Sassen, S., 1997. *The Mobility of Labor and Capital: A Study in International Investment and Labor Flow*, Cambridge, UK: Cambridge University Press.

Sassen, S., 1998. *Globalization and Its Discontents*, New York: New Press.

Saxenian, A.L., 1994. *Regional Advantage: Culture and Competition in Silicon Valley and Route 128*, Cambridge, MA: Harvard University Press.

Saxenian, A.L., 1996. Inside-out: regional networks and industrial adaptation in Silicon Valley and Route 128. *Cityscape* 2(2), 41–60.

Scott, A.J., 1988. *Metropolis: From the Division of Labor to Urban Form*, Berkeley, CA: University of California Press.

Scott, A.J., 1998. *Regions and the World Economy: The Coming Shape of Global Production, Competition and Political Order*, Oxford: Oxford University Press.

Scott, A.J., 2002. A new map of Hollywood: the production and distribution of American motion pictures. *Regional Studies* 36(9), 957–975.

Society for Industrial Archaeology, 1990. *Workshop of the World: A Selective Guide to the Industrial Archaeology of Philadelphia*, Houghton, MI: Oliver Evans Press.

Storper, M., 1995. The resurgence of regional economies, ten years later: the region as a nexus of untraded interdependencies. *European Urban and Regional Studies* 2(3), 191–221.

Sturtevant, L. A. and M. B. Champaign, 2012. *Domestic Migration to and from the Washington DC Metropolitan Area, 1985–2010*, George Mason University Center for Regional Analysis, Working Paper 2012-1.

Temin, P., 1999. *The Industrialization of New England: 1830–1880*. NBER Working Paper Series on Historical Factors in Long Run growth, Historical paper 114.

Vernon, R., 1960. *Metropolis 1985*, Cambridge, MA: Harvard University Press.

Vey, J.S., 2012. *Building for Strength: Creating Opportunities in Greater Baltimore's Next Economy,* Washington: Brookings Institution.

World Bank 2007. *World Development Report: Knowledge for Development*, Washington DC: World Bank.

6 Spatial Evolution of the Megalopolis as a Functional Economic Region

Introduction

This chapter examines the spatial structure of the Megalopolis and how it has been changing. It is organized around two themes. The first is the concept of the Megalopolis as a functional region, which means a space within which a high intensity of spatial interactions exploit complementarities among its spatial subdivisions, making it more than the sum of its spatial parts from an economic perspective. The second is the presence and role of agglomeration within the Megalopolis. The Megalopolis is in itself evidence of agglomeration in the American space economy, accounting for 20 percent of GDP in just 1.4 percent of the land area. Within the Megalopolis, however, we can find more geographically detailed evidence of agglomeration in local clusters of activity, especially in knowledge intensive activities. Given the importance of clustering in the Knowledge Economy, what emerges is a picture of many local agglomerations that are highly interconnected, giving rise to an innovative and resilient functional region. Addressing these themes involves application of techniques of spatial analysis. Technical details of these techniques are provided in a series of appendices at the end of the chapter.

Earlier chapters provide some broad trends in the spatial evolution of the Megalopolis. Chapter 2 describes a long process of decentralization of population and economic activities as the major cities that form the region spread out from their urban cores. The effect of this decentralization has been to fill in the gaps, rather than to supplant the underlying structure. The major cities—Boston, New York, Philadelphia, Baltimore, Washington DC—still define the region from a spatial perspective (see Figure 2.3). While the rapid growth of Washington DC has shifted the Megalopolis' center of gravity somewhat to the south, all the original urban centers remain important anchors in the overall spatial structure.

This structure has been reinforced by the pattern of transportation infrastructure starting with canals and rail that is largely echoed by the later developing highway network (see Figure 3.4) and the patterns of passenger air service. The potential for this highly connected agglomeration of agglomerations to support knowledge intensive industries is illustrated by the Northeast Pharmaceutical cluster (see Figure 2.10).

While population has dispersed, the traditional urban cores have remained strong, especially as employment centers. This is in part due to the strong position of the Megalopolis in finance and other KIBS that tend to locate in urban cores. The enduring strength of urban cores has two broader spatial implications: the preservation of radial commuting patterns centered on downtowns that are conducive to transit service and relatively high population density, which is conducive to non-motorized transportation. This, at least in part, explains the growing shares of both subway and bicycle ridership in the New York metropolitan area (see Figure 3.11). The presence of strong urban cores in a linear, city-rich region provided the ideal spatial structure for the first (and to date only) implementation of high-speed rail in North America: Amtrak's Northeast Corridor Acela Service. Thus, the spatial patterns of population and employment in the Megalopolis both reinforce and are reinforced by transportation infrastructure, technology and policy.

Megalopolis as a Functional Region

Economic geographers define regions in two ways: as formal regions and as functional regions (Anderson 2012). Formal regions are defined as being homogeneous on some dimension. Examples include the Corn Belt or the Bible Belt, defined as comprising subregions (such as counties in the US) that are distinguished by the common characteristics of corn cultivation and conservative Christian population respectively. We can think of the Megalopolis as a formal region where all constituent counties have the common characteristic of a high proportion of urban population.

A more useful conception of the Megalopolis, however, is as a functional region, which is defined as a region with a high degree of spatial interaction within its borders. Metropolitan regions are defined as functional regions because even though their constituent parts are quite heterogeneous—including high rise districts, suburban neighborhoods, industrial zones, shopping malls, etc.—they are bound together by a constant and intense movement of people, goods, and information. (Census agencies generally draw metropolitan boundaries in such a way that people are more likely to commute within the region than across its boundaries.) The Megalopolis is a functional region because it encompasses a hierarchical pattern of spatial interactions within and between its constituent metropolitan areas.

From the perspective of goods movement, the fact that the Megalopolis is a functional region has been demonstrated by statistical analysis of freight flows (Lakshmanan et al. 2006.) A "gravity model" is used in that study to illustrated that freight flows between production regions along the I-95 corridor, which roughly coincides with our definition of the Megalopolis, are higher than expected, even after controlling for the size of the production regions and the highway distances between them (see Appendix 6.1 for technical details). This reflects the industrial history of the Megalopolis and the development of inter-firm relationships leading to the movements of both intermediate and finished goods.

Since the economic revival of Megalopolis has been based mostly on growth in services industries such as KIBS and health care, the movement of people among urban centers within the region is a more important indicator spatial interaction in the functional region. While we do not have comparable data on the intercity movement of people, the high level of travel especially for business purposes is evident from the frequency of service provided by air shuttle services between city pairs within the Megalopolis (Anderson 2007) and the viability of high-speed rail service connecting the major cities.

Both of these transportation options make it possible for people to complete round trips between cities in a single day. This is crucial for connecting up business communities, especially in knowledge intensive industries and occupations where despite the various options provided by IT, face-to-face communication is still important, especially for activities that involve the transfer of complex information (Daft and Lengel 1986; Olanian 1996.) For example, people working for firms located in Boston can, and frequently do, meet face-to-face with financial associates in New York or government agencies in Washington with a minimal expenditure of travel time and no need to incur the cost and inconvenience of an overnight stay. Thus, the Megalopolis is a high powered functional region made up of a number of economically vibrant urban regions, each with its unique advantages and specializations but all linked through forms of spatial interaction that could not be achieved via electronic technologies.

Megalopolis as an Agglomeration of Agglomerations

The various theoretical explanations for why firms in knowledge intensive industries benefit from geographical proximity to other firms in the same industry is discussed in some detail in Chapter 4. Factors such as technological spillovers, transfer of tacit knowledge, the availability of people with specialized skills, and the ability of a community of firms to draw on common inputs and institutions have all been used to explain the phenomenon of spatial clustering of innovative firms.

This type of clustering occurs over a much more local geography than is defined by the entire Megalopolis region. In what follows, however, we demonstrate that the Megalopolis is a broad region within which there is a higher density of specialized clusters than is found in most other parts of the United States. Thus it is an agglomeration of agglomerations.

Measuring the spatial concentration of economic activities and mapping the location and pattern of specific industrial clusters requires specialized forms of statistical analysis. We draw heavily on the work of Song (2009a, b) to provide rigorous evidence of the high density of clusters within the Megalopolis. Technical details of the analysis are provided in a series of appendices to this chapter that review data resources (Appendix 6.2), measures of spatial concentration (Appendix 6.3), and the Local Index of Spatial Association (LISA) method for identifying spatial clusters (Appendix 6.4).

Measurement of Agglomeration

Before addressing the specific economic geography of the Megalopolis regions, we begin by measuring the propensities for clustering in major industries. There are several measures that can be used to compute the geographic concentration levels, including the Locational Gini Coefficient, Spatial Hirschman-Herfindahl Index (HHI), and Localization Index (for a complete review, see Song 2009a). In what follows we use the HHI because in related research we found it to capture most of the information revealed by the more complex Localization Index. The spatial HHI, which is adapted from measures used to indicate levels of concentration across the firms of a particular industry, measures the degree to which economic activity is concentrated across spatial units. Our measure of economic activity is employment by in seven selected industries: apparel, chemicals, electronics, finance, insurance, business services, and legal services. Our spatial unit is the county. The spatial HHI is defined such that a value of 1 indicates that all employment in the industry in question is concentrated in a single county, while a value of 0 indicates that employment in the industry is distributed across counties in exact proportion to total employment. (See Appendix 6.2 for details on county level data and Appendix 6.3 for details on the spatial HHI.)

We begin by measuring the concentration of each industry across the full set of over 3,000 US counties, excluding Alaska and Hawaii. Figure 6.1 shows trends in the spatial HHI for each industry over the period 1977–2005. This figure contains all selected industries but due to the broad variance of industrial results the lines for most industries are clustered at the bottom and therefore not seen very clearly. So an additional Figure 6.2 is added enlarging the five industries that have low values.

The highest levels of concentration are seen in the financial and apparel industries. The financial industry's index dropped from 0.12 to 0.033 in the end of the study period while apparel's increased from 0.007 to 0.05. These trends reflect the spatial dynamics of one expanding industry (finance) and one contracting industry (apparel). The financial industry diffused geographically from a few metropolitan areas to regional centers. In 1977, only 1,005 among 3,079 counties had at least one employee in finance within their boundaries and most of them were in or near big cities like New York, Boston, and Chicago. In 2005, 2,339 counties had employment in this sector. The apparel industry outsourced many of its functions over the study period, especially the routine production activities. This results in loss of workforce and establishments, resulting in a higher level of agglomeration as employment remains in only a few counties. Thus, the agglomeration trends of these two industries demonstrate that the industrial development cycle or structural change can have serious impacts on industrial clustering.

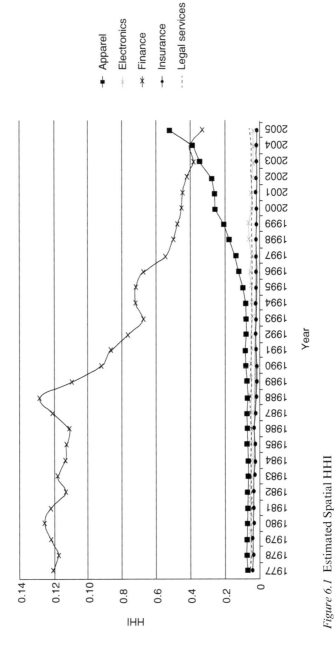

Figure 6.1 Estimated Spatial HHI

Source: Song (2009a) using County Business Patterns, US Census Bureau.

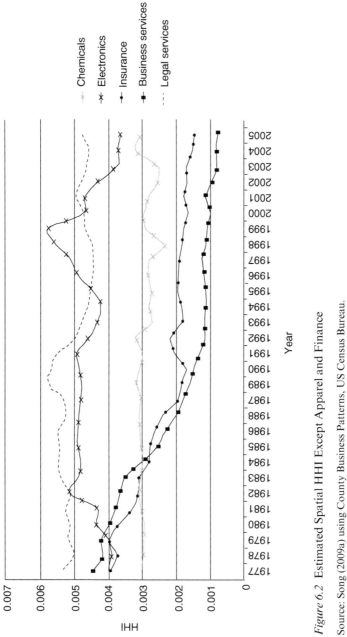

Figure 6.2 Estimated Spatial HHI Except Apparel and Finance

Source: Song (2009a) using County Business Patterns, US Census Bureau.

Two other industries' indices fell over the study period: insurance and business services. These two sectors both expanded in terms of employment and GDP, although not as much as finance. Such expansion could have narrowed the gap between industrial employment distribution and general employment pattern. The HHI also fell for legal services, but not by as much. The concentration levels of other two manufacturing industries do not show any significant long-term trend during the study period. The electronics industry's level fluctuates, which may be related to its fast development in a few regions in the early study period followed by spatial diffusion in the late 1990s.

Overall the trend is for reduced or roughly constant concentration in most US industries over the study period. The sole exception, apparel, reflects a process of industrial decline. We now turn to the question of whether similar trends are found in the Megalopolis region. Figures 6.3 and 6.4 show values of the spatial HHI for 1977, 1987, and 2005 in the I-95 corridor. While it is tempting to compare the absolute value of the measures with those for the entire US, values of spatial HHI defined on different base regions are not directly comparable. It is useful, however, to compare the trends in the Megalopolis and US measures.

Figure 6.3 shows values and trends for the spatial HHI for two manufacturing industries: apparel and electronics. The apparel industry is more concentrated than the electronics industry but not by nearly the same margin as we see in the US measures. In fact the trend from 1987 to 2005 is of dispersion rather than concentration, which is directly contrary to the US trend. The difference in the gap probably reflects the fact that apparel is highly represented in the Megalopolis compared to the US, with its traditional center in New York City, so a measure that includes just that region shows less concentration. The declining concentration, however, suggests that industry is increasingly relegated to peripheral locations. The lower concentration value for the electronics industry may seem paradoxical, given that we might expect such a knowledge intensive activity to benefit from spatial concentration. At the beginning of the study period, electronics manufacturing was a driving force behind the Megalopolis economy, especially in New England. Eventually, electronics hardware manufacturing lost out to other regions. Comparing the trends to the US case, we see a slight increase in concentration, in contrast to the significant decrease in electronics concentration for the US in 2005.

The trends indicated in Figure 6.4 for the three service sectors show a more complex pattern. For the Megalopolis, two categories of service, finance and legal services, are much more concentrated than are the manufacturing industries. In these two industries the trend is toward increased concentration, especially in finance, which reaches a very high level at the end of the period. This is in stark contrast to the sharp decline in concentration of national financial employment shown in Figure 6.1. This reflects the rapid growth in high level financial services that tend to locate in the high rise financial districts of the largest cities—especially New York but also in Boston. Business services become less concentrated, consistent with the national trend, but legal services again run contrary to the national trend and become more concentrated.

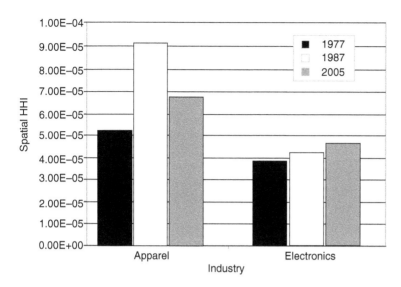

Figure 6.3 Spatial HHI in the I-95 Corridor for Manufacturing Sectors, 1977, 1987, and 2005

Source: Song (2009a) using County Business Patterns, US Census Bureau.

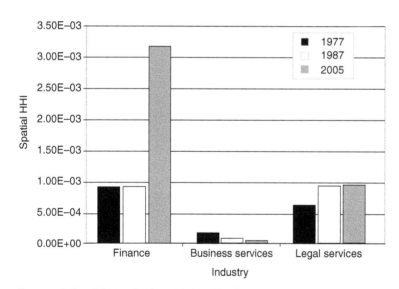

Figure 6.4 Spatial HHI in the I-95 Corridor for Service Sectors, 1977, 1987, and 2005

Source: Song (2009a) using County Business Patterns, US Census Bureau.

While there is a limit to how much we can infer from these comparisons, the general trend of greater, rather than less concentration in the Megalopolis has implications. Especially in the higher order services (finance and legal) the contrast is consistent with a general US pattern of dispersion to follow the pattern of domestic demand, while the concentration in the Megalopolis is consistent with growth in a few major centers to meet national and global demand. But does this suggest a greater overall propensity to economic clustering in the Megalopolis than in other US regions?

Local Indicator of Spatial Association

To address this question we need a way to map out spatial clusters of economic activity to see if their presence and density aligns with our spatial definition of the Megalopolis. A rough impression of the location of industrial clusters may be found with very simple choropleth maps of county employment: a map can show us which counties have relatively high employment in a specific industry and one may be able to say the regions with high values are clusters. But such maps provide only a partial view of clustering. Even a simple choropleth map can show very different spatial patterns of economic activities by the control of display strategies, such as the number of classes and classification methods. Also considering the nature of a cluster, simple mapping can mislead readers. If one county shows very high employment level while neighboring counties have low values, then should we define that region as an industrial cluster? How many high value counties should be located together to be called a cluster?

To answer these questions and to identify the agglomeration pattern from a geographical perspective, we use the Local Indicator of Spatial Association (LISA). LISA has been used to identify clusters in data aggregated into relatively small spatial units, in this case, counties. For example, Simön (2009) applied LISA to locate industrial clusters of manufacturing sector in Spain and found significant clustering for various industries.

The LISA method starts by defining some measure of the concentration of industrial employment in each county. That measure can be raw employment, but that may lead to deceptive results because larger counties will tend to have high employment in all industries, whether they have a local specialization or not. A more appropriate measure is the *location quotient*, which indicates whether a particular industry has a greater than expected employment in a particular county. For example, if the location quotient for business services is 1 for a county, the share of total employment that is in business services in that county is exactly equal to the share of business services in national employment. If an industry is over-represented in a county the location quotient takes a value greater than one.

The LISA method identifies clusters known as "hot spots" as sets of adjacent counties with high values for the location quotient. It also identifies "cold spots" as groups of adjacent counties in which the industry in question is under represented. Mapping the hot spots and cold spots, as in Figures 6.5–6.13, provides a clear picture of the spatial distribution of clustering for each industry. It is important to note that the absence of hot spots on such a map does not indicate the absence of the industry in question, but rather the absence of spatial clustering for that industry.

Figures 6.5–6.7 show the clustering of finance services in 1977, 1987, and 2005. (The broader region is shown in the maps to highlight the higher presence of clusters in the Megalopolis region than in other parts of the eastern United States.) Here the hot spots are shaded in black. It is immediately evident that hot spots are highly concentrated within the Megalopolis. There are isolated hot spots at major urban centers such as Atlanta and Detroit, but only in the Megalopolis do we see such a tight packing of clusters—consistent with the idea of the Megalopolis as an agglomeration of agglomerations.

It is interesting to compare the hot spots for financial services spread out along Megalopolis over the three periods. In 1977, the hot spots are limited to major cities (Boston, Philadelphia, Washington DC) and a broader region around New York. By 1987, additional hot spots appear in New Jersey and by 2005 they extend into Central Massachusetts and Southern New Hampshire. Essentially, the I-95 interstate highway serves as a conduit along which growth spreads in what we might call a process of the dispersion of agglomeration. This means that activities spread out from places where agglomeration is well established to contiguous regions. In this sense, the Megalopolis appears to behave much like a metropolitan area within which some aspects of the most dynamic industries are transferred from the center to peripheral areas that are still accessible enough for daily contact. Such a process is not evident in other major highway corridors, such as the I-85 Corridor from Raleigh—Durham to Atlanta, where hot spots are present only in the Atlanta metropolitan area. This does not mean that there are no concentrations of financial activity (in Charlotte, for instance) but rather that we do not observe clustering of spatial units into broader fields.

Figures 6.8–6.10 display similar cluster maps for the business services industry for 1977, 1987, and 2005. The spatial patterns of clustering in the Megalopolis is similar to that of the finance services, although less pronounced. The patterns for 1987 and 2005 are almost identical, indicating that the spatial extension of business services is more or less complete by 1987. There are more hot spots outside the Megalopolis for business services than for financial services, but they are general somewhat isolated, occurring around major cities such as Atlanta, Cleveland, Detroit, and Cincinnati.

The legal services sector, another knowledge intensive industry, plays an important role in the ongoing structural and organizational transformation of the American economy. Figures 6.11–6.13 show a very similar pattern for legal services. Like business services, a high level of concentration in this activity is well established in the Megalopolis by the beginning of the study period and extends almost continuously along the I-95 spine of the region by 2005.

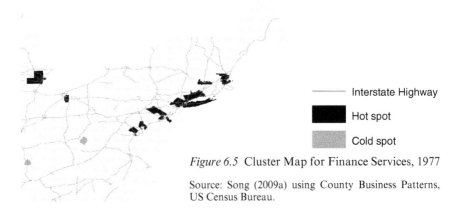

Figure 6.5 Cluster Map for Finance Services, 1977

Source: Song (2009a) using County Business Patterns, US Census Bureau.

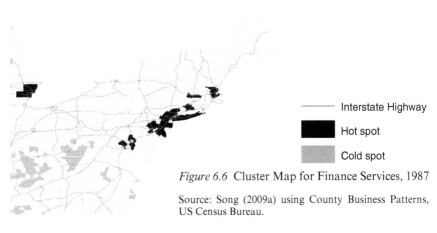

Figure 6.6 Cluster Map for Finance Services, 1987

Source: Song (2009a) using County Business Patterns, US Census Bureau.

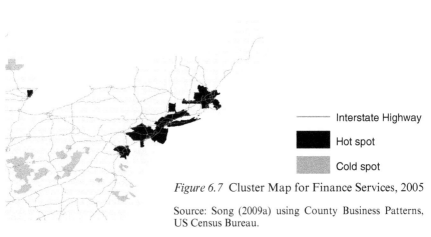

Figure 6.7 Cluster Map for Finance Services, 2005

Source: Song (2009a) using County Business Patterns, US Census Bureau.

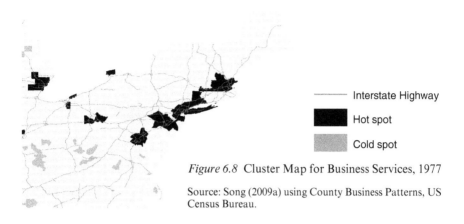

Figure 6.8 Cluster Map for Business Services, 1977

Source: Song (2009a) using County Business Patterns, US Census Bureau.

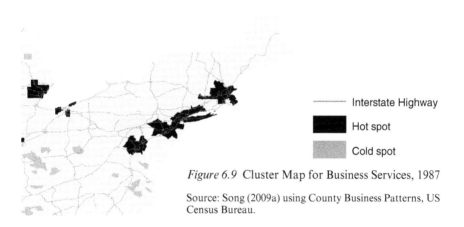

Figure 6.9 Cluster Map for Business Services, 1987

Source: Song (2009a) using County Business Patterns, US Census Bureau.

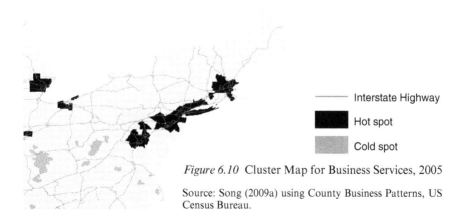

Figure 6.10 Cluster Map for Business Services, 2005

Source: Song (2009a) using County Business Patterns, US Census Bureau.

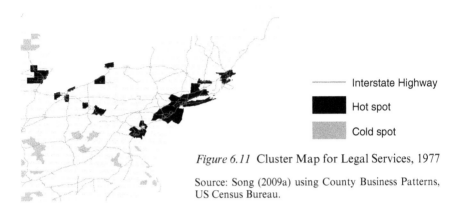

Figure 6.11 Cluster Map for Legal Services, 1977

Source: Song (2009a) using County Business Patterns, US Census Bureau.

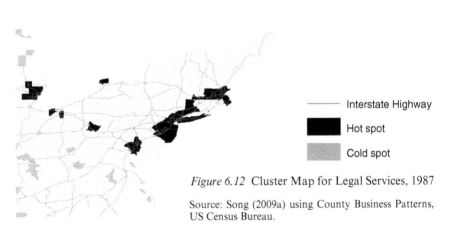

Figure 6.12 Cluster Map for Legal Services, 1987

Source: Song (2009a) using County Business Patterns, US Census Bureau.

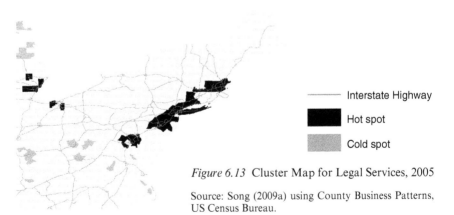

Figure 6.13 Cluster Map for Legal Services, 2005

Source: Song (2009a) using County Business Patterns, US Census Bureau.

The combined results of the spatial HHI and the LISA portray the Megalopolis as a region where the forces of agglomeration are more clearly evident than in other parts of the United States. This is especially true in KIBS where, for example, a national trend to spatial dispersion may be contrasted by a very pronounced trend to concentration within the Megalopolis. The LISA method provides a mapping that illustrates how clusters in the major cities of the Megalopolis that can be observed in the 1970s diffused along the I-95 highway to create nearly continuous hot spots in in finance, business and legal services encompassing almost the entire region.

References

Anderson, W.P., 2007. *Air Transportation in the Northeast Corridor: Challenges for the Future*, Report Prepared for Northeast Corridor Transportation Project, Institute for Public Administration, University of Delaware.

Anderson, W.P., 2012. *Economic Geography*, London and New York: Routledge (Taylor & Francis Group).

Anselin, L., 1988. *Spatial Econometrics: Methods and Models*, Kordrecht: Kluwer Academic Publishers.

Barkley, D.L., Kim, Y., Henry, M.S., 2001. *Do Manufacturing Plants Cluster Across Rural Areas? Evidence from a Probabilistic Modeling Approach.* REDRL Research Report, Clemson University.

Daft, R., Lengel, R., 1986. Organizational information requirements, media richness and structural design. *Management Science,* 32A(32), 554 –71.

Ellison, G., Glaeser, E.L., 1997. Geographic concentration in US manufacturing industries: a dartboard approach. *Journal of Political Economy*, 105, 889–927.

Lakshmanan, T.R., Kuhl, B., Anderson, W.P., Chatterjee, L., 2006. *Highway Development Corridors: Evidence of Growth Effects Along U.S. Interstate Corridors. Phase I Study Report.* A report prepared for the US Department of Transportation, Federal Highway Administration. Office of Policy Analysis. March 2006.

Olanian, B., 1996. A model of group satisfaction in computer-mediated communication and face to face meetings. *Behavior and Information Technology* 15(1), 24–36.

Reynolds, H.D., 1998. *The modifiable Area Unit Problem: Empirical Analysis by Statistical Simulation.* Ph.D. Thesis, Department of Geography, University of Toronto.

Simön, S.M., 2009. Industrial clusters and new firm creation in the manufacturing sector of madrid's metropolitan region. *Regional Studies* 43(7), 949–965.

Song, Y., 2009a. *Global Patterns of Industrial Agglomeration.* Paper 1 of Doctoral Dissertation, Boston University, pp. 7–45.

Song, Y., 2009b. *Local Patterns of Industrial Agglomeration.* Paper 2 of Doctoral Dissertation. Boston University, pp. 46–82.

Appendix: Methods of Spatial Analysis Employed in Chapter 6

Appendix 6.1 The Gravity Model

Gravity models predict flows of people or commodities based on the distances between places and some measure of their sizes. The logic is that larger, nearer places generate movement of people and commodities more than smaller, further away places. The basic form of the gravity model is a log-linearized equation explaining flows of people or goods between two places as follows:

$$\ln Y_{ij} = a_0 + a_1 \ln(M)_i + a_2 \ln(M)_j + a_3 \ln(DIST_{ij}) + a_4(DUMMY) + e_{ij}$$

where the dependent variable, Y_{ij}, is some measure of flows from place i to j, the explanatory variables M_i and M_j are measures of the size (or "mass") of i and j, $DIST_{ij}$ is the distance between them. For our purposes, Y_{ij} is measured as freight deliveries from i to j, M_i is the aggregate freight shipments originating from origin i and M_j is the population of destination j, which serves as a proxy for demand potential.[1] In our specification, a DUMMY variable takes the value of 1 if both i and j are located within a certain highway corridor and 0 otherwise e_{ij} is a random error term. The model was applied to eight US highway corridors, including the I-95 corridor.

Log-linearized gravity models were estimated for each of the study corridors. If the coefficient a_4 is positive and statistically significant, it means that flows within the corridor are greater than flows across the corridor borders *even after controlling for distance and the sizes of origins and destinations.* Such a result identifies the corridor as a functional economic region and indicates a high level of economic integration in the highway corridor region—a potential source of regional competitive advantage.

Data on outbound shipments from Combined Statistical Areas (CSAs)[2] located along study corridors were obtained from the 2002 Commodity Flow Survey.[3] For each of the CSAs along our study corridors, we obtained the value and weight of outbound shipments in 2002 to each destination statistical area.[4] Two data sets were compiled for each corridor, one based on the value of outbound shipments and the other based on the *weight* of outbound shipments.

Distances between principal cities in the origin and destination CSAs are from Rand McNally's driving distances. Population levels of origin and destination CSAs are from the US Census.

For each study corridor, two sets of regressions were run. In the first set, the dependent variable is the natural log of the value of outbound shipments from CSAs located along the corridor. In the second set of regressions, the dependent variable is the natural log of the weight of outbound shipments from those CSAs. The dummy variable in both is 1 for within-corridor shipments and 0 for shipments outside the corridor.

In both regressions, the value of the parameter on the dummy variable was positive for the I-95 corridor, although it was only statistically significant for the regression based on the weight of shipments. Thus the results suggest that from a goods movement perspective, the Megalopolis acts as a functional region.

Appendix 6.2 County Level Employment Data

This study is on the subject of industrial clustering in the US, and a cluster refers to regions showing the same or similar property to adjacent regions. Therefore it would not be proper to include islands or any regions apart from mainland. For that reason, we focus on the continental US, which excludes the states of Hawaii and Alaska and thus 48 states and the District of Columbia constitute the study area.

Many national level analyses have been conducted at the state level and agglomeration studies have been no exception. However, several studies have shown that we may find different result by adopting more detailed spatial level dataset. For example, Ellison and Gleaser (1997) pointed out that their localization measure fell when they used county data instead of state data. This is mainly due to modifiable areal unit problem (MAUP), which cannot be shunned when discrete spatial data are used. There are two sources of MAUP, aggregation and zoning (Reynolds 1998), and zoning effect cannot be avoided or reduced when census data set is used. But finer data may diminish the problem caused by aggregation. County is the finest geographic unit that has aggregate employment and establishment data for the study period. The Census Bureau publishes zip-code level data from 1998 but it does not include industrial employment information. So the spatial unit used here for measuring concentration level is the county and there are 3079 counties in our data set.

This study covers a period from 1977 to 2005. County level industrial data have been annually published by Census Bureau since 1964 and at irregular intervals back to 1946. However, earlier data can be obtained only in printed form, which makes hard to use them in analysis. Digitized data exists only from 1977, so the study period begins in 1977 covering around 30 years, which is a sufficient length of time for a time series analysis.

Since this study aims to see the evolution of industrial clusters as well as to investigate the mechanism of agglomeration, and since county level data are used in the analysis, proper collection and process of the data set are a big task. To save the effort and time required for that process, several industries will be selected based on their growth pattern and theoretical interest in them.

At the county level, the finest industrial category is 4 digit in SIC or 6 digit in NAICS systems. However, the combination of fine area and fine industry results in poor data quality. The Census Bureau withholds data if there is a danger of identity disclosure of individuals. Thereby we consider SIC-2-digit or NAICS-3-digit to be the finest industrial classification level with a high quality of data.

To select study industries, first, general growth pattern in terms of industry GDP, employment, productivity, and so on, are examined. This works as a pre-screening step, and addresses which industries show more dynamic growth or declining patterns. Second, industries that produce transferable goods or services will be selected. If only local customers consumed goods or services produced in a certain region, such industries should not be good candidates since agglomeration level and clusters are defined by a higher level of a production activity than is locally needed. Thus "Eating and drinking places (SIC 58)" is not a good choice while "Business Services (SIC 73)" has possibility to be selected. Then, information from cluster theories is used to determine the final candidates of the study. NEG theory considers differentiated goods, increasing returns and transport costs to be crucial factors in agglomeration process whilst innovation literatures value knowledge intensive sectors.

Most private industrial employment and value added come from service and manufacturing industries in the US and these two are the subject of this study. Most cluster studies have limited their selection to manufacturing sector. However, it is a well-known fact that US industries have become more service and capital-intensive: employment and GDP growth were mainly driven by service sector.

Appendix 6.3 Measures of Clustering

The HHI is normally used as an indicator of the competition among firms in an industry. It ranges from 0 to 1; in a monopolistic market, HHI becomes 1 and in a perfect competition with lot of small firms, it approaches 0. The basic HHI can be derived as following:

$$H = \sum_{i=1}^{n} s_i^{2}$$

where s_i is the market share of the firm i, and n the number of firms.

If we apply the above formula to regional industry data, the calculation would be simpler, but this automatically implies that all the regions have the same size in terms of population, area, economic features, and so on. However, every region is not identical, and a measure that considers the difference in economic size can improve the estimation power. To capture the spatial agglomeration without the disturbance of size factor, minor change in the initial measure is introduced and the spatial HHI is extended as below (Barkley et al. 2001).

$$g = \sum_{i=1}^{n} (s_i - x_i)^{2}$$

where s_i is the share of interested industry's employment in region i, x_i is the share of total employment in region i, and n the number of firms.

This would be a natural measure of the degree to which employment in an industry departs from the overall pattern of employment (Ellison and

Gleaser 1997), which is different from the Gini Coefficient that also considers how much a region's employment pattern differs from other regions. In the calculation of Locational Gini Coefficient, the share of a certain industry in a region is subtracted by that of other regions. But spatial HHI is constructed only by the difference of shares of interested industry and general pattern.

The spatial HHI would be 0 if there were no geographical concentration, and it becomes bigger as concentration becomes intensified. As noticed, this measure assumes that absence of agglomeration is consistent with uniform distribution according to the overall industrial pattern, thus it has limits in identifying randomness in the distribution.

Appendix 6.4 The Local Indicator of Spatial Association

LISA is a tool that examines the local level of spatial autocorrelation and identifies groups of spatial units exhibiting homogeneous characteristics but not following a global trend. So LISA is usually used for identifying the hot spot and cold spot,[5] and is therefore sometimes called by the other name, "hot spot analysis." This analysis can tell us where industrial clusters are located with respect to spatial characteristics.

The local value for each spatial unit, commonly referred to local Moran's *I* value, is calculated as:

$$I_i = \frac{\sum_j w_{ij}(z_i - \bar{z})(z_j - \bar{z})}{\sum_i (z_i - \bar{z})^2}$$

where w_{ij} is a spatial weight corresponding to the observation pair, z_i is the characteristic value of region i, and is the average value of interest.

In spatial analysis, adopting an appropriate weight matrix, w_{ij}, is crucial. A common choice is a geographical distance (Anselin 1988). However, with a broad range of county sizes in the study area, distance based weight cannot be a good candidate here. So weight matrices based on contiguity such as Queen, Rook, and Bishop, are tried in the spatial analysis. We find that they produce almost the same results. Even a second layer of contiguity is applied, but it does not behave any differently. Thereafter only the Queen Contiguity weight matrix is employed in all of spatial statistical analysis here.

By changing the characteristic variable, z_i, we can map different types of agglomeration. We experimented with two variables: the absolute number of employees in a particular industry in each county and the location quotients for the industry in each county. While industrial agglomeration is normally defined from absolute value of economic activities, there is a danger in using only the absolute numbers due to uneven distribution of population and economic activities in the study area: we may find clusters only in most populous areas such as metropolitan areas for all industries. To avoid this problem, concentration measures in previous chapter compared industrial activity share to general economic activity share, and for this geographical study, one more value, namely location quotient, is applied in the place of zi to achieve the same effect.

The Location Quotients (LQ) is defined as below:

$$LQ_{ij} = \frac{emp_{ij} / emp_i}{emp_{nj} / emp_n}$$

A value of LQ_{ij} over 1 indicates that i region's share of j industry is higher than the national average, and in the same vein, higher LQ_{ij} would appear where j industry is specialized regardless of regional economic activity level. Therefore, LISA maps using LQ show us industrial agglomeration with specialization.

If some regions repeatedly appear to be clusters if absolute values were applied in LISA analysis, those regions could be considered to enjoy both externalities from specialization and diversification. This can happen when they have big employment pool in total and many large firms. Metropolitan areas are very plausible candidates for that. On the other hand, if certain regions become hot spots only when location quotients were applied, then we can say those regions are specialized in that industry and can therefore benefit from Marshallian externalities.

Notes

1 A second specification in which population is used for both origins and destinations was also estimated. Since the results were not qualitatively different they are not reported.
2 Combined statistical areas are combinations of adjacent metropolitan and micropolitan statistical areas that have an employment interchange of at least 15 percent.
3 See www.census.gov/svsd/www/02maascii.html, Table 7: Outbound Shipment Characteristics by Destination for CBSA of Origin.
4 For example, there were 6 CSAs located along the I-85 Corridor, namely, Atlanta-Sandy Springs-Gainesville, GA-SC CSA; Charlotte-Gastonia-Salisbury, NC-SC CSA; Greensboro-Winston-Salem-High Point, NC CSA; Raleigh-Durham-Cary, NC CSA; Greenville-Anderson-Seneca, SC CSA; and Spartanburg-Gaffney-Union, SC CSA.
5 The hot spot means an area where high value regions are located together. In other words, it is a cluster of high value regions. The cold spot is the opposite concept of the hot spot indicating an area where relatively low values are located together.

7 Globalization, Tradable and Non-Tradable Sectors, and Widening Income Inequalities in the Megalopolis Knowledge Economy

1. Introduction

This book has advanced a rich conceptual framework which captures the multiple innovations and processes which underlie the multidimensional structural change and evolution embodied in the rise of a Knowledge Economy. It brings together, builds on, and expands the extant literature on the rise of the Knowledge Economy and formulates a much broader analytical framework and a richer model of the rise and evolution of the Knowledge Economy. Further, it has interpreted, in the light of this model, the resilience, structural change, and transition of the Megalopolis region and its component large metropolitan areas in the last three decades or so from a declining industrial economy to a vibrant Knowledge Economy.

In the resulting passage, the globalizing Megalopolis has restructured over the last quarter century *the functional and spatial organization* of its economy. The contemporary production and delivery of goods and services are decomposed into increasing number of value-adding components and the relevant supply chains and value-adding components of economic activities have been increasingly *organized on a global basis*. At the same time, innovations in IT applied in service sectors have created many KIBS. KIBS (comprising financial, legal, accounting, information, and other professional services) enable global corporations to develop and support management innovations that make possible the smooth operation of global supply chains and the integration of global corporate operations. Further, in addition to goods, KIBS also have become tradable.

In the early stages of globalization, global corporations in the Megalopolis moved the lower wage, lower value-adding components of its production activities to low income newly industrializing countries, while retaining the more knowledge intensive components domestically. Thus the upstream knowledge intensive activities (e.g. R&D, product design, capital formation) and downstream knowledge intensive activities (e.g. marketing, after-sale service, brand exploitation) are retained in the Megalopolis, while tasks of fabrication of many components (except the more knowledge intensive components) are outsourced to the newly industrializing countries. At this stage, there is a considerable decline in low wage jobs and some medium wage jobs, and a growth in higher wage knowledge intensive jobs in the manufacturing and other tradable sectors in the Megalopolis. The twofold result of a loss of jobs in manufacturing and other tradable sectors and a rise in value added per job in the more knowledge intensive value chains of production which remain in the Megalopolis in turn yields *rising income inequality* in the Megalopolis.

Over time, however, the nature of global supply chains evolves in response to the pace of economic development in the rapidly industrializing economies of the world—the recipients of the low value-adding components of industrial production outsourced from the Megalopolis. Rapidly industrializing countries (such as China) are accumulating in recent years significant levels of physical, human, and organizational capital, which permit an increasing incorporation of higher value-adding components of global production chains into their manufacturing and other tradable sectors—thereby displacing such components of manufacturing and other tradable sectors in the Megalopolis. In this context of globally linked production, significant aspects of the corresponding production chains disappear in the Megalopolis, which increasingly plays host largely to the high value-adding components such as R&D, design, fabrication of some knowledge intensive components, marketing, and a few post-sales services in production sectors. While overall value added per employee rises in these sectors retained in the Megalopolis, two adverse consequences follow. Powerful market forces operate directly on the tradable sector. More low and medium wage jobs in these sectors disappear from the Megalopolis locations. There are indirect effects on the non-tradable economic sectors of the Megalopolis and the national economy through wage and price effects and shifting opportunities in labor markets. Income inequalities, as a consequence, widen further in the last two decades in the Megalopolis centers of economic activity.

Spence and Hlatshwayo (2011) have carried out an analysis of the evolution of tradable and non-tradable sectors in the US economy and the progress of income inequalities in the nation as a whole during 1990–2007.

This chapter first extends the Spence-Hlatshwayo model to study the evolution of tradable and non-tradable sectors and the progress of income distribution at several spatial levels—*the US, the Megalopolis region,* and its *component major metropolitan areas* for a slightly longer period (during 1990–2011).[1] Second, it documents and interprets the economic changes—consequent to the functional and spatial organization of different tradable and non-tradable economic sectors—in the globalizing Megalopolis and its component metropolitan areas. Third, it documents the widening income inequalities flowing from the ongoing functional and spatial organization of the globalizing Megalopolis economy as evident at the level of the Megalopolis and its major metropolitan areas. Finally, the chapter recognizes that, in addition to processes noted here as driving widening income inequalities, there are additional contributing drivers behind the recent observed sharp upticks in income inequalities in the country and the Megalopolis. Consequently, the final section of this paper sketches a broader context for considering the growing income inequalities—beyond the argument of globalization and the functional/spatial restructuring of the economy presented here—in the nation, in the Megalopolis, and its component metros.

2. Globalization and Transformation of Tradable and Non-Tradable Sectors

The Case of the US

Employment growth in the US in this 22-year period of globalization— depicted in Figures 7.1–7.2—was entirely in the non-tradable sector (reaching

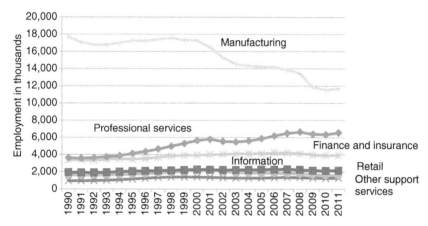

Figure 7.1 "Tradable" Industrial Employment (Major Sectors) in the US, 1990–2011

Source: Bureau of Labor Statistics, US Department of Labor.

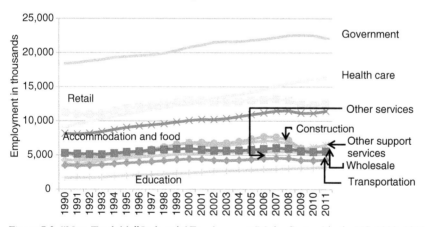

Figure 7.2 "Non-Tradable" Industrial Employment (Major Sectors) in the US, 1990–2011

Source: Bureau of Labor Statistics, US Department of Labor.

about 102 million in 2011). The tradable sectors (led by the manufacturing sector)—with their increasingly globalized production chains—have shrunk in the nation. Business services –which are crucial in the corporate and global spatial organization of the US economy—are experiencing growth of employment and earnings. The non-tradable sectors (led by health and government) are large and becoming larger.

Corresponding to this period's sharp outsourcing and the consequent decline in the manufacturing sector employment in the country, Figures 7.3 and 7.4 display the significant loss of tradable and non-tradable sectors' earnings in the US. The growth of employment and earnings in professional services, and finance and insurance in the country in this period reflects the growing organization of the global economy.

As noted earlier, much of the changes in employment and earnings in non-tradable sectors appear in health, government and the lower wage retail activities.

The Case of Boston Metro Region

The largest tradable sector in the Boston metropolitan area was manufacturing (Figure 7.5). In the recent 22 years (1990–2011) this sector lost about 160,000 employees (45 percent of its total). The average earnings per worker in this sector, however, climbed up from $80,000 to over $91,000 (in chained dollars) in the last 11 years (Figure 7.6). A significant loss of employment accompanied by an upward shift of average wage in that sector in Boston over a decade replicates the pattern of increasing income inequalities

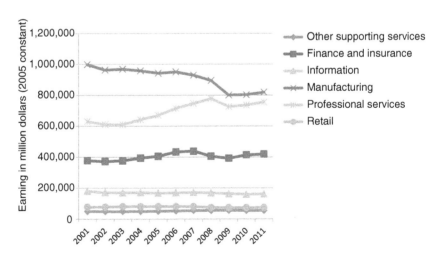

Figure 7.3 Tradable Sector Earnings in the US, 2001–2011

Source: Bureau of Economic Analysis, US Department of Commerce.

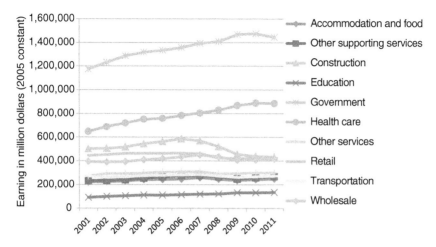

Figure 7.4 Non-Tradable Sector Earnings in the US, 2001–2011

Source: Bureau of Economic Analysis, US Department of Commerce.

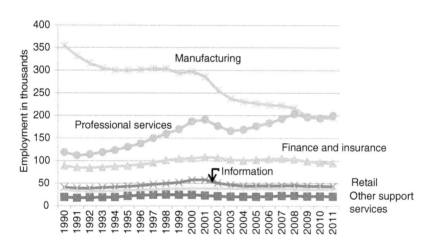

Figure 7.5 Tradable Industrial Employment (Major Sectors) in the Boston Metro Region

Source: Bureau of Labor Statistics, US Department of Labor.

predicted earlier for regions engaged in globally organized production and trade. However, two tradable sectors—professional services and finance and insurance—increased in employment (about 88,000) and high average wages overall per employee—over $140,000 in 2001—climbed up (in chained dollars) 23 percent and 13 percent respectively in in that decade. The result is a drop in tradable sector employment and increasing income inequalities in the Boston region.

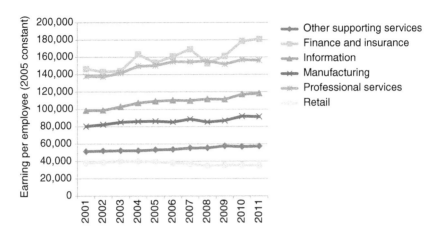

Figure 7.6 Tradable Sectors: Earnings/Employee in the Boston Metro Region (2005 Dollars)

Source: Bureau of Economic Analysis, US Department of Commerce.

Much of the growth in employment in the Boston metro region in these two decades derives from the non-tradable sectors (Figure 7.7). The health services sector is the largest contributor to growth, followed by the government and retail sectors. Indeed, the greater part of the employment growth in the Boston metro region by the year 2011 derives from the three non-tradable sectors of health services, government, and retail. Health and the government

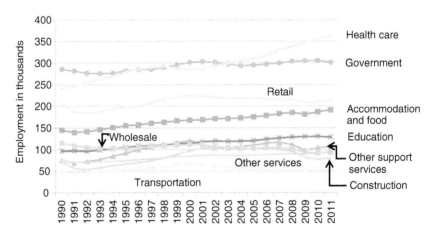

Figure 7.7 Tradable Sectors: Earnings/Employee in the Boston Metro Region (2005 Dollars)

Source: Bureau of Economic Analysis, US Department of Commerce.

sectors have average earnings per employee of about $70,000, while the earnings per employee in the third employment growth sector of retail are low—less than $40,000 (Figure 7.8).

It appears that over the last two decades, employment in the Boston metro region in the tradable sectors exposed to global competition is declining significantly. This development, combined with a rise in average earnings per remaining employee in those tradable sectors, leads to rising income inequalities. Further the dominant (non-tradable) employment growth sectors of health care, government, and retail evidence moderate to low earnings per employee. Clearly, *evolving trends in employment levels and earnings per employee in the globalizing Knowledge Economy of the Boston region over the last two decades indicate increasing income inequalities.*

The Case of the New York Region

Figures 7.9–7.12 on the progression of the employment and earnings per employee in the tradable and non-tradable sectors in the New York region essentially replicate the patterns of changes in employment and earnings (on a larger scale and at a slightly faster pace) noted above in the Boston region.

The two Megalopolis metro regions of Boston and New York also experience a higher percentage loss in the tradable sector of manufacturing than the country as a whole (Table 7.1). They appear to be more advanced in the processes of globalization of the manufacturing sectors in their economies—reporting faster rates of decline than the nation in manufacturing activities.

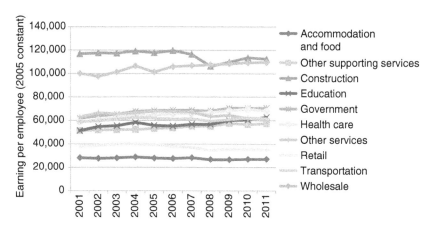

Figure 7.8 Non-Tradable Sectors: Earnings/Employee in the Boston Metro Region (2005 Dollars)

Source: Bureau of Economic Analysis, US Department of Commerce.

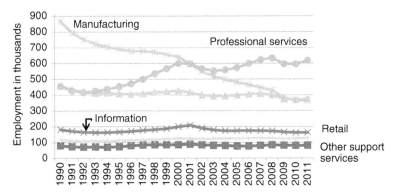

Figure 7.9 Employment in Tradable Sectors: New York Region, 1990–2011

Source: Bureau of Labor Statistics, US Department of Labor.

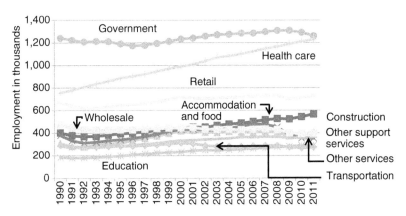

Figure 7.10 Employment in Non-Tradable Sectors: New York Region, 1990–2011

Source: Bureau of Labor Statistics, US Department of Labor.

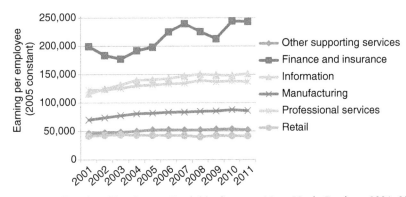

Figure 7.11 Earnings/Employee, Tradable Sectors: New York Region, 2001–2011
(2005 Dollars)

Source: Bureau of Economic Analysis, US Department of Commerce.

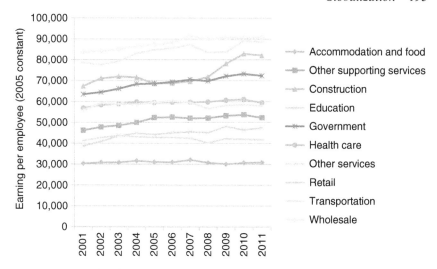

Figure 7.12 Earnings/Worker, Non-Tradable Sectors: New York Region, 2001–2011 (2005 Dollars)

Source: Bureau of Economic Analysis, US Department of Commerce.

Table 7.1 Changes in Employment in the Tradable Sector of Manufacturing, 1990–2011

Geographic Area Percent Change of Employment in the Tradable Sector of Manufacturing	
USA	−33%
Boston Region	−43%
New York Region	−54%

Source: Bureau of Labor Statistics, US Department of Labor.

3. Performance of Tradable/Non-Tradable Sectors in the Megalopolis

A comparative analysis of changes in aggregate employment and earnings in tradable and non-tradable sectors over two decades of globalization and the consequent functional/spatial reorganization of the Megalopolis economy (as gleaned from the performance of its five major metros) and the US can be derived from Tables 7.2 and 7.3.

Over the two decades of active participation in a globalized economy and the consequent functional/spatial reorganization of their economies, both the United States and the four recent *deindustrializing* major metropolitan regions of the Megalopolis (Boston, New York, Philadelphia, and Baltimore) are losing *employment* in the tradable economic sectors—reflecting their active participation in the global economy and the relocation of some of their manufacturing production value chains in the low wage industrializing countries.

Table 7.2 Tradable and Non-Tradable Industries' Employment in Major Megalopolis Metros and the US (in thousands), 1990–2011

	Tradable Industries (000)				Non-Tradable Industries (000)			
	1990	2000	2011	Change (1990–2011)	1990	2000	2011	Change (1990–2011)
Boston	667	721	602	–65	1,559	1,818	1,840	281
New York	2,474	2,425	2,055	–419	5,802	6,405	6,701	899
Philadelphia	828	840	701	–127	1,791	2,046	2,118	327
DC	604	780	823	219	1,920	2,206	2,467	547
Baltimore	341	340	316	–25	922	1,053	1,103	181
US	30,250	33,616	28,503	–1,748	79,237	98,266	102,994	23,757

Source: employment data collected from the BLS covering 1990–2011.

Table 7.3 Tradable and Non-Tradable Industries' Earnings in Major Megalopolis Metros and the US

	Tradable Industries				Non-Tradable Industries			
	2000	2006	2011	Change (2000–2011)	2000	2006	2011	Change (2000–2011)
Boston	71.3	70.4	72.8	1.51	112.0	119.7	120.3	8.22
New York	238.6	254.7	252.4	13.73	431.6	475.6	480.2	48.58
Philadelphia	59.0	61.3	58.0	–1.03	112.7	127.6	127.5	14.82
DC	60.5	73.5	80.6	20.08	149.2	174.4	186.3	37.11
Baltimore	20.0	21.9	21.7	1.69	54.8	65.0	66.2	11.43
US	2,395.3	2,523.7	2,408.6	13.26	5,076.6	5,750.2	5,682.7	606.14

* Earning data is in billions of 2005 dollars.

Source: earnings data from the BEA for 2001–2011.

Proportionately, the overall employment loss in tradable sectors was higher in the Megalopolis (23.4 percent) than in the nation as a whole—in terms of their relative economic size (Table 7.4). This effect is even more pronounced in the four Megalopolis *industrial* metros (Boston, New York, Philadelphia, and Baltimore), which experienced a multi-decade phase of deindustrialization before beginning their passage to the Knowledge Economies. While a positive change in earnings for tradable sectors occurs in four metropolitan areas, Philadelphia reports a decline in this period in earnings as well.

Table 7.4 Changes in Employment and Earnings in Tradable and Non-Tradable Sectors in the Megalopolis and the US, 2000–2011

	Employment (Thousands)		Earnings ($ Billions)	
	Tradable	Non-Tradable	Tradable	Non-Tradable
Megalopolis	–417	2.235	13.26	120.16
US	–1,748	23.757	36.20	606.18
Megalopolis/US	(–23.4%)	(9.4%)	(36.8%)	(19.8%)

Source: Bureau of Labor Statistics, US Department of Labor. Bureau of Economic Analysis, US Department of Commerce.

Washington DC (with a different industrial history to the other four metropolitan areas) actually registers a *positive change* in tradable employment and earnings. Washington DC had very limited growth in the manufacturing industries during the "industrial era" before World War II, and its contemporary growth in tradable sectors stems from its growth in professional services—related to both the governmental and private business services. Overall, this metropolitan region is the only one that registers positive growth in employment and earnings in both tradable and non-tradable sectors in the recent two decades (Figures 7.13 and 7.14).

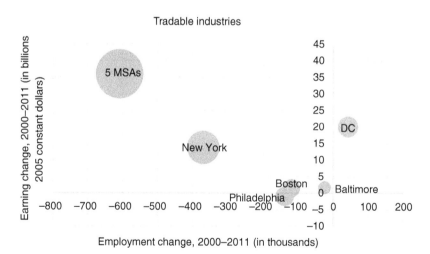

Figure 7.13 Changes in Employment and Earnings in Tradable Industries, Megalopolis, 2000–2011

Source: Bureau of Labor Statistics, US Department of Labor. Bureau of Economic Analysis, US Department of Commerce.

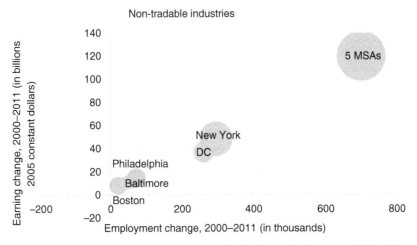

Figure 7.14 Changes in Employment and Earnings in Non-Tradable Sectors, 2000–2011

Source: Bureau of Labor Statistics, US Department of Labor. Bureau of Economic Analysis, US Department of Commerce.

The tradable sector earnings growth in the same period was also *proportionally higher* (36.8 percent) in the Megalopolis, reflecting the increasing higher earnings in the tradable sectors in the Megalopolis metro areas as compared to the nation. Changes in employment and earnings in non-tradable are positive in all metros.

The analyses implemented here of the processes of economic globalization and the consequent functional and spatial organization of economic sectors suggests that these processes are more advanced in the Megalopolis than in the nation. One should expect that the consequent widening of income inequalities should be more pronounced in the Megalopolis as well.

4. Recent Progression of Income Inequalities in the Global Megalopolis

There are many ways of representing income inequality statistically. A common way is to display the Gini Coefficient of the country or the region. Other measures include different ratios of various selected percentiles of income distribution, and various indicators such as the concentration of high income households in the country, the Megalopolis, and its component metropolitan areas.

Table 7.5 displays the Gini Coefficients of household incomes in the country over the last three decades. The last quarter century is a period when globalization has picked up its pace in the US and has actively reorganized the spatial and functional scope of its economy. The Gini has steadily climbed in this period, reflecting increasing inequalities of income in the country.

Table 7.5 Progress of Gini Indices of Household Income in Recent Years in the US

Year	Gini Coefficient
1979	0.414
1989	0.431
1999	0.458
2006	0.470
2011	0.475

Source: Selected Measures of Household Income Dispersion, US Census Bureau.

A comparative analysis of the changes in income inequalities of several met-ropolitan areas (of over 1 million people) in the Megalopolis over three recent decades appears in Table 7.6.

The progression of income inequalities in the nation stretching back over four decades from the present day (Figure 7.15)—as conveyed by three dif-ferent indicators (Gini Index, and two percentile ratios)—suggests that there are two distinct sub periods in this era. The first period (of approximately two decades starting in 1967) appears to have small changes in the three indica-tors of income inequalities. However, in the subsequent two decades or so up to 2009, all three indicators in Figure 7.15 indicate a distinct upward slope. This second period is what has been noted earlier as an active era of globaliz-ing metropolis and national economy.

Table 7.6 shows the progress of the Gini Index from 1979 to 2011 in the US and in selected metropolitan areas of the Megalopolis over three decades. In 1979, income inequalities are more pronounced in the nation than in the

Table 7.6 Gini Indices of Household Income Inequality for Metropolitan Areas of Over 1 Million Population During 2005–2009 in the Megalopolis

Metropolitan Area	1979	1989	2005–2009
New York	0.353	0.385	0.502
Boston	0.399	0.449	0.465
Philadelphia	0.327	0.341	0.464
Providence	0.394	0.427	0.447
Baltimore	0.391	0.412	0.445
Hartford	0.355	0.421	0.443
Washington	0.367	0.380	0.433
United States	0.404	0.431	0.467

Sources: Madden (2000); Weinberg (2011).

Figure 7.15 Progression of Gini, 90th/10th, and 80th/20th percentiles in the US, 1967–2009

Source: US Census Bureau Online Data.

metro areas of the Megalopolis. By 1989, when globalization was underway, the Gini indices (income inequalities) are climbing in the nation and in the metropolitan areas of the Megalopolis. As global organization of business and a finer differentiation of tradable and non-tradable sectors gather speed in the 1990s in the decade of the 2000s, income inequalities widen faster in the rising Knowledge Economies of New York, Boston, and Washington than in the nation.[2] Indeed, the rise of income inequalities is more pronounced in the Megalopolis urban realm than many large regions in the country.

Another measure of urban/metropolitan income inequalities, developed by Bee (2013), is a measure of income concentration, namely the places with the highest concentration of high income households—in other words, the proportion of the top national 5 percent high income households (defined as receiving at least $191,489 per year in the 2006–2011 period) in a metropolitan county. Two of the three US Census regions in the nation with the highest concentrations of such high income households—Middle Atlantic and New England—comprise the Megalopolis.[3]

Table 7.7 lists concentrations of high income households in the highest-concentration Megalopolis MSAs: 2007–2011. A Megalopolis MSA (Bridgeport-Stamford-Norwalk MSA) takes the top place in the nation by this measure of income inequality, and five Megalopolis metros form the top 8 locales in the nation in terms of spatial concentration of the households among the top 5 percent of the national households. Thus the metropolitan areas of the Megalopolis (which exhibit an advanced phase of globalization and the associated functional/spatial transformation of

Table 7.7 Concentrations of High-Income Households in the Highest-Concentration Megalopolis MSAs, 2007–2011

National Rank of Income Concentration	MSAs in Megalopolis	Percentage of MSA Households among Top 5 percent
1	Bridgeport-Stamford-Norwalk, CT	17.9
3	Washington-Arlington-Alexandria, DC-VA-MD-WV	14.1
5	Trenton-Ewing, NJ	11.6
6	New York-Northern New Jersey-Long Island, NY-NJ-PA	10.0
8	Boston-Cambridge-Quincy, MA-NH	9.7
13	Baltimore-Towson, MD	8.0
17	Hartford-West Hartford-East Hartford, CT	7.4
21	Philadelphia-Camden-Wilmington, PA-NJ-DE-MD	6.9

Source: Bee (2013).

the economy) also evidence high levels—indeed among the highest in the nation—of income inequalities.

This study has extended the Spence-Hlatshwayo model to compute and analyze the changing fortunes of tradable and non-tradable sectors in the context of the globalizing economies. This analysis has been at a) the national level (for a 22 year period), and b) at the levels of five major metropolitan regions of the Megalopolis.

The analysis reported in this chapter supports the notion that the Megalopolis is clearly a resurgent economy, restructuring the functional and spatial organization of its globalizing economy (and at a faster pace than the national economy). In the process, the income inequalities are widening in the Megalopolis.

While this premise is valid, a little reflection will suggest that there are other contributors to the process of rising income inequalities in the nation and in the Megalopolis. It is necessary to consider the broader context in which these other processes operate and contribute to the progressively widening income inequalities.

5. Broader Context of Widening Income Inequalities in the Megalopolis

A standard explanation of rising income inequalities in the US economy, where skill-based technical changes occur, attribute such inequalities to differences in human capital levels of the labor force. While this type of approach has a definite merit, some other explanations offer a broader context and a richer understanding of the contemporary patterns of widening income inequalities in the Megalopolis and in the country.

One approach is typified by the work of scholars such as Lawrence Mishel (2012) who, examining market-based incomes, finds that

> the top 1 percent of households have secured a very large share of all of the gains in income—59.9 percent of the gains from 1979 to 2007, while the top 0.1 percent seized an even more disproportionate share: 36 percent. In comparison, only 8.6 percent of income gains have gone to the bottom 90 percent.
>
> (Mishel and Bivens 2011, p. 1)

It has been received wisdom in Economic Geography that *productivity growth* in the economy supports our ability to raise living standards. Recent experience of the last three decades suggests instead that the productivity growth establishes *only the potential* for higher living standards (Figure 7.16). Mishel (2012, p. 7) notes:

> Productivity in the economy grew by 80.4 percent between 1973 and 2011 but the growth of real hourly compensation of the median worker grew by far less, just 10.7 percent, and nearly all of that growth occurred in

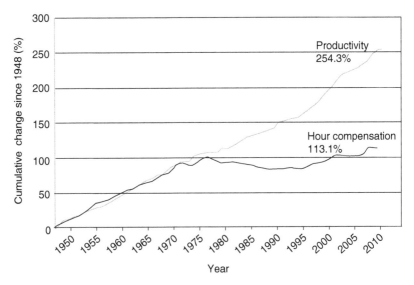

Figure 7.16 Growth of Real Hourly Compensation for Production/Non-Supervisory Workers and Productivity, 1948–2011

Source: Figure A in *The Wedges between Productivity and Median Compensation Growth,* by Lawrence Mishel, Economic Policy Institute, 2012. With permission from the Economic Policy Institute.

a short window in the late 1990s. The pattern was very different from 1948 to 1973, when the hourly compensation of a typical worker grew in tandem with productivity. Reestablishing the link between productivity and pay of the typical worker is an essential component of any effort to provide shared prosperity and, in fact, may be necessary for obtaining robust growth.

This divorce of the gains in wages from the gains in productivity in the last three decades is distinct from the experience of the earlier post World War II period when continuous productivity increases were accompanied by significant increases in income in the different quintiles of income distribution (Figure 7.17).

Levy and Temin (2007) offer a rich analytical framework to view income inequalities in different periods and how the income inequality regimes *are shaped by economic institutions in that era*. Viewed over a long period of a century, the income inequalities—represented by the percentage of the income received by the top 10 percent of the income distribution (Figure 7.18) in the US—display three different periods of income distribution, as influenced by three different sets of institutions supportive of labor and capital to varying degrees:

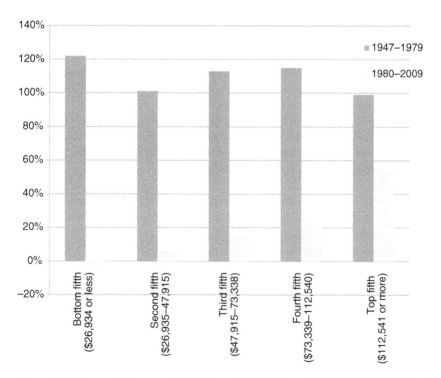

Figure 7.17 Change in Income by Quintiles, 1947–1979 and 1980–2009 (2009 Dollars)

Source: Boston Foundation (2012).

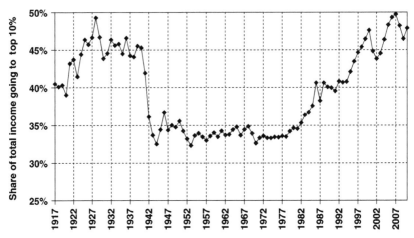

Figure 7.18 Top 10 Percent Pre-Tax Income Share in the US

Source: Piketty and Saez (2013).

1. An early period from 1917 to1940 with the income share of the top 10 percent was around 45 percent; towards the end of this period the onset of the Great Depression and the World War II led to highly progressive taxation when the income share of the top 10 percent began to fall towards 35 percent.
2. The second (1945–1980) era of income growth tied to productivity, and social and economic institutions supportive of increases of incomes of workers (termed as the "Treaty of Detroit").[4]
3. The third era (early 1980s to 2012) of institutions termed "The Washington Consensus" (characterized by *reversals in various factors* which had in the earlier era distributed the gains from growth broadly) and the consequent sharp rise in income inequalities.

Three dynamic processes have thus driven the nature and evolution of income inequality over the last 30 years or more: a) rising inequality of labor income (wages and compensation), b) rising inequality of capital income, and c) an increasing share of income going to capital income rather than labor income (Mishel 2012).

Finally, a new book, *Capital in the Twenty-First Century* by Thomas Piketty (2014), assembles and analyzes a large database on income inequalities in 20 countries stretching as far back as the eighteenth century and uncovers the deep structures of capital. Professor Piketty argues that the few equalizing decades following World War II (noted earlier)—which ushered in the middle class in the US—were but a historical anomaly. Piketty contends that the main driver of inequality, namely, the tendency of returns on capital to exceed the rate of economic growth over the recent two centuries (except for the few decades after World War II), generates extreme income inequalities.

Notes

1 Spence and Hlatshwayo (2011) used a methodology developed by Bradford Jensen and Lori Kletzer (2005). Their approach determined the tradability of an industry based on its geographic concentration—the more concentrated the industry, the higher its tradability (and vice versa). For example, take retail trade: its ubiquitous geographic presence implies that it is highly non-tradable.
2 The latest US Census Bureau data confirm that, overall, big cities remain more unequal places by income than the rest of the country.
3 The third such Census region with such high concentrations of high income households is the Pacific region.
4 The stability in income equality where wages rose with national productivity for a generation after World War II was the result of policies that began in the Great Depression with the New Deal and were amplified by both public and private actions after the World War II. This stability was not the result of a natural economy; it was the result of policies designed to promote it. Levy and Temin (2007) termed this set of policies as the *Treaty of Detroit*.

References

Bee, C.A., 2013. *The Geographic Concentration of High-Income Households, 2007–2011: American Community Survey Briefs*, US Census Bureau, US Department of Commerce

Boston Foundation, 2012. *The City of Ideas: Reinventing Boston's Innovation Economy*, Boston Indicators Report 2012.

Jensen, J.B., Kletzer, L.G., 2005. *Tradable Services: Understanding the Scope and Impact of Services Outsourcing*, Washington, DC: Peter G. Peterson Institute for International Economics.

Levy, F., Temin, P., 2007. *Inequality and Institutions in 20th Century America*, NBER Working Paper 13106.

Madden J.F., 2000. *Changes in Income Inequality within US Metropolitan Areas.* Kalamazoo, MI: W.E. Upjohn Institute for Employment Research.

Mishel, L., 2012. *The Wedges between Productivity and Median Compensation Growth*, Economic Policy Institute, Washington, DC, April 26.

Mishel, L., Bivens, J., 2011. *Occupy Wall Streeters Are Right about Skewed Economic Rewards in the United States.* Economic Policy Institute Briefing Paper No. 331.

Piketty, T., 2014. *Capital in the Twenty-First century*, Cambridge, MA: Harvard University Press.

Piketty, T., Saez, E., 2013. Top incomes and the Great Recession: recent evolution and policy implications. *IMF Economic Review* 61(3), 456–478.

Spence, M., Hlatshwayo, S., 2011. *The Evolving Structure of the American Economy and the Employment Challenge.* Working Paper, Council on Foreign Relations, Maurice R. Greenberg Center for Geoeconomic Studies.

Weinberg, D.H., 2011. *U.S. Neighborhood Income Inequality in the 2005–2009 Period.* American Community Survey Reports, United States Census Bureau, Selected measures of household income dispersion: 1967 to 2010, online data (www.census.gov/hhes/www/income/data/historical/inequality) browsed July 1, 2013.

8 Conclusion

This book addresses two broad questions.

First, it aims to understand the ongoing structural change and socioeconomic transition—over the last three decades in some urban regions—from a mature and declining industrial structure to that of a vibrant "Knowledge Economy." How has this come about? What technologies and other innovations have emerged to promote economic, social, and spatial processes which enable this structural transition to the Knowledge Economy? The success of such a complex structural transition requires major economic, social, and political actors to be engaged—shifting mindsets and behavior in evolving and sustaining innovation, and in maintaining the dynamics of change— developing new institutions and organizations. This book addresses such broad questions and offers a broad analytical framework or model of the rise and evolution of the contemporary Knowledge Economy.

Second, this book attempts to apply this model of the rise and evolution of the Knowledge Economy to the recent experience of growth, decline, and renewal in one of the world's great urban regions: the Megalopolis stretching along the Eastern Seaboard of the United States from Southern New Hampshire to Northern Virginia, including the metropolitan areas of Boston, New York, Philadelphia, Baltimore, and Washington DC Most importantly, it is about the evolution of a huge regional trading and manufacturing economy—one based on the movement and transformation of materials—to an equally formidable Knowledge Economy based on the transformation of knowledge derived from scientific and engineering research into technological innovations, which coupled with institutional and organizational innovations yield high value goods and services for the global market. The second broad question for this book in this context is: to what extent do the observed patterns of economic change and evolution in recent decades in the Megalopolis and its five major constituent metropolitan areas cohere with the scope and predictions of the model of the rise of the Knowledge Economy presented in this book?

For the most part, the recent history of the Megalopolis region is a success story. Consigned by many analysts to perpetual decline in the progress toward a "Snowbelt–Sunbelt" transition in the American economy, the

Megalopolis has become prominent as a key pole in the global network of Knowledge Economies. While it has not developed *extensively* as rapidly as some parts of the United States—and certainly not as rapidly as the emerging economies of Asia—it has developed *intensively* to a level of economic and technological sophistication and proficiency that is matched by only a handful of regions around the world.

But just as the explosion of trade and manufacturing activity in this region during the nineteenth and early twentieth century gave way to economic stagnation in the 1960s and 1970s, the seeds of potential decline are already planted in the apparently thriving Megalopolis. Warning signs are to be found in the imbalance of growth between tradable and non-tradable goods and services and in expanding polarization of incomes. The future is fraught with challenging questions. Will this region maintain its edge in the production, transformation, and commercialization of knowledge? Will an aging and underinvested infrastructure prevent it from fully exploiting its potential?

The economy is always in flux, and since knowledge changes constantly and can be transferred from place to place, a prominent position in the global Knowledge Economy can only be maintained through constant improvement. The future depends on whether the firms, governments, institutions, and knowledge workers of the Megalopolis are up to this task.

1. Rise of a Knowledge Economy

As we said in Chapter 1, the emerging Knowledge Economy is characterized by its ability to generate, share, analyze, and utilize knowledge in the creation of value and wealth. The focus is not merely on expansion of knowledge, but also on *the effective harnessing of different types of knowledge in various sectors of the economy to secure competitive advantage and improved performance*. In exploring the evolution of the Knowledge Economy in the Megalopolis region, we rely on a model of development focused on four broad classes of innovative technologies and processes, and their interactive and cumulative effects:

1. *Transportation innovations* in the form of physical changes such as the establishment of the interstate highways system, the massive move to containerization in global commerce, and the availability of jet aircraft, as well as in the form of institutional innovations such as deregulation and privatization.
2. *Information and Communications Technologies (ICT)* that reduce the cost and difficulty of accessing information and knowledge, sharing information to promote innovative collaboration of a broad spatial scale, and connectivity to global markets.
3. *Innovative processes which a) nurture and commercialize new industrial products and operations and b) promote the structural evolution toward a knowledge intensive service economy*. Notably, these processes give rise to

the emergence of KIBS, which have played a key role in the emergence of the Knowledge Economy in the Megalopolis.

4. *Institutional Innovations*. These include different forms of interaction among and within firms—notably the transition from hierarchies to networks—to facilitate the transfer of knowledge and information, efficiently exploiting complementarities, facilitating joint creative processes, and providing the resilience to adapt to rapidly changing information and knowledge. Public sector and private-social sector innovations, such as new models of urban governance, also fall into this category.

The first two relate to GPTs that support all aspects of the economy in a period of rapid development. Just as steam power and electricity were the GPTs of the industrial era, global transport innovations and ICT are the GPTs of the Knowledge Economy. The second two relate to transformational ways of creating value in the Knowledge Economy, stressing the interactive nature of value creation involving multiple firms and public-private interaction.

Chapter 3, which focuses on the transportation and ICT GPTs (points one and two above), sets them in an extensive literature and explores how they promote economic development. Transportation promotes regional specialization, agglomeration, and global connectivity. In the Megalopolis there is a high density of transportation networks including rapid rail transit within the constituent metropolitan areas, the I-95 highway, high speed rail, and a system of air shuttles connecting the corridor from end to end, and connectivity to America's number one Atlantic port.

While the industrial economies are based on controlling the supply of scarce resources, the emerging (ICT) networked economy creates value by extensively and abundantly connecting individuals, functions, and enterprises across vast spaces around the globe in productive ways and by creating value in the process. The Megalopolis region has been at the forefront of technological development in ICT, and firms in the region have exploited it most effectively in connecting to each other and to the world. The combination of innovations in transportation and ICT make it possible for the extensive corridor to function as a compact economic region and to plug into global economic networks.

Chapter 4 expands to consider all four categories of innovation and how they interact. The relationships among actors in transferring knowledge and creating knowledge-based assets and services are stressed here. The intensity and effectiveness of such interaction depends on different forms of proximity. Physical proximity, defined by the ease of physical movement, promotes agglomeration economies in the form of shared, specialized labor and other resources, knowledge spillovers, sharing of tacit knowledge *via* face-to-face interaction and scale economies. Relational proximity refers to cooperative learning processes. Institutional proximity refers to network cooperation whereby complementary knowledge is exploited by formal supplier relationships and firms are able to monitor and adapt to changing conditions via information that flows through their networks. All three forms of proximity are intensely present in the Megalopolis region. Chapter 4 also describes the emergence of KIBS whereby business functions are contracted to specialized firms who apply advanced ICT and related technology in their provision. KIBS have emerged as a driving force in the Megalopolis Knowledge Economy, not only because they promote efficient internal production but also because they can be exported to the rest of the world.

Chapter 4 also explores institutional innovations. In the Knowledge Economy, the traditional institutions of markets, private hierarchies (firms), and the state are complemented by *economic networks*. With the maturation of the Knowledge Economy, knowledge-rich technologies arrive in various aspects of production—design, fabrication, input and output logistics, marketing, after-sales services, etc. In this increasingly knowledge intensive context, value derives from knowledge, and enterprises seek to add value to their core competencies by taking advantage of complementary assets and capabilities of other enterprises. To this end, networks emerge comprising changing combinations of large and small firms that are adaptable and provide for the efficient production and exchange of knowledge.

Institutional innovation is not limited to the private sphere. New forms of urban governance are needed for cities to thrive in the Knowledge Economy. "Entrepreneurial cities" seek to identify market opportunities for private actors whose exploitation of these opportunities also serves the urban area's growth objectives. There is also an expanding role for SEs in translating the dynamism of the Knowledge Economy into broad welfare benefits.

2. Megalopolis Region

Chapters 2 and 5 provide empirical evidence of the rise and status of the Knowledge Economy in the Megalopolis region. In Chapter 2 we illustrated that by various indicators, this region is more advanced than the US in general in the transition from the industrial economy to a Knowledge Economy. While the region's share of population and employment (especially manufacturing employment) declined over the period from 1985 to 2000, its share in total non-farm earnings remained about constant, consistent with growing per capita earnings and more rapid productivity growth relative to the rest of the country. Most notable is the expansion of KIBS (Knowledge intensive Business Services), whereas the shift of employment from manufacturing to services has led to declining income in many industrial regions, in the Megalopolis it actually represents an upgrading to higher value added activities. Indicators of entrepreneurial activities, such as the concentration of venture capital firms, confirm the reputation of the Megalopolis as a highly innovative region.

Our analysis of knowledge oriented services indicates that the Megalopolis punches above its weight, with 21.5 percent of employment *vs* only 16 percent of population. Even in the knowledge intensive sectors, however, the

Megalopolis share of manufacturing activity is only about 12 percent. But its ratio of payroll to employment is much higher than the national average, indicating that only the highest value, knowledge intensive manufacturing remains in the region.

All of the metropolitan areas of the Megalopolis have higher than the national level of educational attainment. They also have extraordinary concentrations of education sector employment, especially in colleges and universities. Thus, the scientific and engineering research that are key inputs to knowledge intensive production may be locally derived. The entire region also has an extraordinarily high level of health services activities, including industries such as pharmaceuticals, medical devices, and biotechnology.

Our analysis of the five largest metropolitan areas in the Megalopolis region has exposed both commonalities and differences. The Boston region stands out for its history of repeated recovery from periods of decline in seafaring activities, manufacturing, and later a succession of technical industries. Its resilience derives in large part from the extraordinary concentration of research universities that has continually provided technological innovations that have been commercialized by local firms and one of the highest concentrations of elite scientists and engineers to be found anywhere in the world. Industries such as radar, computer hardware, software, and biotech have been closely linked with the university sector, as has the extraordinary local health care industry, which not only serves the local population but also attracts patients from around the world.

New York, which in the 1970s was often derided for civic mismanagement and industrial decline, has re-established its position at the very highest level of the global urban hierarchy. It has maintained and enhanced its position as the world's largest center for financial activities and for high level business services that are exported around the globe. The recurrent ability of New York to remain an economic leader over two centuries reflects both its capacity to exploit technological advances and its "social intelligence," comprising of its capacity to create the institutions, the policymaking, and the incentives that promote continual learning and adaptation in a rapidly evolving context. One of the greatest strengths of the New York metropolitan area is its unrivalled position as a magnet for international migration, drawing both technological skills and entrepreneurial spirit from other countries.

The Philadelphia metropolitan area was once among the largest and most diversified manufacturing regions in America. While a substantial manufacturing sector survives, employment numbers are down. The slack has been taken up by growth in the education and health care sectors, establishing Philadelphia as the quintessential "eds and meds" economy. While these sectors require many highly skilled knowledge workers, they also require large numbers of low-paid, unskilled workers, leading to a polarized distribution of income.

The Baltimore region has shown extraordinary progress from a period of decline in port activities and the heavy industries (steel and shipbuilding) and an acquired reputation for urban blight. Baltimore's period of recovery over the past twenty years may be attributed to a successful waterfront restoration that has made it a favourite destination for tourists and conventions, the expansion of "eds and meds" driven by its legacy institutions, especially Johns Hopkins University, and the spill-over employment from the nearby Washington DC metro area, including the locations of headquarters of several major federal agencies. But there is a dark side to Baltimore's development in an increasingly uneven income distribution and the persistently high and *growing* share of low income population, especially in the urban core.

The Washington DC metropolitan area, which sprawls over large areas of Maryland and Virginia, is by far the fastest growing component of the Megalopolis region in terms of both population and employment. It has a young, highly educated population. While federal employment has stagnated, government spending still drives the regional economy through a process of contracting out of federal services to contractors, many of whom are located in the suburbs and edge cities of Northern Virginia. While employment has been buoyant for many years, there is concern that stagnant or even declining federal spending in the era of "budget sequestration" may lead to a prolonged slowdown. The continued growth of the region depends in large part on whether the human, technological, and infrastructure capital that has been built up to serve government demands can be redirected to more diversified demands outside the region.

Chapter 6 examines the spatial structure of the Megalopolis and how it has been evolving in the context of the decline of the industrial era economy and the rise and growth of a vibrant Knowledge Economy. Two themes animate this discussion. The first is the concept of Megalopolis as a *functional economic region,* which pertains to a space within which a high intensity of spatial interactions promote complementarities among its spatial subdivisions, making it, from an economic perspective, more than a sum of its spatial parts. From the perspective of goods movement, the fact that the Megalopolis is a functional economic region is demonstrated by statistical analysis of freight flows.

The second theme relates to the *presence and role of agglomeration* within the Megalopolis. The Megalopolis space economy—accounting for a *fifth* US GDP in about 1.4 percent of national land area—is the quintessential example of large scale agglomeration. More geographically detailed evidence of agglomeration within clusters of economic activity, particularly in knowledge intensive activities, is offered, within the Megalopolis through the use of many indicators and methods of spatial analysis.

The Megalopolis region has demonstrated an exceptional economic resilience. In the long run, this may be the best reason to be optimistic about its future prosperity. But at the present time there are also warning signals that call that optimism into question. Chapter 7 demonstrates a weakness in the export base that one would expect to drive a dynamic region. It takes the analysis used by Spence and Hlatshwayo (2011) to demonstrate that expansion in the American economy has been focused on non-tradable sectors and applies it to the Megalopolis region. The result is that the decline in tradable employment in the Megalopolis is even more severe than it is in the US overall. All the constituent major metro areas, with the exception of Washington DC, lost tradable employment over the past 22 years. Earnings in tradable sectors, by contrast, grew faster in the Megalopolis than in the nation. This is consistent with the theme of intensive, as opposed to extensive, growth in the Megalopolis. From the late 1980s on, however, the rise of income inequalities was more pronounced in the Megalopolis urban realm than many large regions in the country.

The analysis reported in this book supports the notion that the Megalopolis is clearly a resurgent economy, restructuring the functional and spatial organization of its globalizing economy (and at a faster pace than the national economy). In the process, however, the income inequalities are widening in the Megalopolis.[1]

Note

1 While this premise is valid, a little reflection will suggest that there are other contributors to the process of rising income inequalities in the nation and in the Megalopolis. It is necessary to consider the broader context in which these other processes operate and contribute to the progressively widening income inequalities in the Megalopolis. Such factors include: the divorce in recent decades in the US from gains in productivity from the gains in wages in last three decades, and the changing economic institutions and weakening labor power.

Reference

Spence, M., Hlatshwayo, S., 2011. *The Evolving Structure of the American Economy and the Employment Challenge.* Working Paper, Council on Foreign Relations, Maurice R. Greenberg Center for Geoeconomic Studies.

Index

For Product Safety Concerns and Information please contact our EU
representative GPSR@taylorandfrancis.com
Taylor & Francis Verlag GmbH, Kaufingerstraße 24, 80331 München, Germany

www.ingramcontent.com/pod-product-compliance
Ingram Content Group UK Ltd.
Pitfield, Milton Keynes, MK11 3LW, UK
UKHW020957180425
457613UK00019B/733